What others are saying about *Emotional Value*

"Janelle Barlow and Dianna Maul have written a tremendous book. *Emotional Value* will help speed up the day when businesses provide not only good service but truly engaging experiences, jobs become roles to be characterized and acted out, and workers are paid to self-actualize on the job. Any organization looking to improve the emotional connection between their employees and their customers needs to read this work."

— **JOE PINE** & **JIM GILMORE**, authors of *The Experience Economy: Work Is Theatre & Every Business a Stage*

"*Emotional Value* addresses the key customer service differentiation for twenty-first century corporations. In a well-organized and well thought out manner, it addresses the passion and emotional value required to impact the culture and focus of a corporation. About two years ago, Dell Computer Corporation launched a corporate-wide program focusing on the customer experience as a key differentiation in our industry. It was then and still remains Dell's only nonfinancial goal. Janelle was an instrumental part of our corporate roll out of this initiative. Many of the insights and sensitivities she shared with us are covered in great detail in her book. *Emotional Value* should be a must-read book."

— **MORTON L. TOPFER**, Vice Chairman, Dell Computer Corporation

"This book tackles, head on, the most fundamental yet elusive element of our business. Giving service and meaning it! This is a no nonsense read that provides practical direction punctuated with many humorous yet profound examples. A compelling read with humorous yet practical examples that one can easily relate to and learn from."

— **NIGEL ROBERTS**, General Manager, The Great Eagle Hotel, Hong Kong

"This is the book you've been waiting for! Substantive guidance to understanding your customers and treating them well. Read it. Use it. Benefit from it."

— **NIDO QUBEIN**, author of *How To Be a Great Communicator*

"*Emotional Value* is an extraordinary achievement, destined to become a classic in the literature on customer service. Barlow and Maul have taken a brightly illuminating look into our experiences as customers and service providers and reflected back the true nature of our encounters. *Emotional Value* will forever change how you perceive, provide, and receive customer service. Solidly based in research, this book offers profound content, practical prescriptions, illustrative examples, and compelling stories that will remain with you long after you put it down. . . . I implore you to read this book and immediately put it to use. Your customers' feelings about your organization are at stake, and so is the value they create for you."

—**JIM KOUZES**, coauthor *The Leadership Challenge,* and *Encouraging the Heart* and Chairman Emeritus, tompeters!company

"Just as the emotional health of a person dictates physical well being, the emotional health of an organization dictates its financial well being. Janelle Barlow and Dianna Maul have composed a primer on this important topic. The authors' data and stories paint a compelling picture of why taking care of customer, staff and organizational emotions should be a priority for every CEO/President. It is a must-read for businesses that hope to be on the cutting edge."

—**CHRIS EHLERS**, Organizational Dynamics/Effectiveness Manager Proctor & Gamble

"*Emotional Value* is an awesome guide to understanding human behavior as it relates to the business transaction process. Finally, a practical resource on how to enhance the customer experience . . . an absolute must-read for the staff of any organization interested in exponentially growing their business!"

—**CHRIS STRIPPELHOFF**, Vice President of Member Service, The Municipal Gas Authority of Georgia

"*Emotional Value* redefines customer service—it is the new level. Read this book because delivering emotional value will be the entrance fee for any organization entering the 21st Century."

—**LISA FORD**, author of the *How to Give Exceptional Customer Service* Video Series

"Presidents have to have it. Customers come back when they feel it. Making emotional connections means loyalty. If you want the practical road map for you and your people to take advantage of the experience economy, *Emotional Value* is a must-read. With this book you won't fall victim to change, you can help invent the future of the service industry."

—**TERRY PAULSON, PH.D.**, former President of the National Speakers Association and author of *They Shoot Managers Don't They*

"This book is extremely user-friendly and presents the subject in a way that is relevant, thought-provoking and challenging. I was struck by the realization that we can manage emotional competence in the same way we manage any other aspect of our business—by setting goals, applying processes, aligning rewards and recognition, celebrating success to reinforce behavior, and finally measuring results. This approach to recognizing and managing the role of emotions will help us at ARAMARK to strengthen our customer service programs and will surely result in greater levels of loyalty, retention, and profitability."
  —**TED MONK**, Vice President, ARAMARK

"This gem of a book offering a fresh approach to service. . . . We consider ourselves in touch with service to our member B&B/Country inn owners, but this handbook of practical applications is keeping us on our toes reexamining our assumptions about staff and members. . . . The Applications sprinkled throughout create opportunities to rethink our own approaches in experiential and daily ways. Finally someone talks about emotions in this over-merged, over-numberized society and offers such practical ways to present and understand how to implement them."
  —**PAT HARDY**, Co-Executive Director, Professional Association of
    Innkeepers International (PAII)

"This is the book I wish I had a year ago. Well organized, with excellent examples, this book takes us to a new level of customer relations. Absolutely essential to the customer service professional. I was totally unprepared for the impact this book has had on me. People have milked the customer service/customer satisfaction concept dry. The timing is perfect for *Emotional Value*, which provides illumination from a different source of light."
  —**W. LANDON HEFFNER**, Vice President, Chief Learning Officer,
    Monrovia

"*Emotional Value* will be pure gold for any organization serious enough about delivering solid customer service to pan for the nuggets in this book. The authors place emotion squarely where it belongs—front, center and in the customer service spotlight. As Barlow and Maul declare, emotional memories are more intense and enduring than any other kind."
  —**GAIL M. WEBBER**, Senior Director, Learning & Development, Culture
    & Communications, VANTIVE-The e-customer Company

"Those of us in the customer satisfaction business need all the expertise and new prespectives we can get. *Emotional Value* will ensure that this knowledge is further built upon. If you read only one book on customer relationships this year, read this one."
> —**SIDNEY YUEN**, Chairman, Hongkong Benchmarking Clearinghouse
> & CEO, TeleCare Corporation

"Adopt and practice the five tenets of *Emotional Value*. You will reap the rewards of understanding your customers needs. Don't procrastinate; your competition will be reading this book, too."
> —**DIANNE M. PUSCH**, Regional Vice President, Western Region,
> University of Phoenix

"Understanding the role of emotions in customer service is an essential and often neglected responsibility for our organizations. Barlow and Maul make this clear with real-life examples, and do an excellent job of linking emotional competence to both the business outcomes important to financial success, and to the everyday interactions of our service providers."
> —**ERIKA GWILT**, Northwest Airlines, Inc., Director of Ground
> Operations Education

"This is a very solid book, light reading with hefty insights. And chill out—you can achieve emotional value! I got insight into my own team's service failures. Failures I wasn't even aware of until I read about the emotional needs of our customers. Needs that we may not have been emotionally competent to handle—prior to reading this book."
> —**TONET RIVERA**, General Manager, Avon Products Manufacturing,
> Inc., Philippines

"This book is great. Very insightful. A powerful message with practical application. Not only does it provide a logical approach to a side of the business that is often just assumed to 'work', but it also provides great examples and real-life experiences. The assessment portion of each section is a great way to bring the message home."
> —**RENEE SCHULZ**, Director of Marketing for Worldwide Applied
> Systems Group, The Trane Company

EMOTIONAL VALUE

Also by Janelle Barlow

A Complaint Is a Gift
(with Claus Møller)

EMOTIONAL VALUE

*Creating Strong Bonds
with Your Customers*

JANELLE BARLOW

AND DIANNA MAUL

Foreword by Michael Edwardson

BERRETT-KOEHLER PUBLISHERS, INC.
San Francisco

Berrett-Koehler Publishers, Inc.
450 Sansome Street, Suite 1200
San Francisco, CA 94111-3320
Tel: (415) 288-0260 Fax: (415)362-2512 www.bkconnection.com

ORDERING INFORMATION

Quantity sales. Special discounts are available on quantity purchases by corporations, associations, and others. For details, contact the "Special Sales Department" at the Berrett-Koehler address above.

Individual sales. Berrett-Koehler publications are available through most bookstores. They can also be ordered direct from Berrett-Koehler: Tel: (800) 929-2929; Fax: (802) 864-7626; www.bkconnection.com

Orders for college textbook/course adoption use. Please contact Berrett-Koehler: Tel: (800) 929-2929; Fax: (802) 864-7626.

Orders by U.S. trade bookstores and wholesalers. Please contact Publishers Group West, 1700 Fourth Street, Berkeley, CA 94710. Tel: (510) 528-1444; Fax (510) 528-3444.

Printed in the United States of America

 Printed on acid-free and recycled paper that is composed of 50% recovered fiber, including 10% postconsumer waste.

Library of Congress Cataloging-in-Publication Data

Barlow, Janelle, 1943–
   Emotional value : taking customer service to a new level / Janelle Barlow and Dianna Maul.
       p.   cm.
   Includes bibliographical references and index.
   ISBN 1-57675-079-5
       1. Customer services.   I. Maul, Dianna, 1950–
   HF5415.5 .B3673 2000
   658.8′12—dc12
                           99-086124
                           CIP

First Edition

   05   04   03   02   01   00   10 9 8 7 6 5 4 3 2 1

Copyediting and proofreading: PeopleSpeak
Interior design and production: Marin Bookworks
Index: Leonard Rosenbaum
Cover design: Richard Adelson

CONTENTS

FOREWORD

Emotion: we experience it, we feel it, it affects us, it moves us. Our memories, our relationships, our decisions are all infused with emotion. Emotion is central to our lives as humans, which include not only our families and friends and those close to us but also the many people we interact with every day in the services we use. In the service economy, and more importantly in the new concept of the experience economy, the role of emotion is becoming increasingly recognized as a critical aspect of these interactions and indeed very often comprises the core of the value we receive. Consider the care of a doctor, the helpfulness of a sales assistant, the welcome of a waiter, the adrenaline thrill of a theme park ride, or the poignancy of a theatrical performance. Yet the interest in emotion has not always been the case, and for many, especially in the business world, emotion is still little understood and therefore kept out of the equation. Every business would agree nonetheless that customer satisfaction is vital for success.

Customer satisfaction measurement is now one of the leading performance indicators together with net profit and return on assets. Because we have statistical indices of satisfaction and can monitor and measure it, we often forget that satisfaction is itself an emotional response. We feel satisfied or we feel dissatisfied. But as customers we can also feel excited or relaxed or angry or disappointed or confident. Is this the same as satisfaction? Our own experiences would say no. To say we feel dissatisfied hardly captures the experiential nature of the frustration and even rage that consumers say they feel when customer service doesn't meet their expectations. Staff have to learn to handle complaints that are often communicated in a highly emotionally charged manner so that a complaint is indeed a gift, as Janelle Barlow has previously highlighted. Without question, service providers have to be increasingly emotionally competent and intelligent in their emotional labor.

These many consumer emotions are the focus of a growing body of academic marketing research that is starting to open a window on the consumer experience beyond satisfaction. The study, understanding, and application of consumer emotions is a new and exciting field; the research is already providing fascinating new insights. Academic research eventually informs the practical questions asked and applications demanded by business, but the link has to be made. How do we measure consumer emotions? How do we train staff to recognize and deal with emotions? How do we maximize the experiences of our customers? How do we increase emotional value? This book provides such a link and is one of the first practical applications in this new field of consumer emotions. It is a book for the new experience economy that gives service providers a leading edge into developing customer value beyond satisfaction. Janelle Barlow has brought together these new ideas and sets them within a framework that enables companies to develop emotional value for their customers.

As a researcher, I have had a passion for the study of emotion, particularly consumer emotions, for the past ten years. From the early interest that Janelle showed in my work, and the work of others in the field, to the completion of this book, it is clear that she shares the passion as well. It is a passion to provide real value for customers and the people who serve them. It is a passion to give the reader the tools to do this. The book is timely, its contents very practical yet based on referenced published research. It is a terrific resource for those who want to open the window into the new era beyond customer satisfaction, and I'm sure the reader will share in the excitement of the new view that is presented within these pages. Janelle Barlow and Dianna Maul should certainly feel proud of their efforts.

Michael Edwardson
Consumer Psychologist
School of Marketing
University of New South Wales
Sydney, Australia
October 1999

PREFACE

The authors spend an enormous amount of their time either providing service to clients, staff, and colleagues or alternatively receiving service from others. At times we experience incredibly fine service delivered by sensitive, caring, and emotionally competent humans, so fine we want to tell everyone we just witnessed an Olympic "10" in customer service. Other times—unfortunately all too often—we see the crass underbelly of unacceptable service. As every consumer undoubtedly knows, the space for improvement is immense. All of these experiences, both positive and negative, have rendered the authors fascinated by the role of human behavior and emotions in service, the great underpinning of today's "experience economy."

We have written this book out of our passion for the human element in service and a desire to shape the future of how people offer service to each other. We invite managers and service providers around the world to use the ideas in this book to think about customer relationships in an expanded manner, focusing on the emotional side, the side that can sting feelings if delivered poorly and create lifelong feelings of gratitude if delivered well.

Unfortunately, emotions in service are elusive and are frequently offered without any conscious guidance, positive or negative. It is almost as if the most impactful aspect of service is thrown in the pot without any sense of the flavor it will add. Yet its effect is real. One of our colleagues recently sent us an e-mail describing his poor emotional treatment by airline personnel:

> I was waiting in a queue to board when a lady came and said, "Only business class now," and she said it in such a way that all the economy passengers (I think) felt very embarrassed that they fly economy.

These types of alienating emotional interactions happen all too often and are not improved by simple organizational mandates. A smiling gate agent in the above example could have told the lined-up economy passengers, "Good morning. We're boarding rows one through nine right now. We'll be happy to board rows ten and up in just a moment." But it won't work to just *tell* the gate agent to use these words. The emotional part of service cannot be "fixed" in a piecemeal fashion, which makes its improvement complex. It requires looking at customer interactions as part of the *total* organizational system and culture.

The distinction between customer relationships that have added emotional value and those that are emotionally insensitive may seem trivial, but it is a huge potential-filled room into which many organizations have barely entered, and they are frankly at a loss to know what to do once they get there. While the cost of adding emotional value is frequently minimal in contrast to upgrading the tangible or "hard" side of service, this is not to say that adding emotional value is free or without effort.

By understanding the critical role of emotions, organizations can take their customer offerings to new levels of refinement, compete more effectively, and most importantly, better retain both customers and staff. This book provides an opportunity to create, design, and deliver customer experiences that go beyond satisfaction by focusing on emotional impact. With understanding, careful planning, and diligence, an organization's current level of customer relationships can be defined appropriately for its specific business and then enhanced. Careful consideration of

Emotional Value can guide all who want their customer service to function consistently with the demands of staging experiences for customers.

To add emotional value to customers' experiences, an organization and its staff must engage in five practices, around which this book is organized:

- Building an emotion-friendly service culture
- Choosing emotional competence as the organization's service model
- Maximizing customer experiences with empathy
- Viewing complaints as emotional opportunities
- Using emotional connections to increase customer loyalty

1. Part I: Building an Emotion-Friendly Service Culture. The first part of *Emotional Value* deals with the requirement of building an emotion-friendly service culture. We particularly like Peter Jackson's definition of culture when he says, "Cultures are maps of meaning through which the world is made intelligible."[1] An emotion-friendly service culture can be shaped by understanding the role and power of emotions in business and by supporting emotional awareness among all staff.

2. Part II: Choosing Emotional Competence. Part II explores an argument that has shaped and defined the service economy and is even more critical to the experience economy. This debate focuses on whether service workers labor under emotional duress when they offer friendly customer service or whether they display emotional competency when they deliver positive emotions as part of the service package.

This argument is one that runs deep in business and academic circles. We have positioned this debate with Arlie Hochschild, professor of sociology at the University of California, Berkeley, as a representative for the side that argues service workers, out of necessity, must detach themselves from their own feelings when providing service, and Maureen O'Hara, dean of faculty at Saybrook Graduate

School, as the spokesperson for the side that asserts emotional competency and its expression are positive, personally advantageous, and basic to fulfillment.

We have entered an era where a measure of psychological enlightenment and emotional sensitivity is a prerequisite for competent management. Staff, as well as customers, in today's service/experience economy demand it. The job of emotionally competent leadership is to create and manage the emotional context of business so staff will be aware of and trust their own feelings as they provide service. If we fail to do this, people will begin to lose contact between that which they feel and that which they experience; they will become, in short, inauthentic.

3. Part III: Maximizing Customer Experiences with Empathy. Our third part examines the emotional connections that create positive, shared experiences between staff and customers. The most potent means to maximize customer experiences is with empathy, the common boundary of emotional connectivity. Therefore, to measure an organization's effectiveness with customers requires surveys that assess more than just "satisfaction." Measuring levels of customer satisfaction is barely relevant as a tool for understanding the customer emotional reactions that create loyalty.

4. Part IV: Viewing Complaints as Emotional Opportunities. Part IV deals with the most challenging aspect of customer service: how to maintain positive emotions in the face of service failures. By understanding and working with the emotional dynamics of complaints, companies can use service failures to deepen relationships and strengthen customer interactions, rather than to poison feelings as happens so frequently.

5. Part V: Using Emotional Connections to Increase Customer Loyalty. Our final part examines the emotional drivers of customer loyalty and shows how to increase customer retention by adding emotional value to experience. This requires understanding that loyalty is a two-way street, that customer loyalty is related to staff loyalty, that

loyalty resides in the emotional "extras" of service, and that perceived fairness is a major component of loyalty.

Achieving emotionally competent customer interactions is work that, like quality, is never done. We can take our customer relationships to a new level, an emotionally sensitive level, fully anticipating that another yet unidentified level will emerge. *Emotional Value* does not provide all the answers. It is, however, a prescription for where the service economy and its practitioners need to move next in today's fast-changing business culture.

Orientation of *Emotional Value*

The authors of this book are partners in an international training and consulting firm. As a consequence of heavy work schedules and geographically diverse clients, we spend a tremendous amount of time in airplanes and hotels. For this reason, many of our personal examples come from these two industries. We in no way wish to imply that the hospitality and travel industries are the only places to look for examples of emotional value or its lack. In fact, all one has to do is listen to people talk about customer interactions, and examples will appear throughout every sector of the economy, including government, high tech, retail, education, medicine, and now e-commerce.

We present dozens of ideas, options, and examples of organizations that have already begun to systematically add emotional value to their customers' experiences. We also rely on examples from our personal training and consulting projects. Our intention in writing about these experiences is to share examples with which we are personally acquainted. We apologize in advance to any reader who finds our selection of examples self-promoting rather than illustrative.

This book also contains a set of applications—tools that primarily come from our seminar and training experiences. While this book is not a training manual for using these exercises, we have found that they work very well for us. We have also included a set of "Assessing Your Organization" questions at the end of each of the book's five parts. These are questions we like to pose in our training programs or consulting interventions, or they are questions we have been asked ourselves by our many clients. They are also a means to take the content of this book and share it in discussion with others.

Emotional Value summarizes important and recent research in the service marketing field. We have attempted to survey both popular commentary and academic research and present them in such a way that they do not present a reading burden. While our goal is to walk you through the maze of thought and research on customer emotions, this book was *not* written as an academic text. To keep the text easy to read and yet provide background, this book is heavy with references and additional content in the endnotes and appendices.

The book is best read in the order written, as each part serves as a foundation for the next. The exercises, sprinkled throughout the text, are titled "Application" and are clearly marked in the text. If you are not interested in practical applications, you can skip over them. The same is true for the assessment questions at the end of each part.

ACKNOWLEDGMENTS

Emotional Value sits on the shoulders of hundreds of researchers who have painstakingly toiled in universities around the globe, carefully attempting to capture the essence of customer behavior. We thank you for your efforts and hope we faithfully reflected your conclusions as we translated astute statistical work into language that people who work in the day-to-day operations of business can understand and use.

We also owe a special debt of gratitude to the emotionally sensitive staff, especially Publisher Steven Piersanti himself, at Berrett-Koehler Publishers, Inc. They have become working partners with us as we refined the ideas in this book. Berrett-Koehler is a best-case example of how an organization can add emotional value and in the process create raving fans.

Our TMI colleagues also are to be acknowledged, especially those who read through more than one draft of this work and laboriously gave us their feedback, which we can only see as a magnificent gift. These include Paul Holden, Yvonne James, Chris Lane, Allan Milham, Bill Oden, Peta Peter, Ralph Simpendorfer, Jill Sweatman, and Elcee Villa. The San Francisco TMI staff managed ongoing business as the authors completed this book. Thank you, Lynne Barnard, Jaie Hightower, Jennifer Schmicher, and Lars Spivok for keeping us sane.

We must mention our families, who put up with our difficult schedules as this book was being written. Jeffrey Mishlove should be considered a coauthor in terms of his considerable contributions. Personal thanks to Judith Davison, who provided us with a powerful example of emotions in the health-care industry. We must also thank Sharon Goldinger for holding our feet to the fire to make sure the book's citations are correct and that the English soars. And a special thank you to Maureen O'Hara, who gave us hours of her time in a personal interview. Michael Edwardson has been incredibly generous, not only in writing the foreword for this book but also in sharing his comments and fascinating approach in the field of consumer emotions. In no way should he or anyone else who provided feedback to the authors about this book be held responsible for any errors. But they should receive credit for the things that are right.

Finally, this work would not have the focus it does were it not for all our customers, with whom we have worked over the years and who taught us the true importance of adding emotional value to our seminars and speeches.

ADDING EMOTIONAL VALUE TO YOUR CUSTOMERS' EXPERIENCE

Janelle's dentist recently moved to another town some distance from her home. Nonetheless, she travels to see him because of how she emotionally feels under his care. His rates are higher, and she has to drive almost fifteen miles farther to his office. Does the emotional connection that Janelle feels to her dentist and his assistants contribute to his bottom line? It is difficult, if not impossible, to exactly measure the monetary worth of emotional value, but it is definitely part of what service providers and organizations offer—and it is one of the largest drivers of customer loyalty. The ability to retain customers and sell more to them is, according to many business experts, the single most important predictor of economic success today.

Why does Nordstrom, the big Seattle, Washington–based department store chain, do so well, even with higher prices and fewer special sales, earning more per square foot than other similar operations? Talk with "Nordies" and they will tell you that it is not just their liberal return policy. Actually, many department stores have copied the Nordstrom guarantee on returned merchandise. It's the way customers feel when they return items to Nordstrom. There are few hassles and limited negative emotions.

We define emotional value as the economic value or monetary worth of feelings when customers positively experience an organization's products and/or services. *Emotional value, as much as quality or any other dimension of an organization's worth, can make or break a business.* It is as concrete as that. Cathay Pacific, the Hong Kong–based airline, found that the specific words used to settle lost luggage claims or handle other complaints were more important than the timeliness, accuracy, or compensation of the settlement in determining whether passengers would fly with the airline again.[1] This is a finding that should make everyone involved in business sit up and pay attention.

> Emotional value is the economic worth of feelings.

Emotional value refers to the feelings that customers experience or anticipate experiencing when they deal with organizations and their representatives. These feelings create a desire in customers to want to return to a place of business or go away and never come back. Emotional value is a concept that is ultimately more connected to customer retention than anything else. It is also the value that a company possesses when staff prefer to stay with their employers because of the feelings they have while working. *Both staff and customers tend to stay with organizations that enable them to experience positive, meaningful, and personally important feelings, even if the organizations cannot always provide everything they want or solve all their problems.*[2]

Most customers know instantly how they are emotionally impacted and how they feel about that, if not precisely, then generally, from the moment they walk into a place of business until they leave—with or without a purchase. In order to match the growing and inherent emotional sophistication of customers, service providers must upgrade their own emotional offerings to maintain a distinct competitive advantage.

The Experience Economy

Within easy historical memory, we have seen an evolution from an agricultural to a manufacturing economy. The manufacturing economy, still struggling with quality issues, has given way to the service economy. The service economy is in its early phases, and as we look closely at the service economy and its implications, we see that there are levels and nuances of service that most businesses have yet to attain. These include the careful introduction of competent emotional sensitivity. At one extreme end, service will have to support the orchestrated theatrical experiences referred to by Joseph Pine and James Gilmore in their new and groundbreaking book, *The Experience Economy*. One of the major characteristics of the experience economy, according to Pine and Gilmore, is that customers become engaged in a "personal way," requiring high levels of emotional competency from experience providers.

Pine and Gilmore distinguish the products of the different types of economies in the following way: "While commodities are fungible, goods tangible, and services intangible, experiences are *memorable*."[3] They make a compelling case that more and more of today's customers want and expect to be *positively, emotionally, and memorably* impacted at every level of their commercial existence. Whether or not most products or services in the future will be offered as themed experiences, as Pine and Gilmore use the term, a higher level of emotional competence will be required for the service economy also.

> *Customers want and expect to be positively, emotionally, and memorably impacted at every level of their commercial existence.*

Pine and Gilmore argue that the shift to the experience economy is happening, in part, because large numbers of products run the risk of becoming "commoditized," and commodities in a free-market economy do not enjoy high profit margins. To prevent products from becoming commodities, they contend, it is not enough for an organization to focus on products or services alone. In this book, we suggest that most companies haven't yet fully taken advantage of the power of emotionally sensitive service, let alone evolved to themed productions for customers. Perhaps it will be to an organization's advantage to create themed experiences for its customers, but it first needs to master service that is emotionally competent. It is our assessment that most companies have not

3

taken full advantage of the economic possibilities stemming from retaining customers by adding emotional value.

Customers always form judgments when they interact with organizations and staff. By filtering and processing sensory information, customers form emotional impressions (popularly referred to as Moments of Truth [MOTs]) that help them to remember and distinguish one experience from another.[4] These sensory service clues, many of which have a strong emotional component, need to be understood, managed, and ultimately delivered by individuals. This book focuses on the role of emotions in the customer experience and how individuals can provide emotional value to their customers so they are inclined to return. We assert that adding emotional value to customers' experiences is one of the strongest competitive advantages and *requires not only upgrading staff emotional competency but also upgrading business operations so they positively impact emotions within organizations.*

If we are to move to an experience economy for customers, we have to create an "experience" work environment for staff.

If we are to move to an experience economy for customers, we have to create an "experience" work environment for staff. In the 1980s, the quality concept quickly included personal quality, once organizations understood it was very difficult for workers to produce high quality goods if they did not have high personal quality standards. Likewise, service, as a concept, dramatically shifted once the concept of "customer" included both internal and external customers. Once businesses understood that external customers were treated pretty much the same way as internal customers, they began to focus on "internal service." Retention of external customers has a lot to do with retaining internal staff.

Most jobs in the developed world today are service positions. By the early 2000s, a stunning 80 percent of jobs in the United States will be service related—from fast-food workers, support staff, retail workers, and hospitality and travel employees to highly trained professionals—all demanding huge numbers of staff who can positively impact customers or clients memorably.

We are aware of the confusion regarding service job statistics, some showing very high percentages and others much lower. Part of the disparity in these numbers depends on how broadly "service" is defined. The U.S. government tends to define service more narrowly than some; even so, U.S. government projections are that the highest job growth is expected in four sectors: retail trade, business services, health services, and educational services. These sectors will account for two-thirds of the total number of created jobs in the first five years of the new millennium. At the turn of the twenty-first century, nine of the top ten job prospects in Minnesota will be found in the service industry. In the heavily industrial states such as Ohio and Michigan, the economy is also diversifying and shifting to service, moving away from manufacturing. The farming states are also seeing the creation of more service positions.[5]

No longer can service providers and service systems merely perform functions for customers. To be competitive in today's economy, businesses need to produce a distinctive *personal and emotional* experience for *each* of their customers. As a result, staff need to know how to interact in an emotionally intelligent manner and must possess a knack for listening to people, for showing empathy, and for "owning the problem" of enabling customers to feel positive emotions while using their products and services. They must be competent in delivering the highest quality of emotional interactions and feel good about the time they spend with their customers—whether the experience is a short-lived encounter, such as purchasing a hamburger at McDonald's, or a long-term relationship, such as buying insurance from an agent.

> To be competitive in today's economy, businesses need to produce a *distinctive* personal and emotional *experience for* each of their customers.

When service positions were fewer in number it was easier to hire personality types best suited for the unique demands of people-related work. Just as it once used to be that relatively fewer jobs required workers who could read and write, today most jobs require at least some level of literacy. If literate workers are not available for hire, then organizations must educate for the levels of literacy they require. This is also true for information technology skills. Likewise, with 80 percent of jobs projected to be service related, and many of these forced to support experience-based firms, organizations no longer have the luxury of being able to pick from a huge service pool to hire only the best-suited personality types. They must train, coach, and energize staff once they are hired.

Ari Weinzweig, cofounder of Zingerman's, a $10-million-a-year delicatessen in Ann Arbor, Michigan, describes the positive emotions he wants his staff to create with customers.

> I tell our people that you want the customer to think they're the best thing that has happened to you all day. We're not here to sell a loaf of bread or a sandwich or an apple. We're selling them an experience. It's not enough to sell people a great bottle of olive oil. Who cares? You've got to give them a great experience. People are going to go where they have a great experience, where it's fun, where they feel appreciated.[6]

The kinds of emotions recommended by Weinzweig are not achieved by simple scripting of how staff should address customers or perform their functions or by staff who would rather be anyplace else but at work. As a result of these considerable emotional demands, memorable positive experiences in the service industry are infrequent. Research tells us that over 60 percent of customers have switched service providers, but not because of the quality of products they have purchased—only 14 percent do that. Customers leave because of the way they are treated, or you might say, they leave because of how they feel.[7]

The Emotional Sting of Poor Service

All too often, negative interactions fill customers' emotional memory banks. The emotional sting of poor customer service—especially acute during complaint handling—stays with customers much longer than most service providers realize. We believe these memories of negative interactions stay with staff as well, making it easy to develop an attitude that says to customers, "I'd rather be anyplace else than here serving you, but I need the money." No one benefits in that situation. To quote Harvey Miller, co-owner of Quill Corporation, "People basically

The emotional sting of poor customer service stays with customers much longer than most realize.

6

want to do a good job. I have never heard anybody walk out of this building and say, 'Boy, I feel great! I did a lousy job today.'"[8]

In the past ten years, we have seen a great deal of public interest focused on positive and negative service delivery. Because of this widely publicized attention on customer service, consumers have an increasingly sophisticated understanding of service and are judging businesses by higher standards than ever before. Annual surveys are now available in many countries for all consumers to scan. According to these surveys, regrettably, businesses seem to be getting worse at customer service, rather than better—at least in consumers' eyes.

The University of Michigan's Customer Satisfaction Index's (CSI) annual service score has consistently dropped across all sectors—with the exception of the U.S. Postal Service, where competition has definitely inspired improved offerings. A closer look at the CSI suggests a problem with the people side of service. Year after year, Michigan's CSI finds that the products ranked highest are those that have the least amount of person-to-person delivery contact. For example, soft drinks are consistently ranked at the top of the CSI. Soft drinks are consumed daily by hundreds of thousands of people around the world, yet almost no one has any direct contact with the soft drink companies themselves. When consumers purchase a six-pack of Diet Coke from the grocery store and the checkout clerk is surly, they won't blame the Coca Cola Company for that lapse in customer service.

We summarize it this way: "When people are involved, things tend to get screwed up." This undoubtedly explains why automatic teller machines (ATMs) are so popular. Many customers, anticipating arguments, long waits, and hassles, prefer to limit their exchanges with service providers. The *Wall Street Journal* cites a poll suggesting that with each passing week as Christmas approaches, salespeople report getting "closer to the edge" of losing their tempers at customers, jumping from 18 to 24 percent in just one week's time.[9]

And this seems to be true around the world. Customer Service Benchmarking Australia does "mystery shopping" on 1,300 Australian help line numbers, measuring waiting periods and behavioral patterns. Its findings? A few call centers did well, but most were not inspiring. A worst-case scenario: one company was defensive 50 percent of the time, showed empathy only half the time, listened carefully and understood complaints half the time, and offered solutions none of the time![10] E-commerce seems to face the same challenges. A recent survey of on-line customer experiences suggests that 67 percent of customer purchases are not completed *largely because of lack of customer service.*[11] These findings tell us that there is tremendous room for improvement, and the companies that treat customers right will stake out a strong competitive position.

The Human Aspect of Customer Service

Because of the emotional focus of this book, we are primarily concerned with the human or personal aspect of customer experiences. This is the part of the service Herb Kelleher, CEO of Southwest Airlines, is committed to:

> I keep telling them [visitors to Southwest] that the intangibles are far more important than the tangibles in the competitive world because, obviously, you can replicate the tangibles. You can get the same airplane. You can get the same ticket counters. You can get the same computers. But the hardest thing for a competitor to match is your culture and the spirit of your people and their focus on customer service because that isn't something you can do overnight and it isn't something that you can do without a great deal of attention every day in a thousand different ways.[12]

We do not dismiss the importance of the tangible, or material, side of service. We know the tangibles are critical: the highest product quality, the most appropriate physical environment, and the best technology available to help customers. But, so are the intangibles: the smallest number of communication errors, the highest speed, the best reliability, and the most empathy. We are firmly committed to the notion that all of these factors make a competitive difference.

Nonetheless, research also tells us that organizations are almost always better at the material side of service than at the human side of service.[13] Furthermore, we know that both the "tangible" and the "intangible" sides of service are intertwined with emotional experiences. When a product does not perform, the system that produced it is at fault, and this system is influenced by human and emotional factors—as well as technical factors. It is not a question of focusing on one aspect at the expense of others, though certainly it does not benefit a company to teach staff how to create strong emotional links if none of the material basics are in place.

> *It does not benefit a company to teach staff how to create strong emotional links if none of the material basics are in place.*

After some combined forty years in the customer service business, the authors know that far too many companies put the bulk of their money, time, and effort into upgrading the material side of service. We think this happens because the tangibles, the goods used to deliver the total service experience, are easier to measure and manipulate. This must not lead to the faulty conclusion, however, that the material side of service is more important than the personal and emotional.

The Starting Point

Building emotionally competent relationships with customers starts with love, caring, and respect. Love obviously has different meanings to different people, depending upon the type of love to which they refer: self-love (self-esteem), sexual love, or maternal love. While some people might balk at the notion of using love in a business setting, we think Peter Senge's definition of love, presented in *The Fifth Discipline*, suggests a helpful basis for the relationships among organizations, staff, and their customers.[14]

Senge defines love as a commitment to someone else's growth and development. In a commercial relationship, this would mean that companies focus on how their products or services positively impact their customers. Since businesses receive payment for their services and because exchanging money for goods and services has a significant emotional component

> *Love: a commitment to someone else's growth and development.*

9

to it, we contend that love—*commitment to the betterment of customers*—is a desired basis for that exchange. Defined in Senge's terms, love can serve as the support that takes the powerful emotional component of the service experience into account.

Some cynics might call it hokey, but putting "heart" into customer service is not only good business, it is a necessary, competitive strategy in today's service/experience economy. Love, as defined by Senge, can also serve as the basis for an organization's standard of ethics. Robert Rabbin in his book *Invisible Leadership, Igniting the Soul at Work* puts it this way: "As we open to and embrace this power, this presence of love, we forge a new alliance with life and with work. We can depend upon that power to help us make clear and impeccable decisions."[15]

Even so, love by itself is not enough. Staff need to understand how they interact with and shape customer emotions. They also need practical skills in changing negative emotional states. They need persistence in not succumbing to their own negative judgments of customers, and they need to know how to read emotions in both themselves and others. Finally, staff must know how to tie together the material, personal, and emotional dimensions of the service experience. One could say these are the delivery mechanisms of love.

At its most fundamental level, this book is a call for civility, empathy, and authenticity when interacting with customers. In this regard, we draw from modern commentators such as Harvard Professor Sara Lawrence-Lightfoot, who in her latest book, *Respect: An Exploration*, explores why respect is the single most important ingredient in relationships. Lawrence-Lightfoot sees respect as capable of providing symmetry in unequal relationships, so relevant in the service industry.[16]

We, like Professor Lawrence-Lightfoot, propose that defensiveness, lack of forgiveness, resentment, and a desire for revenge lead to escalations in anxiety, hostility, wasted energy, and a lack of respect on everyone's part. This book takes into consideration that *both* customers and service providers have long memories for rudeness or poor treatment. While forgiveness, empathy, and respect can lead to better relationships with customers, these same responses in difficult service encounters can also create heightened self-esteem, a more hopeful mood, and more positive experiences for service providers. Finally, if customer service is to be delivered effectively, the attitudes and tools in *Emotional Value* must positively add to *both* customer *and* staff experiences.

PART ONE

BUILDING AN EMOTION-FRIENDLY SERVICE CULTURE

The greatest revolution in our generation is the discovery that human beings, by changing the inner attitudes of their minds, can change the outer aspects of their lives.

—William James

Emotions influence every aspect of our thinking life: they shape our memories; they influence our perceptions, our dreams, thoughts, and judgments—and our behaviors, including our decisions whether to return to a place of business, how much we are willing to pay for a product or service, and what we tell our family and friends about our experiences. Emotions are more than mere cognitive processes and indeed more than just feelings.

Emotions influence human reasoning. Emotions shape judgment. And emotions shape behavior. When "customer" is added to these last three statements, they read: *Emotions influence customer reasoning. Emotions shape customer judgments. And emotions shape customer behaviors.* Given this, it is a very good idea to pay close attention to customer emotions and attempt to influence them in the most positive manner.

Emotions in business are even more complex and less readily standardized, measurable, and manageable than previously thought.[1] But as Marta Vago, a family-business consultant, says, "You can't divorce emotions from the workplace because you can't divorce emotions from people. The challenge is not to get rid of emotions but to understand them and manage them in oneself and others."[2] Self-awareness on both an organizational and an individual level is the key to starting the process of adding emotional value to service offerings.

CHAPTER ONE

THE CUSTOMER IS ALWAYS EMOTIONAL

Customers are not always right. They make mistakes; they forget things; they get confused. But customers are always emotional. That is, they always have feelings, sometimes intense, other times barely perceptible, when they make purchases or engage in commercial transactions. Some people dread shopping of any kind. Others define their lives by their purchases. Entertainment for them is a big shopping mall. Indeed, some people spend their vacations at the Mall of America in Minneapolis, Minnesota. They even get married there!

One thing is certain: no one is entirely neutral about consuming. In part this is because money is involved with consumption. British psychologists Adrian Furnham and Michael Argyle, in *The Psychology of Money,* summarize the complex variety of issues surrounding people's emotional attachment to money: "Money is publicly disavowed, and privately sought after; and simultaneously, is the most important quality in the world, but spoken of as having little value."[1]

No one is entirely neutral about consuming.

Consider buying a home. Every real estate broker knows that purchasing a home is invariably an emotional experience for the buyer. Most brokers, as a result, understand that emotional cues can make selling a home a whole lot easier. For example, a subtle scent of cinnamon or vanilla creates a homey feeling, as does the smell of baking bread or chocolate chip cookies. One real estate broker reports, "I had one customer who baked cookies and had three full-price offers in one day."[2] Make customers feel good, realtors advise, and the chances of selling a home increase dramatically.

Ask people why they bought something and you will hear such comments redolent with emotions: "I wanted it." "I needed it." "I just felt like buying it." "I simply liked it." "I figured I deserved it." "John has one, and I had to have it, too." "The clerk told me it looked good on me." "I felt like splurging." "It was on sale, so I grabbed it at a good price." Join a travel writer as she playfully, yet seriously, describes what she calls her *emotional addiction* to the *experience* of expensive hotels:

> Like most addictions, it is full of pleasure, and like most neurotics I feel I have it in hand. I consider it a branch of art appreciation, but of a particularly subtle, interactive kind: for in my view, a hotel and its guests are engaged in a kind of minuet of mutual inference, each responding to the other's vibes and gestures. . . . This is the touch of theater that is essential to the nature of expensive hotels. These people are playacting and are tacitly inviting people like me to join the cast.[3]

Consuming Is an Act of Emotional Engagement

The root definition of *consume* is "to get." The origin of the word *emotion* is "to move." When you put the two words together, you have a situation where in the getting, consumers are moved. Consuming is not an act of detachment. It is an experience filled with emotions, some positive, others negative. And each situation elicits different emotions, depending on what the experience means to the consumer. In reality, emotions are always present, as indicated by University of Southern California

In reality, emotions are always present.

Professor of Marketing Jay A. Conger: "In the business world, we like to think that our colleagues use reason to make their decisions, yet if we scratch below the surface we will also find emotions at play."[4]

Emotions are part of product and service branding. When people are asked what particular brands represent, some kind of emotional identification is almost always made. Scott Colwell, vice president of marketing for Friendly Cafes, which has a strong name recognition in the northeastern United States, describes the essential and emotional part of Friendly's brand: "It's absolutely critical for the business long-term to develop a unique relationship with customers through branding. They need to know that Friendly's stands for quality food and ice cream *in a fun environment.*"[5]

Listen to the emotional richness of life described by Syracuse University Professor of Ethics and Political Philosophy Michael Stocker:

> Emotions . . . are found throughout much if not all of our life, not just in more or less discrete and eventlike emotional goings-on. Emotions and affectivity are found in the backgrounds, the tones and tastes of life . . . various forms and levels of interest, concern, and liveliness. [Emotions] characterize and help make up the ordinary, often unremarkable and often unnoticed, flow of life."

Every great philosopher since earliest times has recognized that emotions are basic motivators for action. In a nutshell, life is about experiencing emotions. Depression, to use everyday language, is a state of flattened or suppressed emotions. In acute states of depression, people will stay in bed all day long staring at the wall, feeling as little as possible. Emotions can become so buried in a state of depression, they barely get out at all.

Emotions are the basic motivators for action.

We suspect some businesspeople would like to do the impossible and remove emotions and passion from the customer experience—perhaps even from the total business experience. A review of a single day of the Money section in *USA Today,* however, reveals hundreds of emotion words to describe business topics.[7] Emotion words are peppered throughout headlines, in ads, and by the dozens in article after article of that issue.

In one such article, Apple Computer's new design for iMac is described as finding the "soul" of the computer. "Capture the feeling of the computer," was the guiding mantra of the designer, Jonathan Ives, as he gave "distinctive personality" to the hot-selling and brightly colored iMacs. "To design an object that elicits the reaction of 'I really want that' is enormously fun," Ives boasted. "We design objects that are totally seductive. A computer absolutely can be sexy; yeah, it can."[8]

This approach has worked for Apple. Regarding its predicted death knell, John Sculley, former head of Apple, says, "The turnaround isn't a fluke. It's back to the future. Steve (Jobs) has done an absolutely sensational job of turning Apple into what he always wanted it to be."[9]

The newly redesigned Beetle (once a "soulful" 1960s car), judged the best car of 1998, is described in that same issue of *USA Today* in evocative, emotional terms by head designer Rudiger Folten: "The shape of the car draws on people's emotions. It makes them feel warm and optimistic."[10] Scott Cook, chairman of Intuit, underscores the role of emotions when he describes the high-tech market: "People don't buy technology. They buy products that improve their lives."[11]

"There is a strong emotional component to the objects themselves that motivates people to buy."

Maine-based Thomas Moser Cabinetmakers puts out a quality product but anchors it into what Moser himself calls "soul." He says, "We don't sell furniture." Rather, he looks at the emotionality in his product. "There's a set of values resident in our furniture that attracts customers. They're not just buying something to sit in, something well made and well designed, or something the neighbors will envy. These are all motivations, but there is a strong emotional component to the objects themselves that motivates people to buy."[12]

Emotions Imply Obligations

While adding excitement, emotions are also messy to manage and they carry implications. Unethical business practices are easily reinforced when there is a lack of emotional sensitivity. Tobacco industry executives and employees do not have to feel responsible for the pain of smoking-related illnesses if they are able to convince themselves that the decision to smoke is a choice on the part of smokers, that addiction doesn't occur with nicotine. Executives of companies that pollute don't have to be concerned about human pain and suffering if they can convince themselves that business decisions are merely "logical" and necessary choices in a competitive world. Nor do medical personnel have to get involved with distraught parents if they stay focused on the technical side of a child's health care.

Accepting the fact that emotions play a part in business transactions might make organizations more sensitive to a whole range of issues and actually make them stronger by integrating the human element in daily work. As we move into the twenty-first century, there is growing support for these ideas. The Hay Group's benchmark of high-performing corporate cultures found them very different from ordinary companies. All the high performers recognize the *priority* of a strong corporate culture; in addition, they focus on "teamwork, customer focus, fair treatment of employees, initiative, and innovation."[13] As a result, they attract the best employees. When high-performing company executives are emotionally aware, they are not afraid to add real emotional value to their internal cultures. Indeed, they view it as a necessity.

High-performing companies view emotional value as a necessity.

Keeping consumer and staff emotions positive through emotionally aware managerial practices is the kernel of continuing success for organizations that offer services and products. Keeping moods positive impacts even ordinary, common service problems such as waiting time. Research suggests that any activity feels shorter when moods are positive and that customers will put up with longer waiting periods when they feel good.[14]

Positive emotions generally create commitment, excitement, and energy while negative emotions may arouse revenge, disgust, and a desire to never return. Keeping emotions as positive as possible is a challenging obligation for twenty-first century organization managers and service providers.

Emotions Matter

Emotions are *not* easy to define, especially if you are looking for a single sentence or phrase to do the job. Nonetheless, most of us seem to know what we are talking about when we use the word "emotions." After all, we experience so many of them so much of the time. Psychologists B. Fehr and J. A. Russell summarize the problem succinctly: "Everyone knows what an emotion is, until asked to give a definition. Then it seems, no one knows."[15]

There are probably as many definitions of emotions as there are different emotions themselves, of which there are hundreds.

There are probably as many definitions of emotions as there are different emotions themselves, of which there are hundreds. (See Appendix A.) One twenty-year-old book lists ninety-two distinct definitions of emotions.[16] Academicians have difficulties defining emotions because each definition carries within it a set of assumptions. As a result, tightly parsed academic definitions of emotions are difficult to apply or even understand in the day-to-day world. One such definition we found is that an emotion is a "valanced affective reaction to perceptions of situations."[17] Imagine frontline staff hearing that explanation![18]

What Do Emotions Tell Us about Customers?

A definition of emotions that we think gets close to being inclusive and yet is understandable for most people is psychologist Erik Rosenberg's: "Emotions are acute, intense, and typically brief psycho-physiological changes that result from a response to a meaningful situation in one's environment."[19] Rosenberg's definition contains three essential elements related to consumers: (1) emotions are about what matters to customers; (2) emotions are relatively brief experiences and provide us with a snapshot view of how customers relate to service, service providers, and products; and (3) emotions are accompanied by body changes. If these body clues are accurately read, they can tell us how customers will likely behave. In short, emotions are brief, noticeable, and important!

1. Emotions tell us what matters to customers. When customers experience emotion, it is because something important is happening to them. If service transactions had no value to customers, customers wouldn't have emotions about them. In the experience economy, this is a point worth emphasizing. Consider the following example.

> *If service transactions had no value to customers, customers wouldn't have emotions about them.*

A woman we know developed breast cancer and in the process of her treatment came to know other cancer patients. One day she went to see her oncologist, whom she shared with a woman colleague who had recently succumbed to her disease. The oncologist, our friend discovered, had *not* been notified of the death of his patient. In an attempt to sort through her searing emotions about this giant health-care corporation, our friend wrote the following:

> By the time I left the doctor's office, I was very upset, although I said nothing to him. He felt bad about Sue's [name changed] death, and his lack of knowledge wasn't through any fault of his own, but rather through the fault of the medical system. . . . Although Sue had been admitted to the hospital on Friday and had been pronounced dead in the same hospital's emergency room on the following Monday, her oncologist who was actively treating her at the time of her death was never notified. It is as if Sue's life, her pain, and her death meant nothing at all to the medical system.
>
> If there is a "colder" example of treatment in medicine, I have yet to hear it. In this age of computers, how difficult could it be for one system to program notification of either your hospitalization or your death to the specialist actively treating you? The answer is that it wouldn't be difficult. The answer is that within this medical system you are nothing but a common animal who pays your premiums and in turn is given an identification number. Sue's story stands as evidence

21

of the haughtiness, coldness, insensitivity, and materialistic values of this system. To think that a person can live and die while actively being treated and never have their doctor even be notified of their death, THAT'S COLD.

Customer emotions, not always stated so strongly and eloquently as the above example, are a clear statement of what is important to medical consumers. The more relevant a situation is to someone's goal, the stronger the emotion is likely to be. In the case of our friend, her strong goal is to survive, rather than to be another forgotten breast cancer statistic. Is it too much for a medical patient to ask that her personal anguish be acknowledged by her caregivers? After all, her emotions are as much a part of who she is at that moment as is her scarred chest.

Customer experiences, as the above example demonstrates, are stories—small scenarios of experience. And customers show up at places of business with their own unique histories, remembering events—many times without conscious awareness—that influence the reality of their current experience. Service providers are frequently forced to deal with strong customer emotions that have nothing to do with the transaction under way. But any displayed emotions are *related to something that currently matters* to the customer, and service providers need to competently interact with the total customer experience—because that is what is occuring at the moment.

> Customer experiences are stories, small scenarios of experience.

Customer emotions are influenced by memories and a wide array of factors, including

- life circumstances (for example, customers wake up elated or they get up on the "wrong side of the bed");

- expectations already formed—largely based on advertising—before walking into a store, making a telephone call, or seeing a professional;

- perceptions of what is happening around them (what they see when they walk into a place of business or visit an e-commerce site, what they hear, what they smell [ambient odor of the site], and perhaps what they taste or touch);

- public reputation or what others have told them about a particular organization;

- the first few seconds and the last few seconds of the interaction with representatives of this business;

- personal pride they feel from their choice of purchases or suppliers;

- quality and intensity of the exchanges they have with service representatives and other customers (easy or problem-filled), promises made to them, words of invitation or exclusion, amount of time spent waiting;

- any follow-up activities.

Service providers do not need to psychoanalyze their customers; at a minimum, however, they need to understand that something important is happening to customers when they display emotions—even if customers never state this directly. Consider the difference this awareness could make in dealing with customers. Frontline staff could say to themselves when interacting with an irritated customer, "Something of importance is happening to this person," rather than "This customer is a jerk ... or nasty ... or uptight." There is a chance of creating positive emotional value when staff are aware of the customer's emotional state, rather than negatively judging customer behavior.

> *Something important is happening to customers when they display emotions.*

One of the authors called a high-volume-flyers telephone line to order an international business-class airplane ticket. Shortly into the conversation, the ticket agent said, "You can't do this." ("This" was an extra loop between two cities the author needed to make.) Actually, passengers can fly any routing they want as long as flights are available; they just have to pay more for the ticket. The author had had a long, hard day, she was prepared to pay a lot of money for this ticket, and she replied to the ticket agent, "We'll have a lot easier time setting up this ticket if you don't tell me what I can't do." Here's the response she got in return: *"Now, don't you get an attitude with me!"* Clearly, the ticket agent saw an irritated customer who needed to be put in her place, rather than a valued customer who had just voiced something of importance to her. The potential cost to the airline: a $7,500 business-class ticket and a high-volume customer.

2. Emotions tell us how customers relate to service providers. When two people are involved in a consumer exchange, a social interaction is taking place. Because of the brevity of many emotions, social interactions can quickly change directions emotionally.[20] By reading emotional cues, it is possible to quickly determine whether the customer and the service providers are sharing a positive experience. If the service provider is seen to be unhelpful, rude, or uncaring—or conversely, eager to help, friendly, and interested—these attitudes matter to customers and they typically respond in kind. In fact, of all the factors that can be measured about how service providers deliver service, the one that most strongly creates negative responses are failures to "meet minimum standards of civility."[21]

If someone had been listening to the exchange with the airline's ticket agent described above, it would have been crystal clear that something negative was happening. Interestingly, we have shared this example with many people, and a few think that the author created the negativity in that situation and is, therefore, responsible for it. "Stop blaming the service representatives when they snap back at you," we were told in no uncertain terms by a "service expert." While we agree that it is "nice" to be a "nice customer," we also believe ultimately *it is the service providers' responsibility to manage the emotions in service exchanges.* Of course, organizations can always decide that they don't want to do business with "direct" customers such as the authors represent, and that is their choice.

> It is the service providers' responsibility to manage the emotions in service exchanges.

It's a costly way to approach customer service, however, and we suspect the airline would rather have had its service representative handle the situation better than lose the sale of that $7,500 ticket.

3. Emotions tell us how customers will likely behave. If customers are angry, they feel threatened at some level and are primed to attack. If customers feel fear, they may be impelled to escape or leave or not come back. If they feel pleased, thrilled, or delighted, they will be inclined to stay longer and return to experience more of that feeling. Emotions, in brief, predict future behavior.

Psychologist Richard Lazarus points out that people are constantly evaluating the situations they experience. An event happens, and then individuals reach conclusions or judgments influenced by internal factors (personality, beliefs, and goals) and by external factors (responses by other people, product quality). These judgments lead to feelings, subjective experiences, reflected in facial expressions or other forms of body language that are available for reading by a sensitive service provider. Along with feelings comes an "action tendency." This action tendency is something that the person wants to accomplish—a goal, if you will.[22]

Psychologist Michael Edwardson, at the University of New South Wales in Australia, has broken new ground in applying cognitive psychology concepts of emotion (as represented by Richard Lazarus and others) to consumer emotions. Edwardson argues that if you can identify the emotion, then you can identify an "emotional script." An emotional script, an idea well established in research on emotions, is a pattern that goes from event, to thought, to feeling, to action. Emotional scripts all have specific goals.

Edwardson writes, "This sequence of sub-events can happen almost simultaneously and not be under conscious control of the person."[23] Edwardson, along with other marketing experts, is beginning to map the scripts that are unique to each emotion. Within the field of customer service, this means it will be possible to logically predict likely customer behavior once specific emotions have been identified.[24] In Edwardson's words, "This concept gives us a framework for research into services that focus on developing, for the first time, a catalogue of emotions experienced by consumers."[25]

Michael Edwardson's interpretation of the impact emotions have on behavior suggests that service providers must not only be able to understand customers' experiences, but they also need to know how to influence emotional scenarios from negative to positive. As Edwardson writes,

> Emotional episodes can flow from bad to good or bad to worse depending on the service person. E.g., bad to worse; impatient—angry—neglected—cheated—upset . . . the customer vows never to return: or bad to good; nervous—impatient—encouraged—happy . . . started poorly but ends positively.[26]

The Link among Passion, Loyalty, and Emotions

Modern academic psychologists believe that the computer is a good model for the mind. Indeed, many academic psychologists describe their work as "mind science," and in so doing they conveniently downplay the "emotional" part of emotions. These influential psychologists describe emotions as "thoughts" about situations in which humans find themselves. Many businesses, in turn, have largely ignored the role of emotions.

There are exceptions, however, to this collective attempt to ignore emotions, notably in the entertainment industry, which clearly understands the selling of emotions. The movie industry carefully studies the emotional reactions of focus groups to help with film editing, sequencing, and even plot endings. Its sole purpose is to create an emotional impact on movie viewers so that large numbers will return to the theater to see the film over and over again, tell all their friends about it, and then buy a video copy for themselves and every tee-shirt, wall poster, and desk ornament representing the film they can get.

Part of the reason why so many academic psychologists have ignored the "emotional" part of emotions is that they believe thinking is logical (hence, scientific), and emoting is illogical (hence, nonscientific). To get around this scientific problem of studying something that is nonscientific, many psychologists describe emotions as *thinking processes*, rather than *feeling experiences*. Unfortunately, this approach removes passion from emotional experience. This is definitely not good to do when an

organization is attempting to build staff and customer loyalty. After all, if emotions, especially passion, are not at the basis of loyalty, what is?

> *If emotions, especially passion, are not at the basis of loyalty, what is?*

Human experience tells us that emotions are
much more than mere thoughts. We can have a
thought about the blueness of the sky, but that in no
way compares to the elation we feel standing on a tall peak basking in the
twilight blueness surrounding us. Personal experience also suggests that
emotions are not always illogical. Indeed, thinking can be illogical, while
an emotional reaction can more accurately reflect a situation. Thought
and perception, in actuality, can be as highly subjective as emotions are.
We look at a red rose and experience its redness both objectively and sub-
jectively. Thoughts, we would argue, are the end result of the processing
of unconscious subjective emotional information—just as emotions are.

Humans constantly seek emotional experiences; our behavior is frequently chosen to either enhance or subdue emotional states. We choose
to view one movie over another in part because of the feeling state the
movie will create. Janelle avoids all scary movies; Dianna loves to be
frightened in the theater. Dianna's teenage daughter paid for and sat
through two showings of *Titanic*, back to back, because of her emotional
reaction to the movie—as apparently did thousands of other young girls
around the world. One could guess, as many have, that life without emotions would be life not worth living. It would be boring, without variety.
And it would just about kill the modern consumer economy.

Valuing the Emotionality in Customer Communications

Customers communicate with their emotions, and service providers
must respond. When customers are highly emotional, service providers
may try to get them to settle down by saying, "Don't get emotional." What
they really mean is, "Don't display your emotions." Many service staff
clearly feel uncomfortable around emotional displays, most likely
because they don't know how to manage such public displays. Frankly,
they're scared.

However, from the customers' point of view, they have just spent time and/or money, and it is difficult for them to not engage in an emotional communication (either positively or negatively) about their situation. When service providers ask their customers to not get emotional, they are telling their customers, "Don't react to the fact that you feel excited, overwhelmed, cheated, used, or mishandled." This is the equivalent of saying, *"Don't get emotional about the emotions you are experiencing."*

Customers are expected to be rational about time and money (that is, nonemotional), when time and money almost always elicit emotions—and very frequently, strong emotions. Service providers may think customer emotions get in the way of solving problems. And from their point of view, this may be the case. *However, from the customers' point of view, emotions are part of the total communication experience, and they must be acknowledged.* Very few customers have a positive response to being told, "Settle down, or I can't help you."

Emotions are part of the total communication experience, and they must be acknowledged.

Take the case of health care. When patients are scheduled for surgery, they want to be seen as human beings by the surgeon, not "the kidney" or some other body part, which frequently is how surgery patients are described. Part of the reason for this is that the patient thinks of himself or herself as more than "the kidney." Logically, the patient may think that if the surgeon thinks of him or her as a specific individual and not just a kidney, the surgeon might have greater concern and the patient would, therefore, receive better personal service. Unfortunately, because many physicians may not know how to manage the intense emotions frequently encountered in health care, they have a psychological need to distance themselves, and they have many strategies for that, including referring to patients as body parts.

We once heard a medical doctor say about a complaining patient, "I don't understand why he was upset. I saved his leg, didn't I?" This doctor was not acknowledging that his patient was more than a leg to save. Perhaps it is easier for the doctor to merely relate to a leg, but this approach is limiting if the doctor's goal is to grow a business. Saved legs don't refer other patients.

The way the event is *handled* has as much significance for the customer as the event itself. Positive feelings about service experiences are much more than simple judgments about service outcomes. Customer judgments about how service is "handled" have a great deal to do with consumers' innate sense of justice. If we order a product that is faulty and we return it to a store, our total feelings are about more than just whether we get our money back. Psychologist William G. Austin writes, "Justice pertains not merely to outcome distributions, but also to how the distribution is arrived at *and* the manner by which it is implemented."[27] While not writing for the customer service field, psychologist Michael Stocker puts the idea in a more poetic form: "For the acts themselves, not just their outcomes, are valued."[28] And it is by an emotional assessment that customers largely place their own *value* on the service transaction. If service providers do not grasp this basic fact, then even after treating customers rudely, making them wait, and embarrassing them in public, they will feel justified in making comments such as "Why are they upset? I gave them their money back, didn't I?"

> *The way the event is handled has as much significance for the customer as the event itself.*

In fact, emotions are as good a basis for customers to make solid buying decisions as any other. When events are proceeding positively, customers, in effect, ask for an enhancement or continuation of their feelings. When emotions are negative, customers most likely are asking for the situation to be changed. The reactions customers receive to their emotions have a tremendous amount to do with whether they will return—and in what mood they will return.

Why should customers go back to places of business if they feel negative? Maybe it's for cheap prices or if there are no alternatives or if they are locked into an incentive program. If customers do not feel strong positive emotions, why not check out the competition? They might feel better with another supplier. Many businesspeople, including Marcy

Wydman, owner of a sheet-metal fabrication and galvanizing business, instinctively understand this:

> If you can figure out what it is that the customers are passionate about, what it is that's important to them, and respond accordingly, and develop a good relationship that's based on more than just providing goods or service, then I think you're going to develop more loyalty and long-term business.[29]

And for this reason, even if emotions are difficult to manage and measure, they must be taken into consideration when attempting to build long-term relationships with customers. At a minimum, if we recognize positive emotional states in ourselves and in others, this helps generate more positive emotions and encourages civilized behavior.[30] There is plenty of research—and just plain common sense—to support the notion that pleasant behaviors are more likely to produce friendships than impolite, unpleasant behaviors.[31]

When we recognize positive emotional states, it helps regulate emotions and encourages civilized behavior.

When Janelle had her first teaching job at twenty-one years of age, she was not very sophisticated about approaching the parents of her students. She would call the parents and tell them their children were uncooperative and poor students—because they didn't turn in their homework assignments. Logically, it was accurate, but it was an emotionally stupid tactic to take with parents. Janelle learned her lesson after two disastrous telephone calls. When she called the next parent, she began her conversation this way: "I need your help." It was hard for parents to turn her down, particularly when she emphasized how capable and smart their children were. Janelle eventually got 100 percent cooperation from the parents to check their children's homework to see that it was finished before they went to bed at night.

Sensitive interpersonal behaviors can serve as the foundation to becoming emotion friendly for both organizations and service providers who want to improve their "customer" relationships, whether these are paying customers or colleagues. Ultimately, if service providers have no awareness of or little concern for the emotional states of their customers, they will find it very difficult to manage customer experiences. A healthy way to view emotions is not as problems to be solved but rather as the basis for forming relationships. As such, emotions have inherent value.

Emotions are not problems to be solved. Rather they are the basis for forming relationships.

CHAPTER TWO

MANAGING EMOTIONS BEGINS WITH ME

In order to deal effectively with feelings, everyone needs to be aware of his or her own full range of emotional states. This will help one to avoid being trapped or hijacked (to use Daniel Goleman's term) by emotions. Goleman, in his bestselling book, *Emotional Intelligence,* defines self-awareness as "a neutral mode that maintains self-reflectiveness even amidst turbulent emotions."[1] The term "awareness" is closely linked to both eastern and western philosophical traditions. Socrates, considered by many to be the father of the field, summarized philosophy with the simple phrase "Know thyself."

Customers come to our businesses riding in on the ship of their own emotions. Service providers join them on that ship. By being aware of the emotional connections within this transaction, service providers can help guide the ship in the best direction for everyone concerned. This requires both self-awareness and other awareness. It also demands involvement and objectivity, control and reaction, self-focus and outer focus.

The Power of Self-Awareness

Awareness: 1. having knowledge of something through alertness in observing or in interpreting what one sees, hears, feels; 2. having knowledge of a sensation, feeling, fact, condition, etc.

Becoming an emotion-friendly organization requires a basic understanding of human emotions and an awareness of personal emotional states. Through awareness we, in effect, become both the actor and the audience. This active participation and observation enables us to better understand ourselves and others. Awareness enables us to experience our emotions while simultaneously creating them; it also enables us to consciously influence our emotional states in a positive direction. Finally, self-awareness lets us delve into a deeper unconscious understanding, making it more likely that we will reduce the impact of unconscious reactions, such as prejudice and hostility. Self-awareness, in short, lets us live consciously.

Often poor service results from behaviors that are not intentional but unconscious, including racial, social-class, and sex-role treatment differences. One study of both male and female sales clerks, for example, found that clerks give male customers more positive expressions (smiling, eye contact, thanks, greetings) than they give female customers.[2] Men tend to get waited on before women, not only in men's departments but also in women's and "neutral" departments, such as luggage sections of stores.[3] The authors, both female, have noted this difference in levels of treatment when they travel. When flying business class, they frequently wait for their coats to be put away and many times are not asked if they want refills on their beverages. One of the authors, while fully awake, was once completely skipped over for meal service. We don't believe service providers do this intentionally, but they certainly aren't operating with a great deal of self-awareness either! TWA recognizes the importance of treating its female travelers better. It has sent 10,000 front-line employees to a two-day training program in part emphasizing bet-

> *Much of poor service results from behaviors that are not intentional, but unconscious.*

34

ter service to female travelers, including how to deal with females' perception that men get preferential treatment while flying.[4]

Psychologists Heath Demaree and David Harrison have looked at how poor awareness of physical arousal and felt emotions increases the likelihood of hostility. In simplest terms, if you don't know what is going on with yourself physically and emotionally, according to Demaree and Harrison, in stressful situations your system reverts to hostility.[5] In the customer service environment, this hostility leads to blaming customers.

> *If you don't know what is going on with yourself physically and emotionally, your system reverts to hostility in stressful situations.*

If a person suffers a severe injury to specific portions of the brain, self-awareness can be considerably reduced. If this capacity is not restored as the brain heals, the patient faces a major barrier to successful social rehabilitation.[6] Self-awareness is more than a modern-age luxury. It is a critical element of healthy human functioning and it is the emotional foundation of service.

By using self-awareness, healthy service providers can avoid hostile and prejudicial unconscious behaviors. Perhaps more importantly, they can be consciously involved in their emotional exchanges with customers and colleagues without denying their feelings and yet without engaging in inappropriate responses with customers. By mastering awareness, the most basic of emotional intelligence skills, service staff can create a solid foundation for authentic (real versus faked) service transactions.

Once we know how we feel, we have several choices available to us. We can (1) accept our mood or feelings and make no effort to change, (2) be overwhelmed by our feelings, or (3) rationally decide if this is the best emotional state for us to be in at the moment and then do something about it if it is not. If service providers can accomplish the latter for themselves, they have a chance of being able to do the same with customers.

▪ Application

Name That Feeling. One of the easiest ways to increase self-awareness is to periodically check how you are feeling. You can think of it as

"Name That Feeling." Start by listing all the emotional words you can. Look up more in a thesaurus if necessary. Some people have just a few emotional descriptors for their conditions: sad, angry, happy, jealous, surprised, or afraid. One could almost think of those six words as categories of emotions, rather than emotions themselves. Sad, for example, could include unhappy, depressed, bummed out, dejected, gloomy, heartbroken, crushed, bowed down, sick at heart, in the doldrums, feeling low, crestfallen, downcast, despondent, mournful, in the pits, miserable, wretched, bitter, joyless, sore, oppressed, sorry, pathetic, crummy, dreary, lifeless, and so on. Each descriptor is a slightly different emotional feeling. Then, using these subtle gradations of emotions, describe exactly what you are feeling. Check in with yourself throughout the day.

Visual Self-Awareness

One aspect of awareness is visual self-awareness. Its power was demonstrated in an experiment conducted in the Psychology Department at Towson State University. Researchers exposed students to music designed to elevate moods. One group was given small mirrors to observe their reactions while background music played; a second group was not given mirrors. The group with no reflection of themselves showed no reaction to the music, while the group that could see themselves reported an elevated mood.[7] This research supports statements we have heard from literally hundreds of call-center employees who say they work "better" if they watch themselves in a mirror.

■ Application

Increase Awareness through Visual Self-Awareness. Place a mirror by yourself when doing some normal activity, whether at work or at home. Get a mirror that is sufficiently large so it will be impossible for you to ignore your reflection. Note your feelings as you periodically watch yourself throughout this activity. Notice the reactions you have to seeing your facial expressions.

A type of visual self-awareness can be accomplished through journal writing. Organizations could encourage exploration of service experiences through writing and in so doing reap the benefits that seem to accrue to people who keep journals.

Researchers at both the State University of New York and North Dakota State University have found that writing about stressful experiences is an effective way to decrease the burden of stress. These researchers found that over half of their experimental groups actually experienced a reduction in a variety of ailments by keeping a journal.[8] Might it be possible for organizations to encourage this practice, perhaps even on electronic groupware so all service providers could benefit from shared insights of those willing to write about their service experiences? We are not aware of any organization that currently does this, but it could certainly be supportive of an emotion-friendly culture.

Awareness in Teams

Awareness can help an entire team provide better service. Staff could point out inappropriate customer treatment by their colleagues so they could be made more "aware" of their behavior and thereby consciously decide whether to continue customer-alienating behavior. Our experience, however, is that most staff do not get involved. Just recently, one of the authors flew from San Francisco to Chicago. She had checked her luggage outside the terminal, and she was in a long line at the gate waiting to confirm her seat. A man at the counter was talking with the gate agent to help his family with their tickets because only he spoke English, though the gate agent hadn't yet figured that out. When she realized that this man was not the passenger, she hysterically shouted at him, "Who is the passenger? I need to talk with the passenger!"

> *Awareness can help an entire team provide better service.*

The Spanish-speaking wife looked bewildered and said something feebly in Spanish. The gate agent, finally comprehending the language problem, then demanded, "Where are the *rest* of the passengers? They all need to be standing *right here!* I need to see *everyone's* identification!" The other passengers were toddlers, who were standing a few feet away playing with their grandmother. "They don't have ID yet," nervously explained the father. The man standing in front of me turned and commented, "That gate agent needs to take some Ex-Lax." Several of us laughed, though what this gate agent needed was a dose of awareness and then a mood adjustment.

Even though the other two gate agents were only a few inches away from the nasty tone of voice, the demands, and the put-downs this gate agent visited upon the hapless family, we understand why they didn't speak up to help their colleague through her unpleasant mood and inappropriate treatment of customers. When someone is emotionally aroused, he or she generally does not respond favorably to criticism. The gate agents probably feared making a bad situation worse. Special skills are needed for dealing with colleagues who act inappropriately, and managers need to address this issue in training or coaching sessions.

▪ Application

Awareness and Team Communication. The next time you observe a colleague mistreat a customer, approach your colleague and let him or her know that the action was inappropriate—without alienating your colleague. To do this, imagine yourself as your colleague. How would you like to be approached so you would maintain an open, receptive attitude to what you were about to hear? For example, perhaps you could start by asking in a supportive tone of voice, "What happened?" It's an open-ended question, and it will give your colleague an unlimited number of ways to respond, which will give you an unlimited number of ways to react. Then listen carefully and follow your instincts. How you approach your colleague will determine whether you "save" the situation or make it worse.

Awareness Is for Managers, Too

Self-awareness can have a major impact on managers as well. Allan Church with Warner Burke Associates compared high-performing managers with average-performing managers. His bottom-line conclusion is that high-performing managers are significantly more aware of their managerial behaviors than are average performers. In short, managers do better when they more closely monitor their own behavior.[9]

> *High-performing managers are significantly more aware of their own managerial behaviors.*

Fortune magazine's lead article in June 1999 was titled "Why CEOs Fail." In this wide-ranging survey, *Fortune* reported: "So how do CEOs blow it? . . . What is striking, as many CEOs told us, is that they usually know there's a problem; their inner voice is telling them, but they suppress it." *Fortune* points out that many CEOs simply refuse to see what is happening around them. *Fortune* concludes: "The failure is one of emotional strength."[10] No doubt this failure of emotional strength at the top is felt throughout the organization. Milt Koult, founder of Horizon Air, used to drive this point home, in his favorite terms, to one to the authors when she worked at Horizon: "The speed of the chief is the speed of the crew."

In order to build an organization that is emotion friendly, senior managers must create an environment where it is possible—and safe—for managers and supervisors to discuss their own emotions. This, in turn, will give permission to staff to consider their emotional issues. A growing but small number of today's senior-level managers purchase this opportunity by hiring personal coaches.

Most psychologists agree that suppressing thoughts contributes to increases in negative moods. Suppressed emotions of service providers can also "leak out" in inappropriate ways, frequently far away from managers' oversight. Nonetheless, the solution is not to turn organizations into therapy sessions. We have to reach a balance between spending excessive time focusing on emotions and silencing them. This demands that conversations about feelings and emotions be a comfortable, regular part of a corporate culture, with the understanding that awareness makes it easier to add emotional value to customers.

Managers need to reach the point where emotions are as much available for discussion as balance sheets, computer systems, product quality, staffing levels, or customer buy rates. Emotions must take on a tangibility that is as real as any other business asset of an organization. No longer should decisions be made that focus merely on speed, cost saving, or efficiency. In an organization with an emotion-friendly service culture, new telephone systems, for example, would be installed only after considering the emotional impact on customers as carefully as the number of years it takes to amortize the equipment. In such an organization, customer value would be considered not just in terms of "value for money" but in terms of "value for emotions" that retain customers.

Emotions need to be as real to staff as any other asset of an organization.

A major retailer in the Seattle, Washington, area recently installed a new telephone system in its stores. When a shopper calls to inquire about the availability of a product, the system asks which department the customer wants, leading the caller through an elaborate menu. Once the correct connection has been made, the caller is forced to wait for an extended period before anyone live picks up the phone. When finally connected, the customer is once again asked which department he or she wants and is then connected to the "right" department for another wait, even though supposedly the menu system should have connected the customer to the appropriate department in the first place.

When Dianna called one of these stores, she was on hold, long-distance, for an inordinate length of time, then finally reached the department she wanted, only to be disconnected when the clerk put her on hold to check on the availability of a product. Having invested a considerable amount of time in the project already, Dianna called back again long-distance, only to go through the entire menu once more. Finally, she reached the same clerk and shared her concerns about the "new" phone system. The clerk agreed, "It's brand new, and nobody likes it." How does a phone system that both staff and customers hate get installed, unless managers neither tested nor discussed the emotional ramifications of the changes? When Dianna asked the clerk to tell the store's management about her reaction, the clerk responded, "Oh, I can't do that; I don't know who handles phones." How does something as important as the telephone system get installed without staff knowing who is responsible for it? As Dianna says, the store thinks it has solved a problem, but in actuality, it is only going to make customers angrier.

In an organization with an emotion-friendly culture, staffing decisions would be made not only by considering profitability issues but also by looking at the emotional impact of any staffing increases or decreases. Positive affect needs to be as real to staff as room temperature. Emotions need to move out of the "virtual" discussion and into the concrete discussion of what they mean to an organization and the people who staff it and buy from it.

Building an emotion-friendly culture places additional knowledge demands on all staff, including managers. Mastery of technological methods or skills does not prepare one to discuss customer emotions. Many businesspeople who have been educated in technical areas will require assistance to reach the bar set as high as Susan Fournier, at Harvard's Graduate School of Business Administration, places it:

> *Building an emotion-friendly service culture places additional knowledge demands on all staff.*

> Understanding consumers' experience means embracing theories of philosophy, communications, counseling, psychology, and religious studies. Even such disciplines as medicine, law, and literature have a lot to offer. Each can give us a new, broad perspective on the emotional lives of our consumers and help us get past the narrow views that training has inured us to.[11]

Application

Ongoing Education for Emotional Competency. Because it is unrealistic to expect that staff will walk in the door with their education and knowledge complete, organizations have to provide such learning in a cost- and time-sensitive manner. Holding brown bag speaker lunches is one way to provide continuing education for emotional competency. You may already have in-house expertise with staff who have studied psychology. Many high-quality videotapes are also available. The teaching staff of a local university may also be available for speeches. Build a library, and link its existence to your corporate strategy of increasing emotional value.

Language literally allows us not only to talk about emotions but also to categorize and understand our feelings more precisely. Infants experience emotions, but they do not know what they are feeling or how to change these feelings. Infants are capable of experiencing their emotions only physically, as bodily states. Eventually they learn language skills so they can recognize various shades of emotional states. As parents help their children identify what they are feeling, anxiety and fear, for example, become distinct gradations of feelings. However, the process of emotional awareness and identification is more than simple language development. It is a means of becoming more sophisticated about feelings in general.

Psychologist Bernard Baars at The Wright Institute in Berkeley, California, uses the theater as a metaphor for understanding consciousness.[12] Consciousness, writes Baars, is the stage on which feelings, thoughts, sensations, and perceptions play to the audience of the unconscious mind. Focus, he continues, is normally at the center of the stage, though it is constantly being pulled one way or another in the drama that is being played out. Sensations and emotions, various competing parts of one's brain, are all tugging on our awareness.

Baar's metaphor applies equally well to both organizational dynamics and customer service. In the service arena, service providers and managers not only watch what is happening onstage but also actively participate in the drama. If customer representatives or managers are not aware of what is happening around them, they can be led by their emotions with little ability to understand or direct them. Customer service representatives can experience a difficult telephone exchange early in the day and hours later still act peeved by what the morning customer "had the audacity to suggest." Just as computer viruses are widely spread when they are not yet identified, the danger of spreading an emotional virus is highest when managers and representatives have no awareness or understanding of what is occurring onstage in the theater of their consciousness.

The danger of spreading an emotional virus happens when managers and service reps have limited awareness.

Application

Dissecting Emotions during Customer Moments of Truth. Organizational leaders need to define the essential mood/emotional states they would like their customers to be in while doing business with them. This can be done by identifying specific customer Moments of Truth, those critical moments in which your organization is being judged. Imagine yourself to be the customer experiencing these Moments of Truth. How would you feel about the level of service you have been offered? How would you like to feel? In order for you to want to return to this organization, how would you have to feel?

Application

Dissecting Emotions during Staff Moments of Truth. Just as customers evaluate the organization at their points of contact, so do staff judge their work environment. What are the critical MOTs your staff experience with you, the manager? Imagine yourself as a staff person reporting to yourself having experienced these Moments of Truth. How would you feel? How would you like to feel? In order for you to wake up motivated to go to work, how would you have to feel?

Organizational Culture and Emotional Awareness

Without the discussion and full understanding of emotions within groups, we have the organizational equivalency of the disorder *alexithymia,* a term conceived by Harvard University psychiatrist Peter Sifneos.[13] Alexithymia is the condition of people who experience emotional states but do not know what they are feeling and do not know how to talk about their feelings. When alexithymics experience emotions, they have no sense of what is happening to them. Psychologists' best guess is that alex- ithymics feel puzzled about what is happening to them. Strong emotions feel "awful" to them, though they can't describe what "awful" feels like. As a result, many alexithymics keep their lives as bland as possible, avoid- ing situations that elicit strong emotions.

Of course, it is not possible to say that an organization is alexithymic. Organizations aren't humans, and many managers attempt to reinforce this reality by refusing to consider the pulsating reality of emotional dynamics within office walls. Other managers pretend to encourage emotional connections with customer interactions by asking their rep- resentatives to use evocative words in their greetings. These can be words that the staff don't necessarily feel. When this happens, the experience of the customer is that of faked emotions.

A friend called the telephone company. The first words he heard from the cheery telephone representative were, "Good morning. How can I offer you *excellent* service today?" "I'd like to order an ISDN phone line," said our friend. "What is your telephone number, sir?" she asked. "I already punched it in when I was first connected to you." There was dead silence on the other end of the phone. This type of exchange is like play- ing at emotions without being able to name them, understand them, and interact with them. It is almost as if managers, through many sincere attempts to improve customer service, create alexithymic customer interactions, which undoubtedly leave both customers and service providers feeling flat. These managers must then wonder why what seemed like a good customer service technique failed.

Most managers understand the necessity of "friendly" service, but they undermine the "friendliness" by too tightly scripting the experi- ence. We suspect a manager or supervisor told the telephone company representative referred to in the above example to start her telephone greeting in precisely that way. However, "How can I offer you excellent service today?" is such an odd opening sentence. Most of us do not normally talk this way. And clearly, the representative did not know what her next lines were to be if someone resisted giving his or her telephone number twice. This situation is equivalent to putting an actor on stage and giving him or her two or three opening lines, and then nothing more—unless you know the actor can improvise. In fact, theater improvisation more closely resembles customer service exchanges than

Most managers understand the necessity of "friendly" service, but they pull the legs out from under the "friendliness" by too tightly scripting the experience.

a stage show. Improvisation is a theater technique in which the scene has been described, but no one has been told exactly what to say. Interestingly, theater improvisation demands three abilities, all of which are necessary in customer service: flexibility, self-confidence, and huge amounts of awareness.

Again, we bring Harvard University's Susan Fournier into the discussion:

> It's startling how wrong we've been about what it takes to cultivate intimate relationships with customers. And it is alarming how quickly and thoughtlessly relationships can be destroyed through the muddled actions we often engage in. We've taken advantage of the words long enough. It's time to think about—and act on—what being a partner in a relationship really means.[14]

■ Application

Easing into Discussions about Emotions. If managers jump too quickly into a discussion of emotions, everyone may become nervous, and some may ask the question, "What new book has the boss read now?" Some staff will be downright suspicious that the manager is probing for information that may be used against them at some point in the future. Building an emotion-friendly culture requires a subtle activation, not a shock. Managers can begin by asking staff, "What do you think about that?" "How do you see that?"

The purpose of inquiring about emotional reactions is not to "pin" staff down, but rather to increase awareness.

These are questions that build to a more direct "emotion" question: "How does that make you feel?" Managers must also recognize that because of the transitory nature of feelings, people may give one answer one day and have a totally different reaction the following day. If managers grasp that the purpose of inquiring about emotional reactions is not to "pin" staff down but rather to increase awareness and to invite discussion, then questions about emotions take on an entirely different slant.

CHAPTER THREE

POSITIVE EMOTIONAL STATES ARE AN ASSET

Even though books, audiotapes, and speakers on the power of positive thinking have become a regular part of modern life, it has become almost stylish to poke fun at motivational speakers, "positive thinking" authors, and their ideas. The motivational industry is a billion dollar market in the United States alone, and one of the best-selling books of all time is Norman Vincent Peale's *The Power of Positive Thinking*. Yet the disparagement of positive thinking continues.

Part of the reason for this is that most academic studies of psychology have focused on negative emotions. Positive emotions are considered lightweight, yet without positive emotions we have little hope of attracting and retaining customers. A new body of research, recently summarized by psychologist Barbara L. Fredrickson at the University of Michigan, has started a credible and serious discussion of positive emotions, such as joy, interest, contentment, and love.[1] The bottom line of Fredrickson's argument is that positive emotions open up the mind to think in more directions, which means the positive thinker has more choices and resources available to him or her than the negative thinker. The applicability of this idea to customer service and consumer spending is stunning.

Fredrickson says that if we can keep our positive emotions dominant, we can be more effective in just about everything we do. If we add the word "customers" to her concept, it becomes "We can be more effective with our customers if we remain positive." Some would say that this is patently obvious. Yet look at how frequently this advice is not followed by customer service representatives. Indeed, it might not be too strong a statement to say that most failed customer service situations are a direct result of service representatives failing to remain emotionally positive.

Customers have higher positive attitudes when they think businesses are involved in customer-focused behaviors and service quality.

The same applies to sales. To create a more open "buy" mentality in the sales process, for example, selling needs to be experienced by customers as solving their needs and building relationships, rather than as "selling behavior." Customers have more positive attitudes when they think businesses are involved in customer-focused behaviors and service quality than when they think they are being sold to.[2]

Fredrickson explains the natural bias toward negative emotions and her preference for positive emotions. As we consider customer service and customer retention, these reasons and their implications are worth exploring.

1. *Languages favor negative emotions.* We have fewer positive emotion words than negative emotion words in our languages. What this probably means is that we haven't yet differentiated positive emotional states as fully as we have negative emotional states. As a rough indication, a popular thesaurus, *The Synonym Finder*, has three inches of words for "anger" and only about half as many words for "joy." Paul Ekman has reduced the vast array of emotions to a basic six-pack: anger, fear, surprise, disgust, happiness, and sadness. Only happiness is definitely positive. Surprise can be either positive or negative. None of us would consider anger, fear, disgust, and sadness as positive emotional states, even when they are appropriately felt.[3]

2. *Negative emotions are more compelling.* Part of the attraction for focusing on the negative, says Fredrickson, is that problems are more compelling than enhancement of the positive. Many of our own consulting clients are initially more interested in learning how to handle upset customers than in what they can do to prevent the upset in the first place. This is not the best way to build the foundation for emotional added value. When we lead exercises in our workshops about good and bad service, there is considerably more attraction for groups to discuss "bad" service examples. The room gets noisier, and people definitely become more animated than when discussing examples of "good" customer service.

3. *Negative emotions narrow thinking.* Negative emotions narrow our thinking possibilities. For example, if you see a huge, vicious dog charging at you with ears flat against its head and teeth bared, it is a good idea for you to have a negative thought: *This dog may attack me.* If you don't have that conscious thought, you will probably do nothing to protect yourself. If you can imagine the dog attacking you, all of your consciousness is organized to survive the canine attack.

   When service representatives see customers coming at them with narrowed eyes, tight mouth, and tense muscles, the natural tendency is to think, *Here comes trouble.* Immediately the brain begins to narrow its focus. Avoiding or defending against this attack is pushed to the center of the consciousness stage. Under most circumstances, nothing positive happens when service providers become defensive or want to give up in disgust.

   Nothing positive happens when service providers become defensive or want to give up in disgust.

4. *Positive emotions open thinking.* On the other hand, positive emotions widen our thinking possibilities. When we are filled with joy, for example, possibilities abound. We can play, joke around, engage in fantasy, open up emotionally, intellectually, and socially. Danger is absent in a condition of joy. This leads us to ask: Why *shouldn't* we

work for deepened customer and staff relationships, get to know these people better in order to form healthy long-term partnerships? Why shouldn't we fight off emotional viruses that have infected our customers? Customers can more easily be taught in a condition of joy. They are more open to suggestions. If customers experience positive interest, they will more readily consider how products and services can help them. Their attention will not be on why products won't work. Furthermore, when customers are contented with the experiences they have had, they are more likely to return, seeking to experience more of the same feeling of trust.

Cebu Pacific, a Philippines air carrier, allows passengers to serenade each other through an in-flight karaoke system. Its flights also have a "bring me . . . " portion. To win a coffee mug or tee-shirt, passengers are asked, as in a treasure hunt, to find improbable items, such as a baby picture of oneself. The impact? Cebu Pacific enjoys a very profitable 80 percent passenger load factor; that is, eight out of every ten seats are booked on the routes the company flies.[4] When customers experience positive emotions for an organization's services and products, no doubt commercial relationships will be more secure.[5]

5. *Positive emotions help regulate negative emotions.* Positive emotions definitely help change negative reactions. Substituting joy for cynicism can help staff spend their time at work in a much more contented state. Consider the energy that could be released for everyone (staff, management, and customers) if, instead of "Thank God It's Friday," we could experience contentment over a week's worth of positive work. Does anyone gain from hating his or her job?

Researchers have also found that positive moods tend to generate more creative thinking, better inductive reasoning (problem solving), and greater flexibility in approaches.[6] Salespeople in this frame of mind will more authentically express enthusiasm for a customer's purchase. They will undoubtedly be more creative in finding products that best meet cus-

Positive moods tend to generate more creative thinking.

50

tomers' needs. Rarely are people sickened, diminished, or isolated by positive emotions. Creating an environment in which people can learn how to adjust their emotions is basic to emotional foundation building for adding emotional value.

> *Rarely are people sickened, diminished, or isolated by positive emotions.*

Application

Conditions for Positive Emotional States. Generate a list of everything you can do to positively improve your outlook. Which of these could be used at work? Which ones are more suited for home? Can you practice them until you are as capable of switching your mood from negative to positive as you are capable of switching a light on or off?

Shifting to Positive Emotions

Substituting positive emotions for negative mental states starts with awareness. It then requires a conscious decision to shift or alter emotions. The ability to shift in and out of mood states is one of the most important skills for managing emotions. Consider the computer. When it sends an "error" message, it generally also tells you to save your documents and then restart. When you experience negative moods, your biocomputer is telling you *not* to ignore your emotions but to shift or restart your mood.

Janelle remembers her son Lewis as a very young child awakening one morning in an extremely sour mood. He marched into his parents' bedroom complaining about everything. His father said, "Lewis! What kind of a 'good morning' is that?" Awareness struck. Lewis stopped and dejectedly walked back out of the room. Two seconds later, a small knock was heard on the door. Lewis stuck his little head in the room and pleaded, "Can I start over?" Too bad that most of us don't know how to do that as adults.

Mood "restarts" include five shifts, described below—geographical, solution, attention, meaning, and physical. Service managers and service providers can think of these five shifts as an emotional skill set. Knowledge that these shifts are possible, and then regular use of them, will enhance their effectiveness.[7]

1. Geographical shift. This strategy involves reducing negative emotions by physically moving away from the work site. If a service representative deals with a difficult situation, such as loss of a major client or a highly upset customer, negative emotions will undoubtedly ensue, and a geographical shift might be called for. Staff could be encouraged to briefly walk away from their desks or counters after confronting a challenging emotional experience. If used with awareness, a short time-out can quickly alter moods. Managers can enhance this mood shift's effectiveness by saying, in effect, "We know you are going to have emotional reactions. We don't deny this. We want to make sure that you manage them in a positive way so one difficult situation doesn't rub off onto the next. If this means leaving your desk or phone station for a short period of time, we encourage you to do so." It is a realistic, solid position for managers to take. To do otherwise is to say that we expect our staff to become alexithymic, to deny the emotions they experience.

If used with awareness, a short time-out can quickly alter moods.

◼ Application

Take Breaks from Upset Customers. Awareness of a negative attitude, and the residual effects of it, happens best when physical distance can be created between an emotional event and the person affected. In offices, this means getting up from one's desk to go to another location. Awareness, in itself, helps create mental distance. But to create that mental distance, sometimes we need physical distance. Awareness and physical space combine to expand the felt distance. Most people need only a couple of minutes away, but those brief moments can be a lifesaver. Those few minutes, however, will be taken only if staff believe they have the support of their managers to do so.

▧ Application

Create Mental Space by Avoiding Quick Judgments of Your Customers. A geographical shift can also involve visualizing space between one's self and an immediate emotional reaction. For example, when a customer makes a mistake or does something unacceptable, don't immediately assume the customer is trying to be difficult. Create space between the event or behavior and your judgment. It's just possible the customer made an honest mistake—even possibly by following instructions of one of your coworkers.

---

2. Solution shift. Problem-focused coping is the essence of the second emotion shift. It involves looking for solutions so attention is focused on problem solving rather than the original stressor. The operant question here is, "What can we do to fix this?" Believing that nothing can be done about the situation keeps one focused on negative emotions and narrows the thinking process.

Most customers face the same customer service problems over and over again. For organizations not to know which are most prevalent and not to educate staff how to handle them is the equivalent of sticking one's head in the sand—a useless variation of psychological denial. Not only do repetitious situations need to be identified and then addressed, staff also need support in understanding and coping with the emotions they experience during repetitive situations.

For example, staff in Hawaiian hotels tell us they don't like hearing guest complaints about bad weather. They especially don't like to hear that it is raining because they feel they can't do anything about it. Despite how beautiful Hawaii is most of the time, it does rain. Think of the impact on customer loyalty if staff could be made aware of their own resentment at hearing this bothersome complaint, understand its underpinnings, and then be coached to commiserate with hotel guests and offer bad weather alternatives. Both the service providers, who feel unnecessarily picked on by being blamed for the weather, and the customers can talk themselves out of their cloudy moods through problem solving.

■ **Application**

> *Staff Discussion.* Use these questions to begin a discussion. What are the most common problems presented by our customers? Do we all know the best ways to solve these problems for our customers? What can we learn from someone else on staff who might have handled a similar symptom of customer distress? Do we know how to handle these situations positively? What are the alternatives or options we can offer our customers under these circumstances?

3. *Attention shift.* Shifting attention basically means distracting oneself. Some people learn to distract themselves through self-talk. Others distract themselves by losing themselves in their work. Because children haven't learned how to amplify their moods but mostly react, it is fairly easy to distract a child. Every parent has had the experience of being with a crying toddler and doing something as simple as shaking car keys to distract the child. A smile appears, even while tears are still coursing down chubby cheeks, as tiny hands reach for the jingling keys. It is possible, though a little more difficult, to distract an adult. One powerful way is through humor.

One powerful way to distract adults is through humor.

One of the authors talked with an Internet data bank sales representative from whom she had purchased an "unlimited" user's contract. The sales representative had been told by his manager to call the author because she was using her "unlimited" access "too much." When the author pointed out that unlimited access logically couldn't mean "too much," the representative agreed. "They made me call you," he whined. "Well, I'm out of here—real soon. They don't pay me enough to do this, anyway."

This salesperson probably did not have the opportunity to discuss the emotions that were being created as a result of what he was "made" to do. As a result, his inappropriate emotions leaked out to the customer. We can almost imagine the manager saying to any objection his staff raised about first talking customers into an unlimited access contract and then calling them back to tell them they were abusing the unlimited nature of the plan, "Just call them. Just do it, and I don't want to hear any of your objections about it." Psychologist Kenneth Kaye says listening is crucial, especially at times like this. "If you try to shut somebody down when they're angry or emotional, they will feel not heard, and they will feel more upset, more angry, and perhaps more irrational."[8]

> *"If you try to shut somebody down when they're angry or emotional, they will feel . . . more upset, more angry, and perhaps more irrational."*

An attention shift might have been utilized if the manager had asked the sales representative to focus on how to get the customer to sign up for a different plan, given her usage volume. They could have discussed the humor in trying to get a customer to "limit" the "unlimited." From there, the manager and service provider might have discussed the best language to use with the customer to encourage her to use a more suitable plan.

■ Application

Schedule Time to Discuss How Staff Feel about Interacting with Their Customers. Schedule regular times to allow staff to talk about their reactions to the demands of customer service work. Don't allow the discussion to dwell on and reinforce negative feelings, as groups can easily reinforce negative aspects of customer exchanges. Instead, use the discussion to enhance an awareness of emotions, and then coach staff how to use distractions to shape moods and subsequent behaviors.

4. Meaning shift. According to British psychologist Brian Parkinson, "the ways in which organizations define emotional reality may directly shape emotional responses to it."[9] The positive way to perceptually change a situation is to change its meaning. Some people refer to this as reframing. It involves understanding that what you see may have an entirely different story attached to it than the one you currently perceive. For customer service providers, utilizing the meaning shift can involve understanding a situation from the customer's point of view. This strategy is as close to "walking in the customer's shoes" as any we know.

For example, does the telephone representative see an aggressive businessperson or a customer who is being asked to yet again change a telephone number and reprint all stationary and business cards? Does the hotel check-in clerk see an unpleasant customer or someone who has had a difficult day, including missed flights, long waits for taxis, lost luggage, and now another long line at the check-in counter? Does the medical clinic worker see a rude patient or a parent who is deathly worried over the unfavorable test results she just received about her only child? Does the marketing assistant see an uptight, out-of-control colleague who wants information or an employee who has been put under heavy pressure by a manager and asked to do impossible tasks with limited information? Does the grocery store checkout clerk see an exasperated, demanding customer or someone who has faced disappointment all day and is now faced with changing a dinner menu at the last minute because needed ingredients are not available?

When we see someone who is angry, what does it mean? If we interpret the anger as an attack on us, then it is more difficult to maintain a positive mind-set. If customer anger is seen as an increase in emotionality (albeit not a pretty one!) with the intent of being heard, the anger will not be taken so personally. If service providers view themselves as problem solvers, then the appropriate self-question becomes, What signals do I send to let customers know they are being heard?

> *If customer anger is seen as an increase in emotionality with the intent of being heard, anger may not be taken so personally.*

5. *Physical shift.* This strategy requires a direct influence on one's physiological response by either relaxing or exercising. It could involve taking a short, brisk walk. In our workshops, we encourage service representatives to get up from their desks, grab a piece of paper so they look like they are making a delivery, and then quickly walk around the office to release tension. With that piece of paper in hand, they will look like they

are on official business and won't have to explain that they are taking a stress break. In this case, geographical and physical shifts are combined. And we ask managers to support this behavior.

A physical shift could also be putting a smile on one's face, stepping out into the sunshine (not to lament the fact that you can't spend the entire afternoon there but to enjoy the warmth at that moment), taking a deep breath of air, or relaxing one's shoulders.

Imagine if organizations made it a regular practice to discuss these strategies for restarting one's mood. Imagine that all staff were as knowledgeable about personal mood regulation as they are about where to get photocopies made. Think of the impact this could have on adding emotional value to both customers and staff.

> *Imagine that all staff were as knowledgeable about personal mood regulation as they are about where to get photocopies made.*

■ Application

Physically Changing Your Mind-Set. Ask your colleagues to generate a list of activities the organization could encourage everyone to use to change one's mind-set. Everyone gets upset from time to time or experiences moods that may actually infect everyone else's moods (in the same way a flu virus is passed about the office). We have done this exercise with several organizations and each team of people generates remarkably different lists—each, we have concluded, fitting the participants' unique corporate culture. At times this exercise elicits the response "I didn't know you could do that." Many people, especially those newer to the organization, have no idea what is possible in taking care of their own emotional needs.

ASSESSING YOUR ORGANIZATION'S EMOTION-FRIENDLY SERVICE CULTURE

Answer the following questions:

1. What practices are in place so that positive emotions can be easily discussed in your organization?

2. What messages does your organization send about the appropriateness or inappropriateness of discussing emotions?

3. What prejudices may be slipping through to your customers because you don't discuss or understand them? Can they be identified and then discussed? For example, if a service representative meets a customer who reminds him or her of a hated relative, how is this handled? Without awareness, the service representative will probably respond in some way as if dealing with the hated relative. Self-awareness can allow the service representative to acknowledge the similarity and then not allow his or her unconscious tendencies to control the customer interaction.

4. Do you believe that to be professional is to be unemotional? If so, what impact does this have on your customer service and/or managerial style?

5. What is the impact of your organization's overall marketing plan on the emotional state of individual customers? What impact does your advertising have on customers' moods when they first interact with you? How does this affect sales and customer service representatives?

6. What beliefs does your management team hold about displaying emotions? What impact do these beliefs have on the rest of the organization?

PART TWO

CHOOSING EMOTIONAL COMPETENCE

We see things not as they are.
We see things as we are.

—Anais Nin

Organizations have a choice about how they view their service relationships. Some see service as little more than a necessary evil, while others view service relationships as the magnet that keeps customers coming back over and over again. Some see service as emotional labor; others choose to view it as emotional competence.

In today's world, high-tech companies charge for service, even offering different packages for different levels of service. Airlines have long done this with coach-class, business-class, and first-class distinctions. The assumption these companies make is that service competency has intrinsic value and can be charged for. While businesses may not be able to advertise a specific charge for added emotional value in the same way that high-tech companies can enumerate a price for twenty-four-hour service or airlines for the lay-back seats in first class, it is a memorable component of the customer experience and therefore has value.

It is not an easy task for organizations to create a culture of emotional competency and link that to customer service, but it is a competitive edge—especially in the developing experience economy. It does not happen by accident and requires full support from management to ensure that emotional competency is chosen as the foundation for the organization's service philosophy.

> *Emotional Labor:* 1. requiring staff to produce an emotional reaction in the customer, such as satisfaction or delight; 2. employing voice or facial interaction with customers; 3. requiring staff to display a set of emotions that differs from the emotions they feel.

> *A nineteenth-century child working in a brutalizing English wallpaper factory and a well-paid twentieth-century American flight attendant have something in common: in order to survive in their jobs, they must mentally detach themselves—the factory worker from his own body and physical labor, and the flight attendant from her own feelings and emotional labor.*[1]
> —Arlie Hochschild, *The Managed Heart*

Emotional Competence: 1. knowing one's emotions; 2. managing emotions; 3. motivating oneself; 4. recognizing emotions in others; 5. handling relationships.

> *On the positive side, imagine the benefits for work of being skilled in the basic emotional competencies—being attuned to the feelings of those we deal with, being able to handle disagreements so they do not escalate, having the ability to get into flow states while doing our work.*[2]
> —Daniel Goleman, *Emotional Intelligence*

EMOTIONAL LABOR OR EMOTIONAL COMPETENCE?

Maureen O'Hara sits in an old-fashioned office chair, dressed all in black, looking resolute as she is interviewed for the brisk-selling business magazine *The Fast Company*. Dean of faculty at San Francisco's Saybrook Graduate School and postmodern psychologist par excellence, Dr. O'Hara makes a strong case for the necessity of emotional skills at the turn of the twenty-first century.

> Everyone must become a student of human nature in all its glorious complexity. Exercising new psychological muscles—tolerance, flexibility, empathy—becomes part of developing competence at work.[1]

Exercising new psychological muscles—tolerance, flexibility, empathy—becomes part of developing competence at work.

Contrast this message with that of Arlie Russell Hochschild in *The Managed Heart*, as she discusses emotional labor:

> This [emotional] labor requires one to induce or suppress feelings in order to sustain the outward countenance

that produces the proper state of mind in others—in this case, the sense of being cared for in a convivial and safe place.[2]

Are these two viewpoints, expressed over a period of fifteen years, with one seeing emotional competence as a "glorious" skill set and the other viewing it as a emotional "burden," merely two different opinions about service work? Or do O'Hara and Hochschild, the spokespeople we have chosen to represent these two points of view, speak to *fundamental* and *divisive* beliefs about the nature of service? We think it is the latter.

In fact, we contend these points of view reflect a chasm that puts management and service staff on opposite sides and is so deep that it *must be* acknowledged and bridged if organizations are to gain the participation of their staff in effectively offering emotional value to customers. Hochschild contends that service providers are alienated from their own emotions in a service economy and that they, therefore, cannot experience meaningful relationships in the service exchange. We would say that it is up to managers to create a context for meaningful relationships to develop. This context requires choosing emotional competency over emotional labor to define service offerings.

> *It is up to organizations to create a context in which meaningful relationships can occur in the service exchange.*

If customer-staff relationships are structured so value is experienced by *both* customers and staff, then service providers can see themselves as adding value in their work, rather than merely laboring under the weight of service requirements. The "reality" of service work can be a positive definition that we choose and one that benefits both the supplier and the receiver. Or it can be a burdensome definition, one that gives little value to either customers or service providers. As Anais Nin implies in her quotation—"We see things not as they are. We see things as we are"—the choice is ours.

Do Employers Have the Right
to Demand Emotional Participation?

Arlie Hochschild's 1983 work brought attention to the concept of emotional labor. She pinpointed a point of view held yet today by many who believe that workers are demeaned, basically under the thumb of managers and customers. They are, in Hochschild's world, taken advantage of. Hochschild's point of view is based on assumptions that need to be revisited. This is particularly true as we transition from a service to an experience economy. Genuinely expressed emotions, or as we call them, authentic interactions, are in even greater demand today in order to create memorable experiences, the touchstone of success in the experience economy.

Authentic interactions demand more than merely giving personal attention to customers. Authentic interactions demand emotional connectedness and require some level of emotional disclosure.[3] While civility is better than rudeness, scripted politeness or forced friendly behavior will not add sufficient emotional value to create the experiences out of which loyalty is deepened. To use the words of marketing experts, "it [authenticity] involves a relational exchange that requires emotion work, real giving on the part of the provider."[4]

This creates a conundrum. You can't force emotional transactions of this type, and yet this is precisely the type of interaction organizations must encourage and even expect their staff to create with customers. Consider managers who supervise staff with little sense of teamwork. To fix this problem, managers may attempt to create a functioning team by hiring team-building experts. Team builders, with exercises, discussions, and reflection, attempt to change team dynamics from within the team. They don't just tell the staff to be a team and expect that will happen. They start with the assumption that staff won't function as a team if the individuals don't want to be a part of that team. They also assume people will like their work more when they function as a team. A group of people cannot be forced to operate as a team, but they work better when they do.

> *If managers force service workers to engage in friendly transactions with customers, a real disservice will be done to frontline staff.*

In the same way, if managers *force* service workers to engage in friendly transactions with customers, not only will these commands be countereffective, but a real disservice will be done to frontline staff, as Hochschild points out. The only means to bridge this chasm is for everyone to shift perspective and see the value that is present for *both* customers and service providers when authentic exchanges occur. In short, to gain the full benefit for everyone, service needs to be redefined as emotional competence, rather than emotional labor.

Hochschild bases her notions about emotional labor and the service economy in a reality rooted in the industrial age. Her analysis is grounded in Marxist theory, which says that workers are *necessarily* alienated from their own labor in a manufacturing society. That is, the Marxist line goes, industrial line workers can have no meaningful relationship with the goods they produce. This is in contrast to the craftsperson who carefully carves a piece of furniture from start to finish and in so doing identifies with the outcome of work.

Service workers become similarly alienated, Hochschild writes, when they can't express their "true" emotions, when they must "transmute" their feelings of hostility into a smile—all for the purpose of increasing corporate profits. If service providers are upset with customers, she asserts, they dare not snap back because that action would interfere with the economic goals of their organizations. Actually, we wish she would tell more service workers they can't attack their customers. We see all too many instances of scolding, arrogance, and flat-out rudeness—and they do interfere with the economic goals of organizations.

Hochschild further argues that workers who once sold their labor in the manufacturing economy could at least retain some sense of self or individuality at the end of the day. Because workers could be angry at their situation, they retained personal dignity and worth, even if their assembly line work was devoid of meaning. Angry workers couldn't be fired for expressing their attitudes, as Hochschild assumes they can be today.[5] (This probably wasn't true even in the early industrial period, unless workers were protected by a union.) Industrial employees were asked to produce goods under difficult conditions, Hochschild concedes, but they didn't have to endure the onerous and stress-filled burden of forcing smiles on their faces or being nice to customers or colleagues when they didn't feel like it.

This point of view undoubtedly romanticizes events from the industrial past in its criticism of the service economy. Hochschild assures her readers that selling emotional labor is more demeaning than selling physical labor. We suspect that most laborers who were "authentically" angry while chipping coal in mile-deep mines or standing on their feet in sweltering steel mills or performing the single task of tightening the same screw on every passing automobile might happily have changed places with modern service workers. Hochschild makes a big assumption when she states that the service workers' "public faces" are *necessarily* not the service workers' "authentic selves." To the degree that we accept this viewpoint as a "real" description of the modern service world, we undermine the entire field.

The Positive Challenge of Service Work

Maureen O'Hara, on the other hand, promotes the idea that learning the skills of human interaction in all their magnificent complexity is an honorable task, a blossoming of individual potential, rather than a diminishment. O'Hara sees a positive challenge in service economy work:

> All this puts pressure on people to be a lot more psychologically flexible than ever before. People need what I call group empathy. That encompasses a whole set of higher-order mental skills; openness to learning, a capacity for self-criticism, low defensiveness, and the ability to process multiple realities and values.[6]

Daniel Goleman's term for the empathy that O'Hara refers to is "social radar."[7] Goleman suggests that without this empathic radar, people become blunt and inappropriate with each other. Nonempathic people don't know how to effec-

Without empathic radar, people become blunt and inappropriate with each other.

tively ease the bumps and pressures that naturally occur in social communication.

Consider the following example of botched empathy reported in a customer service newsletter. A woman called a mail-order catalog company to order a scanty undergarment. She was a little nervous about spending money on something she feared was frivolous so she told the man who took her order, "I don't know whether I should be buying something like this." His task-focused, nonempathic response to her comment, delivered in a flat tone of voice, was "Credit card number, please." The woman was upset enough to write about the incident to an electronic newsletter. The clerk's non sequitur comment, totally lacking in empathy, will never nurture customer loyalty and may even drive business away. Any sales organization would certainly not want this to continue.

This type of exchange happens all the time, all over the world. A friend went to fill a prescription at a local drugstore that prides itself on its quality customer service. He was asked, "How is your day?" "Fine," he responded. "How is yours going?" "Don't get me started," the clerk answered. "It's a lousy day. I have to stay in here and work all day long." *(Unspoken message: waiting on you is no fun.)* She continued, "Here's my philosophy. First you work all your life—and then you die." The management of this particular store may argue that it is difficult to hire staff who, for a low hourly wage, like to wait on customers or that there is no time for training or that staff turnover is ridiculously high. Perhaps. But then stop advertising your store as an establishment that treats customers as number one—as this particular drugstore does.

The emotional labor point of view is that if the order taker and sales clerk are required to engage in reassuring behaviors to customers when they don't want to, they are somehow selling their souls. O'Hara, in contrast, would say that the organization and the employee are facing a challenge of empathy, and the service provider needs enhanced skills. If empathy involves learning to read one's own emotional signals and those of others and then acting out of compassion with this information, under what circumstances could this be negative? Perhaps only if the service provider took this job as a last resort or faked attitudes during the interview process or believes that showing empathy for customers/ strangers is more than can be reasonably expected for a salary.

There are positive examples where both customers and staff seem to benefit. Another friend went to a drugstore. He is forty-four years old and bought some beer. The female clerk said in a coy manner, "How can I be sure you're old enough to buy this?" He laughed and responded, "I'll show you my ID, but first I want to know how old you think I am." She said, "About thirty-four." Flattered, he told her his real age, to which she said, "Well, if you're married, you tell your wife that you've still got it. You've *definitely* still got it!" When our friend related this exchange, he said, "Can you imagine how lucky this store is to get someone like her working a checkout stand? She makes me want to go back in there and get more of her sunshine."

> *"She makes me want to go back in there and get more of her sunshine."*

Creating Customers

Peter Drucker proposes, in a deceptively simple statement, that the fundamental purpose of business is to "create customers." Obviously, there has to be a needed, offered, and available product or service in order to create a customer. But products or services alone won't create customers, unless you happen to have them forced into your lap. Loyal customer relationships require nurtured, personal connections and generally don't happen by accident.

Imagine the benefits if every organization could enjoy the results of all staff working to create these relationships whenever the opportunity arose. What could happen to the bottom line of an organization if all new hires clearly understood that the reason they were hired was to create customers, to spread sunshine? Yet how many times is creating a customer about the farthest thing from a service provider's mind? Maybe the boss is on the staff's mind, perhaps the difficulty of the new software program, possibly the long queue of customers waiting to be helped.

Creating customers can occur at the emotional, human level any time, any place. It happens when customers walk down grocery store aisles and an inventory stocker turns to smile at them, when a genuine

> *"Creating customers" can occur at the emotional, human level any time, any place.*

voice of concern is heard at the other end of the line as they express frustration over another computer glitch, or when an item is accepted for return with a smile.

Dianna recently checked out of a hotel. The desk clerk, while asking all the appropriate questions to ensure a speedy checkout, remained consistently involved with his computer, didn't look at Dianna except as she stepped up to the counter, and then gave her a weak smile when he finished looking to see who was next in line. He made no attempt at all to engage Dianna as she was leaving.

This desk clerk thinks his job is to check people out of the hotel. He doesn't have a picture in his mind that his job is to "create customers" for this hotel. The purpose of a concert pianist is not simply to play a piece of music. It is to create an experience for the audience. To the degree that the pianist and the service provider are able to explore the full possibilities of their work experience and their subsequent impact, they also create customers.

Hochschild uses the word "transmutation" to describe suppression of feelings. It's a word we like—but with a different twist. Hochschild uses the term to mean "selling out" one's true feelings. Transmutation also refers to the supposed Middle Ages alchemical practice of converting base metals into gold and silver. What if service providers thought of their work as converting base (normal, everyday) emotions into gold and silver (customer-creating) emotions? Would the undergarment mail-order clerk and the drugstore clerk referred to above perhaps see and then perform their work differently than when they see their tasks as simply filling orders or earning a paycheck? Would they find some sunshine and deliver it to their next customer?

British psychologist Brian Parkinson summarizes it this way: "In more general terms, the ways in which organizations define emotional reality may directly shape emotional responses to it."[8] If service staff, with the support of management, do not embrace emotional skills and see them as a positive addition to their own competencies, they will indeed find themselves with Hochschild's "commercialized feelings." Furthermore, if organizations fail to move from emotional labor to emotional competence, they will unconsciously nurture an "us" (service providers) versus "them" (customers and management) attitude.

Does Giving Diminish Us?

Some cultures struggle with the concept of service because of its connection to the word "servant" (L. *servitium servus*, a slave: see *serf*). In these cultures, service implies "over" and "under" positions. The dictionary supplies other meanings as well: "the serving of God, as through good works; an act giving assistance to another; friendly help; also, professional aid or attention."[9]

A more modern view of service is that in today's world of fluid roles, all of us offer service and assistance *to each other* at one time or another. There is a profound difference between being a good service provider, being a server, and being servile.[10] When the authors present a seminar to hotel staff, they are in a service provider position to everyone in attendance at that course. Later in the evening, if one of the members of the class goes to the authors' rooms and provides turndown service, the daytime course participant has become the service provider. The next morning, back in class, roles are shifted once again.

A more modern view of service is that all of us offer service and assistance to each other.

It used to be that servants remained servants twenty-four hours a day in relation to their employers. Many were born as servants and died as servants. The concept of "internal customer," introduced in the 1980s and gaining wide acceptance by the end of the twentieth century, has had a tremendous influence on adding fluidity to roles in modern organizations.[11] A staff member's internal customer is his or her boss. At the same time, a boss's internal customers are his or her staff. They are customers of each other at different times, roles switching throughout the day.

Hochschild implies that when workers are placed in a service role for which they are paid they are somehow dirtied. This attitude is remarkably prevalent among a substantial percentage of service providers themselves, and fundamentally it suggests that service work is not valued. Yet everyone understands that if an organization delivers poor service, it will be hard-pressed to retain customers. If an organization disparages its service work and workers in any way, service providers will play out this reality and deliver inauthentic service exchanges, with smiles that involve only the mouth and tones of voice that could never be criticized for being rude but contain not an ounce of friendliness or compassion. It's almost as if they are saying, "I'll give you a smile on my face, but you'll get nothing else from me." We think it reasonable to conclude that no one is ennobled under these circumstances of pretence, that the service worker is indeed being servile. Most customers are not taken in by this lack of authenticity.

Another view of the role of service providers is provided by Naomi Rhode, one of America's foremost public speakers. As a past president of the National Speaker's Association, Rhode developed the theme "The Privilege of the Platform" to remind speakers of the great opportunity and responsibility they have to impact people's lives. Of course, speakers are placed in a service role for which they are handsomely paid. However, in illustrating her theme, Rhode chose to use the example of a waitress at a busy airport restaurant who provided an outstanding experience while serving a cup of coffee. This waitress, Rhode remarked, understood that the coffee counter was her *platform.*

We have also received similar outstanding service from a toll taker at the Golden Gate Bridge who makes every perfunctory transaction memorable to us and his other customers—even if the contact is only a few seconds. His outstanding attitude has even been the focus of a *San Francisco Examiner* article.

Service Relationships versus Service Encounters

Service today is offered via encounters or via relationships. Service *encounters* are relatively short-lived exchanges, mostly with strangers, such as in the fast-food industry, in department stores, or with a telephone operator. The service level of an encounter generally doesn't depend upon specialized information that the service provider has.

Service encounters are thought to be more or less "one size fits all" kinds of service. Service *relationships* are entirely different. A service relationship might be one's relationship with an insurance broker, banker, pharmacist, doctor, or baby-sitter. Generally relationships are experienced more than once, take more time, and require a degree of tailoring.[12]

Organizations use service encounters as much as possible because they are less expensive to deliver, can be standardized, and aren't as dependent upon staff forming long-term relationships with customers, making staff turnover not as big a detriment. Encounters also make more sense because increasingly larger numbers of people live in heavily populated urban areas; they move easily from one shop or restaurant or business to the next, rarely forming relationships along the line. Internet shopping, which is very distant and encounter-like in its nature, is also booming in popularity.

People want faster, standardized service across the world, twenty-four hours a day, so they can enjoy the limited personal time they have. Many more people travel today and conduct business at all times of the day and night, so service companies are forced to have several providers, not just one, interact with the same customer. The challenge for businesses is to make service encounters feel like service relationships.

> The challenge for business is to make service encounters feel like service relationships.

Hochschild sees an inherent problem with service encounters. She argues that people can be who they authentically are in their personal family and friends relationships, while in their work *encounters* they can't. Staff have to "put on a face" at work when they are in the business of service encounters, and this is laborious, Hochschild contends.

In reality, people regularly compromise to aid their social interactions—whether at work or at home, whether they have personal encounters or personal relationships. If people behaved as they truly wanted to all the time, they would no doubt find themselves without families or friends. Indeed, we know many individuals who find emotional giving at work a relief compared to coping with the emotional demands of their families. Emotional competence requires learning which of our fundamental values—at work or at home—should never be compromised and at the same time learning how to get what we want without having to fight battles all day long. We disagree with Hochschild that emotional labor is just a work-related issue.

> *Emotional competence requires learning how to get what we want without having to fight battles all day long.*

Parents who easily lose their tempers and physically abuse their children need to seek help so they avoid acting out destructive feelings. They must practice emotional strategies to make being around children easier for them. Are parents less authentic because they don't hit their crying or messy children? Hardly. Conversely, Hochschild assumes that when we modify our responses in a *paid* environment we have "sold out." She writes that when service workers transmute or squash their feelings so many times during the day, they run the risk of losing the function of feeling altogether. Couldn't the same charge be made of parents with small children?

We don't want to be overly harsh in our judgment of the "emotional labor" point of view ably represented by so many. Hochschild's book is important, as is British business psychologist Sandi Mann's latest book, *Hiding What We Feel, Faking What We Don't.* We recommend these books along with the entire issue of the January 1999 *Annals of the American Academy of Political Science*, devoted to this topic.[13] They speak to challenges in the service industry that must be addressed. In fact, Hochschild's book has helped us crystallize our own approach to customer service.

If we buy into the thesis, however, that service workers necessarily sell out their feelings when they provide service, then we will have created a reality where service work is, by definition, emotional labor in the worst sense of the term, and we will have no means to escape it. To the degree that businesses create or allow the emotional environment that Hochschild has described, they are ultimately doomed to suffer its consequences. We think a better approach is to choose and nurture a philosophy of service that recognizes and compensates for the value of emotional competence, rather than focuses on the burden of emotional labor.

We agree that many flight attendants (the group that Hochschild focuses on) find it difficult to work flight after flight in crowded airplanes with unhappy, rushed, stressed passengers—and still maintain a happy countenance. But what about the alternative? Would Hochschild encourage flight attendants to express frustration at passengers who don't move quickly to their seats? (Actually, they sometimes do.) Or should they shout back a cynical response to a passenger who dares to ask for yet another cup of coffee? (This happens, too.) She does not recommend this, by the way, though she does not offer any alternatives either. In fact, while she admires the airline training programs that help flight attendants cope with their jobs, she also disparages the airlines as taking advantage of women, since most flight attendants and other frontline staff are female.

Maureen O'Hara, on the other hand, acknowledges that learning to be empathic can be difficult and cause stress. People in business and on the front lines definitely know it is not without costs. Managers can help by designing customer-friendly systems and by offering service training about coping with relationship demands. In this way, service work can be experienced as a challenge, rather than as a burden, and as more than "grunt" work. We've heard participants in our programs say, "I can hardly wait until a customer blows up at me so I can try out this technique." If service staff are appropriately supported, they are excited to try out a new competency.

Service work is best viewed as requiring emotional sophistication, just as writing computer code requires programming skills. Someone who does not possess the emotional competence to deliver emotionally competent service needs to be placed in a position with more limited human demands, just as someone who cannot learn to use a computer needs a position where a computer is not required.

Can Technology Save Us from Emotional Labor?

Is it possible to avoid the challenge of emotional demands placed on service staff by using more technology? In other words, is it possible to avoid the stress of emotional labor by substituting technology for personal contact? Certainly technology can help. In some limited ways, computer technology makes it possible for brief service encounters to possess more of the feeling of ongoing service relationships because enormous amounts of customer data can be stored and quickly accessed by staff. This allows any service provider to be seamlessly connected to whoever last interacted with the customer.

Some companies are getting very good at enabling customers to help themselves to products on the Web. In 1997, a single Cisco customer reportedly bought a hundred million dollars worth of equipment without talking to one Cisco employee![14] As more and more people, particularly the younger generation, become comfortable with technology, examples of this type will abound. We do not believe, however, there will ever be a perfect substitute for human contact.

Janelle Barlow and Claus Møller reported in *A Complaint Is a Gift* that some companies use tape recordings for the opening words of telephone greetings.[15] A perky tape-recorded "hello" is delivered in an interested high-energy voice so that the customer hears a positive service provider answer the phone. This saves the service provider from expending unnecessary energy on the first few words of greeting. The service provider then shifts into real time. The customers get that important first impression delivered electronically, though customers would never suspect they just heard a tape recording.

The notion that technology can save us from negative emotions is based on the faulty assumption that the feelings customers experience when dealing with machines are minimal.

However, the notion that technology can save us from negative emotions is based on the faulty assumption that the feelings customers experience when dealing with machines are minimal. Anyone who believes this has not experienced a computer crash destroying three hours of painstaking work. People have been known to tip over vending machines when they eat up coins and do not deliver a product. We have seen people pound on ATM machines when they are depleted of funds.

There is no reason not to use technology to help ease the burden of service providers, but at some point humans need to be present, especially when persuasion is necessary to complete a transaction. When one considers that over half of the interactions companies have with their customers take place over the telephone, the importance of managing the emotional impact of this technology is immense.[16]

In fact, the demands on service providers may increase because the first contact many customers have with an organization is a machine. By the time customers get to talk with a person, many of them are already upset. This especially happens with voice-mail systems that present dozens of looped menu options, not one of which involves talking to a live human being. It is not uncommon for service representatives to hear customers say when they finally reach them, "My God, I can't believe I actually got through to a person!" That's not a very positive beginning to a service experience. In fact, consulting firms are now beginning to suggest that Internet companies, many of which limit customer contact with their staff, must learn from the traditional businesses against which they have been competing. Issac Lagnado of Tactical Retail Solutions concludes, "Progressively more and more of the e-players will have to hire people and train them."[17]

The Challenge of Burnout

There is no magical solution to the challenge of constantly dealing with emotions. Choosing to see service as emotional competence over emotional labor can help, but intense emotional involvement with limited opportunities to escape hassled customers can still cause burnout. The "opportunity" question for organizations is, How can service workers learn to deliver service hour after hour, day after day, without becoming alienated and paying a health price?

Burnout, as an idea, has mostly been used to describe people in the helping professions (social work, nursing, psychology, and child care). Sociologists have long assumed that the helping professions required intense emotional involvement, and, therefore, people in these fields were the ones who would most likely suffer burnout's negative effects. To the degree that an organization expects staff without any coping skills to

There is growing recognition that burnout can also dramatically affect service providers.

offer "experiences," burnout will also surely take its toll on the modern service/experience worker.

Signals of burnout include fatigue that does not go away with more sleep, low motivation for just about everything, and a cynical attitude.[18] Burned-out, exhausted nurses, for example, might stop caring about how their patients feel or even whether they live or die. Burned-out service/experience providers also stop caring whether their customers walk away with a positive attitude, whether they get their needs met, or maybe even whether they live or die as well! Most readers of this book have probably suffered through desperately needing something from a business, only to be told in a completely flat, cynical, disinterested voice, "Sorry, there are none left." And if a customer protests, explaining the genuine need for this product, he or she may be told by a service provider who cares not a bit for the customer's personal situation, "Look, you're not the only one."

We know of airline gate agents who have gotten into shouting matches with passengers over cancelled flights. A group of gate agents at San Francisco International Airport actually requested "cages" to work behind so they could be protected from their customers. This request speaks to a high level of cynicism among the gate agents or perhaps a level of frustration with their management that they are reluctant to voice directly. So they take it out on the customers.

Flight attendants in the United States have asked for special federal legislation, called "air rage laws," to protect them against unruly passengers. It could be that airlines (both management and cabin crew) need to look at how to make the whole flying experience more friendly, rather than blame their customers of which it is estimated only one in three million engage in air rage. In the case of the San Francisco fiasco, an airline grossly oversold cheap tickets for the last flight of the day between San Francisco and Los Angeles. Who knows what impact this had on the individual lives of the passengers who couldn't get where they had counted on going?

Cathay Pacific flight attendants in early 1999 threatened to refuse to smile for one hour on every flight to show their unhappiness over management plans to eliminate automatic pay increases.[19] That's not exactly "creating customers" behavior. Their action raises several interesting questions. Are the flight attendants saying that it is easier for them to deliver their service without a smile? When workers go on strike, they withhold something of value—namely their labor. So in the "smile strike," should Cathay Pacific flight attendants be paid less for that one hour's flight time? Should the passengers get cheaper tickets because they endured one hour of no smiles? How do the flight attendants prepare themselves for this hour? Do they put little reminder signs up: "Remember, don't smile"? Do they let the passengers know they are entering into an hour-long smile-free period? Do they tell the passengers their somber faces have nothing to do with the passengers but are a message to Cathay Pacific management? If the flight attendants felt like smiling but were in their one-hour smile strike, would they think of negative emotional situations so they could hold back automatic smiles?

What if a group of New York or London actors decided to engage in an "emotional" strike in the middle of a stage performance? Would such withholding make it easier for them? Undoubtedly not. We suspect that when people lose themselves in the sheer joy of performance, work is easier, not more difficult. It can take a lot of energy to be negative.

Blaming bad behavior on senior management's refusal to grant automatic pay raises shifts responsibility away from individuals, where we believe responsibility for personal behavior lies. At the same time, some senior managers make decisions and communicate these decisions in a way guaranteed to create unhappy staff. Some managers also try to script every move of their employees in an attempt to "get it right," telling staff what to say, when to smile, and how to behave in every situation—in short, treating staff like machines that happen to look like humans.

Is Cathay Pacific in the transportation business, or is it in the "creating customers" business? If it is the latter, how could management have communicated with staff when an automatic pay increase was not possible during a period of economic downturn so staff did not feel inclined to take it out on Cathay customers? The answer has a lot to do with how a company handles internal emotional discontent and how it defines its reason for existence. It also has something to do with being emotion friendly and choosing a service model of emotional competence.

Becoming emotion friendly can be done in part by focusing on voluntary partnerships in every aspect of the business: partnerships between staff and their coworkers, partnerships between management and staff, and partnerships between staff and customers. Partnerships will never work if they are forced. We will indeed have emotional labor under those circumstances. When this happens, not only will we have alienated and former staff, we will have "former" customers as well.

> *Partnerships will never work if they are forced.*

Emotional competency is extremely valuable in an increasingly crowded, interdependent society. It is the role of management to describe it, explain it, set up systems to make it easy to deliver, and then honor it as genuine added value. Hans Selye, "father" of the modern concept of stress, wrote about contributions years ago, "If you want to live a long life, focus on making contributions."[20] Selye's message applies to both staff and managers.

Teaching staff stress management techniques is a strong antidote to burnout. Stress management can show staff how to maintain peak performance levels while operating in high-stress environments. Instead of using energy to deny emotions, staff can learn to work cooperatively on teams and with customers while not denying their emotions. Acknowledging feelings is one of the best ways to avoid burnout and is a powerful stress management strategy; it also enables service workers to maintain contact with their own emotions. No one wins if service providers go home in the evening burned out and numb to feelings.

Years ago, Janelle was invited by a hospital to conduct a stress management program. The program organizers asked an unusually large number of probing questions regarding program content. Finally, Janelle asked them if something negative had happened that prompted them to ask such detailed questions. The woman replied that they had had a previous "stress" speaker who urged the surgical nurses to just say "no" to the surgeons if they didn't like the way they were asked to hand over surgical equipment. That would never work in a crisis or operating room environment. Unfortunately, some people believe that there are only two strategies for dealing with stressful situations, both of which are extremes: either debase yourself by giving in, or simply refuse to cooperate. There is middle ground, and it is up to managers and staff to find this shared space with each other and with customers.

Acknowledging feelings is one of the strongest antidotes to burn out.

Organizations must likewise develop systems that do not put staff in impossible and demeaning situations, while simultaneously understanding that emotionally hostile customers are very upset about something that matters to them, feel desperate, or sense they are not being heard. Understanding the emotional needs of customers requires open staff discussion. Staff must be recognized as being capable of making legitimate contributions to how their teams can best operate. If we expect staff to emotionally connect with customers, the organizational structure itself must reflect this approach by valuing staff connections with the organization.

We know of organizations that provide their staff with zero opportunities to discuss emotional responses to their work. In support of Hochschild's thesis, some managers definitely deny the impact of operating in an emotional environment all day long, whether these emotions are generated by interacting with customers or colleagues or from losing automatic pay increases. In Part I, "Building an Emotion-Friendly Service Culture," we discussed the importance of allowing staff to discuss the frustrations inherent in their work. These discussions need to be held within the context of a larger organizational philosophy so that staff walk away with the feeling that customers are not a burden but can make work enjoyable.

CHAPTER FIVE

MANAGING FOR EMOTIONAL AUTHENTICITY

Twenty-five years ago, in his book *Bureaucracy and the Modern World,* Victor Alexander Thompson described a phenomenon most people instinctively recognize as the major challenge for the service/experience economy: *"synthetic compassion can be more offensive than none at all."*[1] Authentic exchanges are noticeably different from synthetic communications. Authenticity has to be felt and driven internally, and unless one is a very, very good actor, faked attempts at authentic communication are quite obvious.[2]

> *"Synthetic compassion can be more offensive than none at all."*

This raises an obvious question: How do organizations get their service providers to deliver authentic customer service when they can't command it?

Senior-level managers who are reading this book know this task is not easy. In fact, it is so amorphous, so difficult to measure, that many do not consider it at all. They also are aware that coaching "authentic" service workers necessitates a revised set of supervisory skills. Yet some do look at these challenges. An AT&T executive describes the emotionally competent supervisor's role in the new economy as essentially absorbing uncertainty for staff, something that most of us are not very good at.[3] Author and president of Edventure Holdings, Esther Dyson, underscores the point that emotional skills are even more critical for today's leaders than ever before:

> As change becomes constant, leaders must have the flexibility and vision to handle it. . . . You have to fire people up and calm them down, resolve disputes, uncover the key points in a conflict or a strategy, make firm decisions. All these traits and capabilities inspire confidence and lead a company forward. These traits are the least definable—and their impact is the most visible.[4]

Harvard Professors Leonard A. Schlesinger and James L. Heskett put it in even stronger terms:

> In virtually every large-scale change effort we have studied, one of the most stubborn problems is resistance from middle managers. Many people call them the concrete layer and tell endless stories of how they get in the way of progress. The plain fact is, in this new service model, they often do get in the way.[5]

Fortune magazine goes so far as to say that *the prosperity of the entire United States economy depends upon how well managers manage their frontline staff.*[6]

We recommend two broad managerial approaches for implementing emotional competence as a service model. First, enable staff to see that managing emotions in the best manner possible not only is a critical part of job requirements but also is to everyone's personal benefit. Second, systematically teach staff to understand feelings and to recognize the importance of the emotions behind customers' behaviors.

> *Service work must not be viewed as "selling out" one's authentic self.*

Service work must not be viewed as "selling out" one's authentic self. Emotionally sophisticated staff can maintain contact with their feelings while managing customer experiences in a positive way. Obviously, this doesn't happen automatically, and some people are better at this than others. Managers must staff, train, and then coach their service providers on an ongoing basis to make sure their staff know what to do emotionally and then are supported in their choices. A strong, supportive human resource function is necessary as well.[7]

The management team itself must also be committed to a customer focus. Managers must know that they are taking the entire company to an intangible goal: *We are committed to adding emotional value in order to develop long-term customer relationships.* The intangible goal, if properly planned and executed, can lead to the tangible goal of profits realized from repeat business.

Managers also have to ensure that business policies and practices do not compromise staff positions. The experience economy will not allow managers to engage in shady business practices and then expect frontline staff to "fix" impossible situations. We know one communications company that makes it virtually impossible for customers to pay their bills on time, so a late fee is invariably attached to the next billing period. It's a small amount, so most customers say nothing or perhaps don't even notice the extra charge. But for the hundreds that do notice and care about the fee, frontline staff have to put up with vicious monthly attacks. When the issue was brought to the attention of senior management, the decision was made to retain the practice because of the sizeable revenue stream it creates. Expectations of adding emotional value by even the most emotionally competent frontline staff are unreasonable under these circumstances. Attention to the ethical behavior of an organization becomes essential in the experience economy. An entire book could be written on this critical topic alone.

Unethical practices create cynical customers who become increasingly difficult for each subsequent service provider to handle. Many consumers fear being taken advantage of or being swindled. They wonder if the salesclerk is being honest in saying that a product is a great buy or looks wonderful on them. Today's customers find it challenging to make the

> *Attention to the ethical behavior of an organization becomes essential in the experience economy.*

best buying decisions, especially for big-ticket items, because so many choices are available. As a result, customers become even more dependent upon salespeople. Consumers may be suspicious that they are being encouraged to buy items that are not selling well or items for which the clerk earns a larger commission. Consumers also wonder if the repairs they are asked to pay for are really necessary or are just excessive. And some even suspect that food that has fallen to the floor is sometimes picked up, brushed off, and served to diners.

Focusing on emotions is the obvious next step for service organizations that want to transition to the experience economy.

Focusing on emotions is the obvious next step for service organizations that want to transition to the experience economy. To do this, everyone in the organization has to come to grips with the reality of emotions in business. The organization's *total* service system must focus on emotional value for staff and external customers.

The following sections outline six strategies for implementing emotional competency as a service model.

- Fostering Positive Interdependency
- Dealing with the "Always Right" Customer
- Hiring for Emotional Competence
- Defining the Emotional Requirements of Service Jobs
- Understanding the Necessity of Ongoing Education
- Encouraging Staff Autonomy and Emotional Competence

Let us re-emphasize, however, that both tangible and intangible approaches must be utilized. We have seen too many instances of limited success when organizations attempt to "fix" service providers while continuing to make unrealistic marketing promises to the public, set grueling work schedules for their staff, and refuse to invest in technical upgrades. As we continue to reiterate, emotional competence by itself will take you only so far.

Fostering Positive Interdependency

We live in a world of interdependence within our families, cities, work teams, organizations, national government institutions, and global community. Most people spend the bulk of their time in interdependent commercial and organizational relationships. As we plunge into the new millennium, all this time spent leads to a consequential question: What should the best commercial and organizational relationships look like? Maureen O'Hara, champion of emotional competency, provides an answer. She says that if we do not reach for the level at which two human beings are connected in a system of mutual honoring and respect, we become people who spend most of their lives simply performing tasks for each other—outside the context of relating.

> *Most people spend the bulk of their time in interdependent commercial and organizational relationships.*

If clerks and customers do not reach for a level of human connectedness, customers are "people who mess up the merchandise," and clerks are "people who are never around when you need help." If technologists and customers do not reach for a level of human connectedness, people are "stupid users who never read their manuals," and technologists are "arrogant nerds who always start off by asking, Is your computer turned on?" If flight attendants and passengers do not reach for this level of human connectedness, passengers are "job tasks" to flight attendants, and flight attendants are "the people who bring coffee" to passengers. There is little that is satisfying in these types of relationships. And certainly there is not much pull for customers to return to such relationships or for staff to bring enthusiasm to their work.

Leonard L. Berry, who introduced the term "relationship marketing" in the 1980s, pointed out that organizations benefit when "customers form . . . relationships with people rather than goods."[8] Yet it is interesting that we still use economic models based primarily on exchange theory—monetary value is based on scarcity and value of the product or service as determined by consumers—which in turn emerges from the concept of rational consumption. We undoubtedly need new models that take emotional factors into consideration, models that Frederick

Webster suggests "focus on the relationships themselves, not just on the market exchanges."[9] Most people acknowledge that business relationships include emotional components, but this value is neither well understood nor easily measured. As a result, most businesses focus on "reciprocity" or tangible exchanges. It is easier to measure something concrete, such as how quickly the telephone is answered, than to account for the emotionally driven behavior of consumers.[10]

> *Some service situations are ". . . so influenced by emotional forces that rational ones barely come into play."*

Marketing Professor Barbara Stern at Rutgers, the State University of New Jersey, points out, "Emotionally-driven consumption is the *polar opposite* of economic rationality." She even goes so far as to state that some service situations are "so influenced by emotional forces that rational ones barely come into play."[11] This is particularly true in the entertainment industry.

Task-Oriented versus Emotional Relationships

Talk with Maureen O'Hara for more than a few minutes and you quickly view relationships as a matter of being. And once you move into a "being" world, then it is possible to achieve relationships that last only moments and yet are as authentic as any we experience. It is these moments of experience that most people remember as the poignant memories of their past. In fact, we hunger for them.

Some would argue that it is too much to ask for happenstance, commercial relationships to be anything more than task oriented. We disagree. Most customers prefer some level of relationship even in their brief encounters. We want to feel that we are interacting with a human being and not just a service robot. Since we live in a world where more and more services are being delivered as brief encounters, the challenge is how to transmute these encounters into experiences that take on some of the attributes of relationships, instead of relegating them to commodities. Transformation of commercial relationships into personal relationships requires a full understanding of the dimension of experience—within the power of the transaction moment.

O'Hara points out that we live in a society of affirmation deficit, leaving people hungry for connectedness. Most of us don't have enough feelings of worth, which today are *primarily* achieved from a narrow set of socially defined signs of accomplishment: money, status, and power. If people do not have enough of these, then they begin to search for other sources of respect and affirmation. We all like to see someone's eyes light up when we walk into a room. It is one of the reasons that people hunger for relationships with their small children. It does not matter how much success you have in the world, a small child will love his or her parents unconditionally, just because they exist.

This is why some customers will go to a place where they are affirmed, even if these encounters are transitory. And service providers, if they enter into these relationships with an open mind, can also get affirmation from their customers. It doesn't take a lot of time for someone to be disparaged by another; likewise, affirmation can be achieved in split seconds. It's a question of how managers envision the service experience and then communicate this vision internally so it is displayed by staff to customers. Managers are directors of the "experience" product.

Affirmation can be achieved in split seconds.

Value Exists in Connections

O'Hara sees the service provider–customer relationship as complementary. It is win-win in her estimation. Both customer and service provider can be affirmed by the other. They can get value from each other, as in martial arts, where both participants honor the other's attempt to win as an opportunity to get better. Service providers and customers need each other to be excellent; we need each other to be of value. In fact, O'Hara says that *we are of value primarily in our connections.* This need for affirmation, for valuing from other people, is so fundamental, according to O'Hara, that to say, "it is exploitative to attend to it, is to say that is like exploiting someone's hunger when you feed them."[12]

Richard Farson, leadership expert, tells "people connection" stories he has collected by asking people about their most significant memories of childhood. He makes the point that people almost always remember small shared emotional experiences of connectedness with other members of their community or family—and not major events. For example, he tells the story of a young girl in a family of extremely limited means. Her mother invited relatives who were much better off financially over for dinner. To stretch their meager resources, she told her children that when the chicken was served, they were to say, "No, thank you. I don't want any," thereby saving the costly and rarely served chicken for the guests. All went according to plan. However, when it came time for dessert, the mother scolded her children, "Since you didn't eat your chicken, you don't get any dessert." The children hadn't been told about this. The woman relating this story of her childhood said in that moment her mother looked at her across the dinner table. In those few seconds of shared nonverbal communication, she understood what her mother was forced to do to maintain family pride and what this had cost her emotionally. She said she never felt closer to her mother than at that moment.

Forming Relationships Is the New Competency

O'Hara says knowing what relationships mean is part of the new emotional competence required in today's world. Depth is not the only measure, but neither is time nor blood relatedness nor who is paying. These are all dimensions, but no *one* is the overriding dimension. In our experience world, we negotiate these dimensions all the time. You can say a relationship with a salesclerk, a toll taker, a nurse, a teacher, a bank clerk, or a flight attendant, for that instant, is all there is. You can see it either as an exploitative experience or as a deeply human moment. It is your choice. Managers have to prepare all their representatives to make this choice.

Knowing what relationships mean is part of the new emotional competence.

One question we frequently hear is, Can we spend our time dealing with issues like this and still be economically viable? Certainly, *avoiding* these issues doesn't guarantee economic viability. Paco Underhill, who has literally invented the "science of shopping" field, points out that the amount of time a shopper spends in a store is perhaps the single most important variable in determining how much will be purchased. And shoppers leave when they are uncomfortable. Furthermore, the more contact there is between shoppers and employees, the greater the likelihood of a sale.[13] Research also suggests that changes in a salesperson's customer-respect orientation help to increase sales.[14] Ultimately, every organization *chooses* whether it will tend to these issues.

Many companies are beginning to find that if they do not pay attention to forming relationships, do not build these competencies into their corporate cultures, they lose their best workers. Successful companies aim to be listed on *Fortune* magazine's "best companies to work for" list. When the economy is strong, staff will literally walk out the door if they are treated badly or placed in emotionally untenable situations. And the best employees will always be able to get employment elsewhere. If an organization needs the best staff to be competitive, then it has to create the same positive moods for staff that it uses to develop long-term customer relationships.

Unisys Corporation has made its primary service goal to become the preferred employer in its line of business. Company leaders figure that if they can get that right, everything else will fall into place. Over the past five years, the authors have personally experienced the difference this has made to Unisys, and they have watched a growth in Unisys's stock value as well.

There is a call today for all of us to be more sophisticated about our inner worlds than we have ever needed to be in the past. To accomplish this goal, managers need to encourage staff to understand and feel comfortable talking about their strengths and their weaknesses and then encourage support of each other. It has nothing to do with exploitation. Few staff "own" customers these days. It's more of a team effort, and people on teams have to learn how to help each other. No one gets along best with every customer. If we can create this context, then staff are not paid to endure but to do what they are good at and what

> *There is a call today for all of us to be more sophisticated about our inner world than we have ever needed to be in the past.*

they love to do. Managers have to understand that emotional sophistication and competence is not a luxury. It is a necessity.

How do managers get staff to this level of emotional sophistication? First, they have to change current staff's emotional frames of references. And the necessity of emotional competency must be accepted by staff when they join an organization. New hires must understand that they are going to be trained not only with technical skills but also with emotional and social skills. If people are to see contextually what is required in service positions, this starts from having a different mind-set toward how they feel about the people they are relating with—customers, teammates, and managers.

> *The necessity of emotional competency must be accepted by staff when they join an organization.*

■ **Application**

Building an Attitude of Positive Interdependency. Changing attitudes within organizations is never easy. Here are five procedural steps organizations can take to better achieve positive interdependency.

1. *Identify a team of organizational leaders and champions for the idea of positive interdependency.* Ask the team to carefully define positive interdependency as it relates to your organization's mission statement and customer service goals. For example, some companies define it as "seamless service."

2. *Empower the team to prepare general staff to adopt this attitude and shift in behavior.* This could include training, education, information sharing, and any other ideas the team can conceptualize.

3. *Set success scores that will tell you when you are achieving your goals.* Share these scores with staff on a regular basis. Success scores can include formal feedback systems or customer- and staff-retention statistics.

4. *Collect and share anecdotes of events that happen as a result of implemented changes.* Sometimes a strong anecdote can be more powerful than a whole raft of statistics.

5. *Celebrate your successes.* Then set new emotional competency challenges and new positive interdependency standards.

Dealing with the "Always Right" Customer

The phrase "The customer is always right" is used a lot. It is one of those phrases that demands discussion because, of course, the customer isn't always right. Sometimes customers make mistakes, get confused, and forget things. They misread documents, or they don't read the instructions at all. They even misinterpret what they have been told. One Toronto-based consulting company specializing in customer satisfaction measurement systems found that as high as 40 percent of the time, customer dissatisfaction is caused by problems customers create themselves.[15]

So what exactly does the phrase "The customer is always right" mean? In part, it acknowledges an organization's financial dependency on customers. *Ultimately, however, it's a phrase that every company has to interpret for itself.* Here's how one restaurant owner put it: "When we say the guest is never wrong, we mean the server should never question a guest's judgment and perception."[16] "The customer is always right" does not advocate that staff put up with unacceptable behavior. There are limits to what customers can do in their exalted role of "always being right." They can't show up naked. We'd cover them up and send them away. They can't steal our goods. Thieves are charged with shoplifting. They certainly have no right to become physically abusive. Laws and security systems protect us from attack. Drunk customers can be asked to leave. Some restaurants require certain dress. It is their right to do so, and it limits the number of customers they will get. At the same time, it may encourage the very diners a restaurant has decided are its target market.

> *Ultimately, "The customer is always right" is a phrase that every company has to interpret for itself.*

Some organizations have standards about the type of language customers can use. Swearing at staff is forbidden if you want to use their services. We do not necessarily recommend getting rid of customers because they swear, primarily because swearing is so much a part of modern culture that many people have no idea they are using offensive language. It is just part of their expressional style. Again, each organization has to make decisions about limits on customer behavior.

Contrary to Hochschild's assertion that "it is often part of an individual's job to accept uneven exchanges, to be treated with disrespect or anger," we believe that adding emotional value does not require a *subservient* "the customer is always right" attitude. In fact, most customers would find that distasteful. They generally prefer an exchange between peers. Social transactions that result in wins for both customers and providers are mutually advantageous. Again, it is up to managers to coach for this attitude and to teach staff how to handle customers who become heavy handed. One of the most important emotional competencies for service providers is how to help customers through bouts of strong negative emotions. They need to do it without being debased in the process, taking the burden of those emotions on themselves, or attacking the customers.

> *Adding emotional value does not require a subservient attitude toward customers.*

Our own experience is that service providers who sincerely reassure their customers they will do everything possible to help them are able to get most customers to settle down. Customers hope that service providers are not their enemies. In fact, they want to believe this. Customers do not enjoy going to a place of business walking in with a cynical attitude or anticipating a fight. And when they do get upset, and perhaps pull "the customer is always right" rank, most appreciate being helped to positively change that attitude.

Service workers need to learn to use language such as "I need you to . . . " instead of "You have to . . . ." or "I'll be able to help you better, if . . . " instead of "I'm not going to help you if you don't . . . ." Getting heavy handed with customers almost never works. So it's not a good idea to order customers around unless someone's life is at risk or you want to lose customers.

▪ Application

What Are We Telling Our Customers? Gather a group of people in your organization and make a list of the different ways you phrase requests to your customers. Can you find alternative ways of speaking with customers to respect the role they play, while at the same time gaining their cooperation?

Service providers are not asked to manage hostile, overbearing, always-right customers eight hours a day, five shifts a week. It is instructive for staff to remember that most customer interactions are neutral or lean toward the positive. Many customers will even go out of their way to help other customers or their service providers. For those who spend much time on airplanes, it is truly amazing how frequently one sees passengers being civil to each other—especially after spending five hours crammed together in a sold-out coach-class section on a U.S. East to West Coast flight at the end of the day. Customers often pitch in to help improve a tricky situation. We have watched men help female passengers with their overhead luggage. We recently saw a passenger be very gracious when she was was bumped from her first-class seat because the airline made a mistake. The passenger helped console the flight attendants. All left that situation with smiles on their faces, including the other passengers who were onlookers.[17]

> *It is instructive to remember that most customer interactions are neutral or even lean toward the positive.*

▪ Application

The Customer Is Always Right. Discuss in groups the phrase "The customer is always right." Managers should explain their philosophy about the phrase and then listen to team members' interpretations as well. They should also invite analysis of specific customer service experiences in which customers were abusive. Once managers have had this initial discussion with staff, it will become safer for staff and managers to discuss difficult customer interactions. It will also be easier for managers to handle staff interventions when customers complain about rude treatment they have received from service providers.

Hiring for Emotional Competence

Even though few people would agree that everyone is suited for the emotional demands of service work, the service industry is renowned for hiring "warm bodies" to fill vacancies. "Just get coverage," seems to be the norm for many service organizations. In many areas of the United States, finding and retaining staff can be more taxing than finding customers. According to the late 1990s Michigan Retail Index survey, 36 percent of Michigan retailers said hiring and keeping staff was their biggest concern. In contrast, only 18 percent said attracting and keeping customers was their number one concern.[18]

The service industry is renowned for hiring "warm bodies" to fill vacancies.

These "warm bodies" hired to simply "fill" a position must surely find the burden of emotional labor onerous. Not all adults make good parents, even if they can procreate. And not everyone is suited for the emotional demands of service work, though just about anyone can get hired to these positions. Most can learn how to better develop their emotional skills, but it will be a struggle for some.

Nordstrom recognizes this. As one of its interviewers says, "We're selective, and a lot don't make it. You prove yourself at every level, or you leave."[19] Oren Harari, professor at the University of San Francisco and customer service expert, states the lesson in very strong terms: "Employees, unionized or nonunionized, must understand that their job is not to simply perform a set of tasks but to act in such a way as to create value for the customer. Nobody's entitled to a job anymore."[20]

Creating value for the customer in the service environment and experience economy is quite different from creating value in the manu-

96

facturing environment.[21] In the service industry, the service provider is always part of the product and in many cases is the bulk of the product. This is even more true in the experience economy. And frequently, it is the emotional part of the service encounter that creates the greatest amount of customer satisfaction or dissatisfaction.[22] As indicated earlier, the University of Michigan's Customer Satisfaction Index reveals a basic rule of thumb: service industries that have the most contact with customers (Federal Express being the one exception) tend to have the lowest satisfaction ratings.[23]

A shipping company's employees would be removed from positions requiring repetitive heavy lifting if their back muscles were unable to withstand the strain. So, too, should organizations consider the reasonableness of not allowing people to continue in service positions when their emotional "muscles" do not enable them to authentically express desired emotions.[24] If the expressive behavior that the organization wants displayed is carefully defined, then staff who match these requirements can be hired and then trained and coached to further improve skills.

> *If the expressive behavior that the organization wants displayed is carefully defined, then staff who match these requirements can be hired.*

Some companies are beginning to hire based on relatively simple personality profiling tests. One such consulting group based in Colorado has worked with 5,000 companies around the world administering profiling tests. The group's founder, Bruce Hubby, believes that people should be placed in positions that build on their strengths and where their personalities match the emotional and behavioral requirements of the job.[25] Some organizations might argue this is a luxury they cannot afford; we would suggest it is a necessity that no organization can afford to ignore.

Southwest Airlines, recognized for both its profitability and its customer service, spends what many other companies would consider an inordinate amount of time finding the right people for its positions. It once interviewed thirty-four people for a single ramp agent position.

The airline uses its own "model" employees and its frequent flyers to help make final hiring decisions. CEO Herb Kelleher describes the process:

> We also give prospective employees strange tests because we want to see what kind of attitudes they have, what kind of sense of humor. Sense of humor is a sense of proportion to a great extent. You don't make mountains out of molehills. When one pilot class came in, we said, "Take off your pants. We don't interview people in suit pants just in shorts. Southwest Airline shorts." This may sound strange, but what we look at are the reactions. The pilots who got a kick out of it and saw the humor in it were the ones whom we hired.[26]

■ Application

Hiring Staff to Fill Required Emotional Skill Sets. Your hiring functions may need a complete overhaul if they are to be emotionally upgraded. If you are lucky, perhaps all they need is a fine-tuning. One way to determine this is to list all the emotions you want your customers to experience while doing business with you. Then describe the emotional abilities your staff will need to encourage these customer emotions. Now assess your hiring procedures to see if they are likely to identify staff who meet these criteria. If not, devise simple tests that will let you know if potential staff have these capacities. For example, if you hire for telephone positions, at a minimum, spend time talking with potential staff on the phone! Listen to the emotional tone of their voices and the messages they convey on a nonverbal level.

Defining the Emotional Requirements of Service Jobs

Emotional competencies for service jobs need to be delineated with as much detail and care as technical competencies. For example, airplane pilots have to have near-perfect vision; waiters must be able to take food orders accurately; fire fighters need to be able to physically pull and lift heavy equipment; stockbrokers and floor traders must be able to concentrate in the midst of chaos.

We are only just beginning to precisely define the emotional characteristics required of service people. Among these characteristics are, to use O'Hara's term, "higher-order mental skills." These aptitudes include the ability to read body language, communication flexibility, the ability to stay involved in situations of high emotionality, empathy, and the capacity to establish rapport. If these competencies are

> *Emotional competencies for service jobs need to be delineated with as much detail and care as technical competencies.*

defined and people are hired with these abilities, then emotional requirements will more likely be perceived as a challenge, rather than a burden.

Service positions require varying levels of emotional labor. Experiences of short duration generally do not require as much sophistication as longer customer relationships. In fact, short-duration customer encounters can be scripted to a limited degree. A position that involves greeting customers and directing them to a specific location does not call for a great deal of psychological competency. A position that requires detailed knowledge of someone's finances, however, such as a loan processor, would mandate additional skills, including managing upset, anxious, or aggressive customers. The factors listed in the following chart, depending on their strength and frequency, determine the amount of emotional content in the service experience.[27]

This scale can help rank the relative emotional demands of service positions. Positions with higher numbers need staff with more developed emotional competencies. For example, the position of an organizational trainer who offers customer service courses would have extremely high numbers, suggesting less scripting is possible. The job of order taker in a fast-food restaurant chain would have lower ratings, requiring less empathy. Job turnover in positions with higher emotional content is more costly to organizations. Staff who handle high emotional content positions well are a genuine loss to an organization when they take employment elsewhere.

Lower Emotional Content						**Higher Emotional Content**			

Product or service is of less importance to customer / Product or service is of higher importance to customer

1	2	3	4	5	6	7	8	9	10

More supplier alternatives / Fewer supplier alternatives

1	2	3	4	5	6	7	8	9	10

Interaction of shorter duration / Interaction of longer duration

1	2	3	4	5	6	7	8	9	10

Greater distance between provider and customer / Spatial closeness

1	2	3	4	5	6	7	8	9	10

Simple process / Complex process

1	2	3	4	5	6	7	8	9	10

Employee delivers product / Employee is the product

1	2	3	4	5	6	7	8	9	10

Less information about customer is known / More information is known

1	2	3	4	5	6	7	8	9	10

Less public / More public

1	2	3	4	5	6	7	8	9	10

Smaller range of emotions needs to be expressed / Greater range of emotions required

1	2	3	4	5	6	7	8	9	10

This chart can also be a guideline for suggesting strategies for increasing the emotional content of customer interactions. For example, smaller spatial distances between staff and customers can be built into the layout of a shop, thereby encouraging more contact between customers and staff. And organizations can design a more expressive style into their product offerings, such as Disney does in its parks and Southwest Airlines does on its flights.

■ Application

How High Is the Emotional Content of My Job? The above scale can be used in a variety of ways. Human resources departments can map service positions based on these standards. Individuals can map their own positions, perhaps using the scale for different aspects of their work. Some parts of a job may have lower emotional content and other parts of the same job, higher. As a team-building exercise, ask individuals to fill out the scale about themselves, and then have everyone score everyone else's job as well. In this way, individuals can see how teammates assess the emotional content of their work.

Understanding the Necessity of Ongoing Education

Some organizations do not provide emotional training and coaching for their frontline staff. Instead, they fire when staff don't perform. "You can't get good staff anymore" is the way we have heard managers default on their responsibility to hire and then train appropriately. We believe it is the responsibility of management not only to support staff in difficult service situations and to honor the significance of their work but also to properly educate for the emotional challenges service staff will face.[28] Many high-tech companies are diligent in educating about complicated computer technology, but they haven't been as committed at bringing staff along on the emotional side.

The most common reason we hear for inadequate training is lack of time. When organizations use this excuse, in effect they say it is less damaging to continue with the same problems they have with their staff so they can ensure coverage than it is to factor in training time as part of the cost of retaining customers. We know one company that spends multimillions on technical training but balks at emotional competency service programs that will cost it less than 1 percent of its total training budget.

> *It is the responsibility of management to properly educate for the emotional challenges they will face.*

Training programs must be based on both the technical demands and the emotional demands of each service position, some requiring more instruction than others. Some service staff must learn how to contain emotional viruses and become adept at crafting connections with customers. Others need innate "emotional capacity" and require additional training to develop their emotional muscles.

We know of individuals who, in their desperation to get employment, feed into this competency gap by lying in their job interviews. "I love people," many will say—until they have to start serving them or dealing with upset customers. This misfit must be at the root of the frequently heard phrase "Hey, what do you expect! I just work here." Sandi Mann in her latest book, *Hiding What We Feel, Faking What We Don't*, devotes an entire chapter to providing tips for faking emotions so people can get one of these emotionally draining jobs they don't want in the first place.[29]

The Emotional Competence Gap

Nordstrom seems to grasp that the level of emotional maturity required to function in an emotionally upgraded business environment is higher than most people have, and perhaps even higher than many people will ever have. Almost half of Nordstrom new hires are gone after one year.[30] Maureen O'Hara says examples of this type are evidence of an "emotional competence gap," though she sees the gap as not a matter of simply lacking interactional skills. Rather, she says people haven't fully developed emotionally. Most adults recognize this about themselves. We know that our emotional maturity in our forties is definitely different from that achieved in our thirties. In our sixties, we are more developed than in our fifties.

Robert Kegan, in his book *In Over Our Heads: The Mental Demands of Modern Life*, talks about the need for continuing development: "It may still remain for us to discover that adulthood itself is not an end state but a vast evolutionary expanse encompassing a variety of capacities of mind."[31] In short, when we reach the age of twenty-one, we aren't finished developing mentally or emotionally. Development is a lifelong process, and this has consequences for the field of service.

Kegan writes about the challenge of getting adolescents to change behavior, saying, "When it comes to sexuality and adolescents it may be that the way we will 'get *them* to change' their behavior tomorrow will depend on our changing the way *we* think today."[32] Let us reword Kegan's statement to make it applicable to the field of service. "When it comes to providing emotionally sensitive service, it may be that the way managers will get service providers to change their behavior tomorrow will depend on managers changing the way they think today." The challenge may be more in the way managers approach the emotional competence gap than in the actual lack of emotional competence.

Most adults aren't finished developing mentally or emotionally; it's a lifelong process, and this has consequences for the field of service.

If this gap isn't in some way bridged, then staff will experience anxiety in their jobs because what is demanded of them emotionally is more than they can deliver—at their stage of development. This gap represents learning challenges, and if they are managed well, managers can help staff take their next development steps. A big question is whether managers can speed up this learning process. We have noted in our complaint-handling classes that most participants find complaint handling much easier as they age. However, we think it is possible to, in effect, "age" entry-level staff by teaching awareness sensitivity and specific skills about effective complaint handling.

One of the highlights of teaching emotional competence is that at some point, seminar participants comprehend that they are being given a skill that is for them, that it can never be taken away, and that they can use it in all aspects of their lives. In fact, we maintain that unless people apply these emotional competencies throughout their lives, they will rarely be used with customers. Once seminar participants recognize the global applicability of emotional competency skills, enthusiasm and commitment dramatically increase. We have a corporate client that recognizes the importance of this, in part measuring the efficacy of our training programs by the number of comments it sees on feedback forms that read "Great program. I can use it at home as well!"

▨ Application

Developing an Inclusive Customer Service Style. If your business consists primarily of brief encounters with customers, staff should be aware that they probably unconsciously engage in behaviors preventing customers from feeling like partners. When stranger after stranger enters a place of business, it is easy for staff to develop an "in group" and "out group" set of feelings. By discussing this reality with staff, you can help them avoid acting out the natural dynamics of encounter exchanges.

Help your staff relish the relationships they form with repeat customers, even if the exchanges are brief. Regularly ask staff whether individual customers have been in lately, even if you don't know their names. Ask staff how they can acknowledge remembered relationships. Customers remember the last time they were in a restaurant, for example, and at some level are disappointed that service providers don't recall them from their last visit.

Identify ways staff can greet customers so there is a feeling of being welcomed back, even when the service provider doesn't remember the individual. At the Mandarin Oriental Hotels in Manila, doormen are told who is arriving in hotel cars from the airport. This way they can deliver the emotionally engaging message, accompanied with a gracious smile, "Welcome back, Dr. Barlow. Welcome home to the Mandarin." It's a very powerful greeting for creating loyalty!

Encouraging Staff Autonomy and Emotional Competence

A growing body of research suggests that when service providers are given greater freedom in determining the nature of their relationships with customers, they experience less conflict between the emotions they display and the emotions they feel.[33] The greater the dissonance between felt and displayed emotions,[34] the more likely employees will experience the worst aspects of emotional labor.[35]

This is particularly important when customers behave inappropriately toward staff, such as when they make unwelcome sexual advances. Some staff find it easy to engage in friendly banter with inappropriate customers and at the same time establish firm limits. Other staff need supervisorial help.[36] Therefore, an additional task of management is not only to hire and train appropriately for service positions but also to ensure that staff have adequate *control over* or *support for* their reactions to customers.[37]

In an attempt to address control issues, some companies give staff very simple instructions, leaving it up to individuals to determine how to carry them out. TMI Systems Design, a small but highly successful North Dakota cabinet manufacturer, has only one policy instruction to its employees: "Do what any caring person would do."[38] Jerre Stead tells a similar story of simplification while at Square D, an industrial control products maker. Stead says, "These rules [in thick policy books], aimed at 1 percent of employees, handcuff the other 99 percent.

> *When service providers are given greater freedom in determining the nature of their relationships with customers, the less conflict they experience between the emotions they feel and the emotions they display.*

Nobody can do all that stuff in the book, so people end up following just one unofficial objective: Keep the boss happy."[39] He disposed of two thick policy books and replaced them with eleven rules designed to take the focus off management and place it on the customer.

Some organizations have simplified empowerment because their customers expect it. Ritz-Carlton Hotels empower to very high levels because customers who pay several hundred dollars a night for a room expect that everyone they deal with will be able to solve their problems. It is important to note that Ritz-Carlton doesn't use empowerment as a stand-alone technique. "They have service sewn into their inseam," is how one competing and admiring hotelier put it. Empowerment is but one piece of Ritz-Carlton's total service approach.

Other companies carefully monitor almost every employee interaction with customers. At the turn of the millennium, several articles have been written about Safeway grocery stores, with their strong California presence. Safeway staff are required to stop what they are doing and escort customers who ask where food items are; they are not allowed to just tell the customer where to go. They are also required to use the customers' names at the checkout stands. If customers are members of the Safeway Club, their names are printed out on their receipts. Checkers

Choosing Emotional Competence

glance at the receipts and thank the customers by name for having shopped with Safeway.

Janelle, living in California and shopping in Safeway stores, has had a chance to study their impact. When the practices were first instituted, not all Safeway employees were comfortable with their execution. When clerks used customers' names at checkout stands, at times it felt forced and uncomfortable. But a year or so later, it is part of the routine, and most Safeway staff have integrated the practice so it feels normal and friendly. The practice of escorting customers to the food location is very helpful. Telling customers that some item is on Aisle 3 is not all that useful when there are hundreds of items on Aisle 3.

Sometimes careful monitoring of expected practices can backfire. We are acquainted with a telecommunications company that aims for a twenty-second completion rate with customers who call for directory assistance. Not all telephone numbers are so quickly found. In an effort to please managers, staff watch the monitor clocks carefully, and if they can't find the number in twenty seconds, they pass the customer off to a colleague, where the clock starts again. Staff at this company tell us that they sometimes pass customers around four or five times, each new operator starting over with the customer, but they beat the twenty-second clock. Management hasn't a clue that its monitoring is resulting in worse service, say the staff. And we would agree because we had the opportunity to talk with the "management" of this telecommunications company, who insisted nothing like this was happening.

Excessive supervision of service providers can also create an oppressive atmosphere. Some companies monitor the number of computer keystrokes per minute or the number of phone calls per hour or time away from the computer in call centers. Many employees report a strong negative emotional reaction to this kind of Big Brother supervision. Here's how one employee described the feeling of oversupervision: "The monitoring makes you feel like less than a child, less than a thinking human being. . . . You have to stop and think from time to time that your ancestors did not cross the ocean in steerage and come through Ellis Island to be treated like this."[40]

Federal Express has made a conscious decision that excessive monitoring is bad for business. It has developed a "people first" approach, instead of a "measurements first" methodology. According to Fed Ex, this change in emphasis has resulted in higher worker productivity and performance than when workers were closely monitored.[41]

Application

Empowering Staff with Emotional Competency. Empowerment, or focused freedom as it is at times called, rests on four legs.

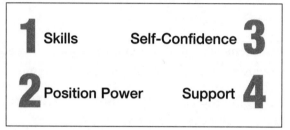

To adequately empower staff, all four legs must be addressed, or empowerment runs the risk of backfiring. First, staff need certain skills. Second, in order to make communication easy, they and everyone else in the organization need to know what particular positions are empowered to do. Third, staff need self-confidence in their ability to take appropriate action. This confidence comes from practice and adequate skill development. Finally, managers must support the empowerment with the necessary tools to do the job. Otherwise, staff will think that managers are using empowerment primarily to delegate problems down the line.

Choose two positions in your organization and list possibilities for empowering these positions. List what needs to be changed to ensure the four empowerment pillars are in place and sturdy.

ASSESSING YOUR ORGANIZATION'S SERVICE PHILOSOPHY

Answer the following questions:

1. Do all people in your organization know what emotional skills are required for their positions?

2. How many of your customer interactions are "customer encounters," as compared to "customer relationships"? Have you analyzed your "encounter" experiences to see if they meet the relationship needs of your customers?

3. What measurements could you put in place to let you know whether customers are excited about doing business with you?

4. Has your organization defined its customer service goals? Can you state what they are? Can all staff do this?

5. What is your organization's approach for handling situations when customers say one thing about how they were treated and service providers claim something else happened? How can the handling of these situations be improved?

6. If your organization were truly committed to being staffed with emotionally competent staff, what changes would have to be made in your hiring process?

7. Do training programs in your organization always cover aspects of emotional competence—regardless of the subject matter? For example, when a new telephone system is being introduced, are staff encouraged to discuss how they and customers will react to the changes?

8. How much autonomy is allowed for your frontline positions? Is autonomy considered as important a variable in equipping staff as making sure they have the necessary tangible tools to handle the demands of their jobs?

PART THREE

MAXIMIZING CUSTOMER EXPERIENCES WITH EMPATHY

A high degree of empathy in a relationship is possibly the most potent factor in bringing about change and learning.

—Carl Rogers

We place two interrelated questions on the table. One, do customer satisfaction surveys reliably measure anything that is meaningful? That is, do they give us any kind of consistent data? *Generally not.* Two, do satisfaction scales tell us anything about what an organization should do once it has measured customer satisfaction? *Almost never, in any precise, meaningful way.*

In order to better understand our customers, we need to get closer to their emotional reactions, and satisfaction surveys simply don't tell us enough about emotional reactions to guide organizations in the experience economy, let alone in the service economy. The entertainment industry has understood this from the beginning. Entertainment is about emotional reactions. Only now do other industries seem to grasp how critical this element is in their businesses as well—even for those businesses that do not sell an "exciting" product. Such businesses, nonetheless, are eliciting emotions as they "create" their customers.

On the operational side of customer service, getting close to customers' emotionality requires empathy. The challenge for organizations is to ensure that staff are capable of reading customer emotional communications and can then appropriately and empathically interact with them in order to emphasize positive reactions.

CHAPTER SIX

SATISFACTION ISN'T GOOD ENOUGH— ANYMORE

It doesn't take long before you realize that Michael Edwardson is saying something important, something different, something almost startling in the field of customer service. Yet as a listener, you find yourself accepting his thesis from the very beginning. Edwardson, a tall, articulate Australian on the faculty at the University of New South Wales, says point-blank that setting goals to increase customer satisfaction is essentially meaningless.

> *Setting goals to increase customer satisfaction is essentially meaningless.*

That, of course, is exactly what countless numbers of organizations do. This focus on customer satisfaction, according to Edwardson, "seriously limit[s] . . . our discovery and understanding of the total consumer experience."[1] In terms of creating loyalty, the most important aspect of customers' experiences is emotional rather than satisfaction based. Harvard researchers Thomas Jones and Earl Sasser put it in operational terms: " Customer satisfaction surveys cannot supply the breadth and depth of information about the customers needed to guide the company's strategy and product innovation process."[2] This statement is pointedly relevant for the experience economy.

Edwardson reminds us that we don't go skiing to get satisfied; we want to be thrilled, just as we do when we go to see the latest Hollywood blockbuster movie. If the only choice we are given is satisfaction or dissatisfaction, our judgment of the weekend of skiing might be high on the satisfaction questionnaire we were asked to fill in as we left the ski slopes, but our emotional state could be less than thrilled. And without the thrill factor, we might never go back to ski again at that resort, given the time, effort, and money it takes to spend a weekend on the slopes.

When we feel angry, using "dissatisfaction" to describe that emotion is completely inadequate. The last time Janelle's luggage—containing all her work for a presentation she was to make in two hours to a critical client, and over which she had slaved for three full days—did not arrive at Chicago's O'Hare airport, dissatisfaction would have been a pathetically weak description of the stinging rage she felt. After insisting Janelle check her suitcase, and all the while assuring her it would be in Chicago on her arrival, the agent sloppily tagged the luggage for a 6 P.M. departure, rather than the 6 A.M. flight Janelle actually took. And the O'Hare baggage assistant actually reprimanded Janelle in a scolding tone of voice, saying, "Now don't get upset." That might be good advice, but it was hardly an empathic comment at that moment.

There is disagreement as to whether satisfaction is an emotion.

Humans experience hundreds of emotions. Yet the service industry still relies mainly on one—satisfaction—to measure what customers feel. In fact, there is even disagreement as to whether satisfaction is an emotion. Some would argue that satisfaction is a judgment about emotions.

What if we used only one measurement of fitness, such as weight, for our indicator of physical health? It would tell us something, but as an overall measurement of health it would be inadequate and incomplete. In the same way, if organizations want to consider total customer experiences, satisfaction by itself is a weak measurement.

While we do not have the final answer as to what is the best measurement of customer emotions, there are a number of interesting possibilities. In fact, there may be no single best measurement because the emotional connection between the service provider and customers is context dependent. Furthermore, this context is heavily laced with empathy, not one of the easiest emotional exchanges to quantify.

Emotional Accounts and Empathy

A vibrant and context-dependent metaphor of customer emotions that we think helps to explain a lot of customer behavior is that of emotional accounts. This idea, called "emotional bank accounts" by Steven Covey in his work on habits for families, paints an easily comprehensible picture of deposits and withdrawals. To a large degree, Covey's emotional bank accounts metaphor refers to goodwill within our personal relationships. When the metaphor is applied to commercial relationships, its meaning is more demanding. Personal relationships come laden with social and family values that do not create the same constraints as in commerce. For example, a spouse who tolerates a roving partner may be considered a forgiving and courageous person willing to put the importance of maintaining the family above personal feelings. No one admires a customer who continues to go back to a supplier in the face of mistreatment.

Emotional accounts in commerce have to do with a reservoir of strong, positive feelings that are deposited and literally stored in customers' memory banks. Each strong positive emotional experience (both material and personal) helps connect the customer to the organization until the customer reaches such a point of connectedness that it is a rare experience for that customer to purchase anyplace else.

When there is a negative experience, a withdrawal is made against that reserve of positive emotions, and it must be repaid—with interest. Even neutral experiences probably make small withdrawals from long-term loyalty. At a minimum, they do nothing special, making it more likely that customers will at least be open to other suppliers. As long as

As long as the total account is in the strong, positive range, there is a much better likelihood customers will stay where they are.

the total account is in the strong, positive range, there is a much higher likelihood customers will stay where they are.

Emotional accounts is a useful metaphor for staff to use if they also see the purpose of business as "creating customers." Every time they have a customer interaction they can ask themselves whether they added to or subtracted from a particular customer's emotional account.

Strong, positive emotional feelings are most likely to be created when the customer–service provider interface is empathic—when, in other words, emotions are shared and mutually understood. Consider the following example from the trust and estate business. An in-depth survey revealed that 84 percent of trust beneficiaries felt their trust professional did not understand the pain they were going through while handling financial arrangements necessitated by the death of someone close to them. Of that 84 percent, 78 percent (or a total of 65 out of 100!) expressed a desire to switch financial institutions, *primarily motivated,* as they said, because of the lack of compassion offered by their trust officer.[3]

Many trust professionals think their accountability ends with meeting fiduciary responsibilities, the collection and disbursement of financial assets. Yet it is not uncommon for trust officers to spend time with clients or relatives of clients who tell them, "I no longer feel like living now that my husband has died." Still, trust experts Janine Smith and Gaylon Greer write that in most trust and estate offices, no one "acknowledges [client] death[s] as anything other than a business event."[4]

As a result, they publicly express little emotional response at the death of their own clients, even though many of them get quite close to clients in the process of setting up trusts and wills. The power of empathy teaches us that customers are not best served solely by accurate dollar calculations, but as Smith and Greer put it, "if trust industry employees are to participate in the full experience of providing service to customers they must be willing to share those customers' fears, weaknesses and pain associated with illness and loss."[5]

Empathy does not mean that service providers become embroiled in their customers' emotions. Empathy implies sympathetic listening, without becoming consumed with the problem. As a result, staff must learn not only how to feel genuine sorrow for their customers' plights but also how *not* to take those feelings of concern as burdens on themselves, perhaps carrying them home in the evening, where they prevent restful sleep and rejuvenating interaction with family and friends.

Empathy necessitates a careful balancing act for service providers. We want our medical personnel to care about us, and yet we do not want them to be disabled by their caring. We expect firefighters, police officers, and medical personnel, among others, to be able to put aside strong emotions and cope with the emergencies at hand. Computer technologists must be able to cope with the frustration of a customer whose system has just crashed and yet provide accurate technical information. And a doctor's office staff must manage lengthy physician delays, balancing the difficulty this creates for patients who show up on time for their appointments while being responsive to the reality of medical emergencies.

One branch of Barnett Banks Trust Company, in Clearwater, Florida, has taught staff how to manage patient grief without assuming their clients' emotional burdens. As a result of this special training, staff no longer view spending time with grieving customers as a threat but as an opportunity to share support and knowledge. When customers open trust accounts, staff now give as much priority to personally getting to know their clients as they give to understanding their clients' financial situations. These behavior changes have impacted Barnett Banks' customers, who now report that they not only feel safer with the bank but also believe they will benefit from their relationships with trust officers.

> *After staff grief training, customers reported they feel safer and expect good things will happen.*

Barnett's training program puts flesh on its vision statement, which reads in part: "Barnett people are caring and proud. We improve the lives of our customers and the well-being of our communities. We help each other succeed, and make our customers feel like they belong."[6] This vision statement is not all that different from many company statements we have seen. *But Barnett, through its training programs, helps staff understand how empathy resides in those words and in so doing maximizes customer experiences.*

Timothy Firnstahl, owner of Satisfaction Guaranteed Eateries, Inc., understands the power of empathy. When his restaurant staff call customers and ask them to rate their recent dining experiences, they give the customers the following choices: lousy, OK, good, very good, or excellent. Firnstahl says, "If they said 'OK,' that meant 'lousy' to us, and they got a letter of apology, a certificate for a free meal, and a follow-up phone call."[7] Firnstahl, in the process of surveying his customers, demonstrates empathy by assuming "OK" is an inadequate emotion for someone who has paid to dine out. Through their survey process, Firnstahl's staff puts something back into customers' emotional accounts after a withdrawal has been made by an "OK" dining experience.

Even though they don't use the phrase "emotional accounts," a growing group of marketing experts, including Michael Edwardson, is among the first to address this tricky but important issue.[8] As previously discussed, this group is charting new ground by combining concepts from social psychology, consumer behavior, and the study of emotions to better understand and measure customer experiences that are inadequately described simply as satisfied or dissatisfied.

If all we do is look for satisfaction, we won't focus on understanding the emotional meaning of the service experience to them.

If all we do is look for satisfaction, we won't focus on understanding why customers feel drawn to return to organizations or the emotional meaning of the service experience to them. Furthermore, if staff rely on customers to report when they have experienced negative emotional reactions, service providers won't be looking for subtle emotional communications that may not be expressed verbally. If service providers understand, however, that customers are building emotional accounts, then they will more likely try to enhance service experiences when situations are going well and turn around negative emotions when service experiences go awry.

Emotional Reactions and Satisfaction

We have an opportunity to bury the widespread notion that satisfaction is by itself an adequate measurement of customer retention—even if it feels right on the surface. A high-tech client has a customer who buys a lot of the company's equipment and then calls repeatedly with one problem after another. He is persistent. After several years of this, the company told the customer that perhaps he should consider buying products from another company because obviously our client wasn't able to satisfy him. The customer declined this offer. "You're too good a company to produce poor products. I like your products, and I want you to get better," he argued. "I'm going to continue buying what you make, and I'll keep calling when something goes wrong," he concluded.

Isn't it interesting that a customer beset with problems and dissatisfied with product performance is, in this case, a strongly loyal customer? How do we explain such behavior in terms of the satisfaction/dissatisfaction scale? Obviously we can't. But the emotional account metaphor goes a long way in explaining how someone can have one bad experience after another and still feel loyal. Somewhere along the line, this customer experienced enough positive emotional deposits that he wants to continue doing business.

Isn't it interesting that a dissatisfied customer can be a strongly loyal customer?

Edwardson has measured the emotional reactions of people who fill in customer satisfaction surveys. He correlates ratings on 1-to-7 satisfaction scales with emotional reactions that he ascertains through in-depth interviews. His findings should be enough to make all managers focus even closer attention on the limitations of satisfaction surveys.

If customers' statements of satisfaction were truly related to their emotional reactions, we might expect that customers who check "1" as their level of satisfaction (on a scale from 1 to 7) would have a lot of negative reactions to whatever happened. If they checked "7," that would logically indicate mostly positive emotions. In fact, if satisfaction ratings and emotional reactions were exactly correlated, they would be related to each other as illustrated in the following graph, labeled "Logical Customers."

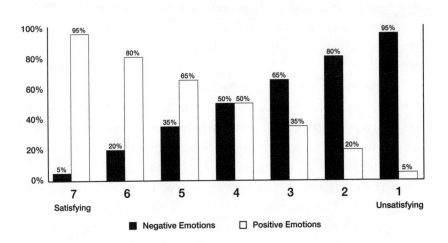

Logical Customers

Based on his research, Edwardson has found that the emotional reactions of real customers, as they relate to satisfaction evaluations, look quite different from the "Logical Customers" graph.[9] As illustrated in the graph below, at the low end of the rating scale (1, 2, and 3), negative emotions are consistently higher than expected. At the midpoint (4), negative emotions considerably outweigh positive emotional reactions. According to Edwardson's research, customers who check the midpoint of satisfaction surveys still have almost three times (74 to 26 percent) as many negative reactions as positive emotional reactions. In fact, when someone checks "5" (in the upper half of the scale), the amount of negative emotions is still higher than the amount of positive emotions (55 to 45 percent). At "6," the customer finally shows more positive emotions than negative. It is only at "7" that customers experience

> *It is only at the highest levels of satisfaction that customers have more positive emotions than negative.*

118

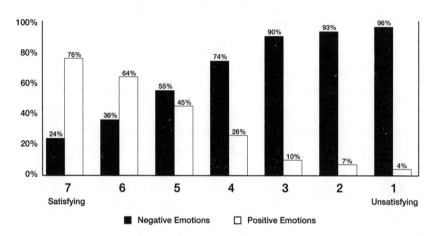

Real Customers

**Percentage of Positive and Negative Emotions
for Different Levels of a Satisfaction Scale**

Encounters - 325

Source: Michael Edwardson
University of New South Wales

significantly more positive emotions than negative. Even at "7," however, the negative emotions are still considerable (24 percent).

Many customer service managers we work with are extremely happy to receive "5" ratings from their customers on a 7-point satisfaction scale. It's not enough. Based on Edwardson's research, midline satisfaction survey ratings (4 and 5) suggest no intention to repurchase. There's not even enough positive emotion stored in customers' emotional accounts at "6" to create much loyalty because of the strength of negative emotions.

Midline satisfaction survey ratings are not good indicators of intention to repurchase.

Professor Prashanth Nyer, at Chapman University's School of Business and Economics, has demonstrated that the felt emotions of anger, sadness, and joy are the best predictors of consumers' future behavior. Experiences of joy mean repurchasing is likely, while sadness and anger indicate repurchasing is unlikely. Dr. Nyer also found, as has Edwardson, that "emotional responses *[are] distinct* from the evaluations

119

that subjects [make] about the product."[10] This research makes a lot of sense. A diner can have two meals, essentially identical from the standpoint of food quality, speed of seating, ambience, cleanliness, and price. Yet one dining experience could be pleasant and the other personally embarrassing or disappointing, depending on the behavior of restaurant staff.

Some organizations attempt to steer away from problems inherent in the satisfaction/dissatisfaction scales by choosing measurements they think are important and then asking their customers whether they delivered. Depending on the type of questions they ask, this approach can end up creating much the same situation as traditional types of satisfaction surveys. For example, we've seen hotel surveys that ask guests about the importance of items such as "service provider was polite" or "hotel room was clean" on one-to-five scales. Customers are then asked to judge how the hotel performed on each item. If you put any thought into it at all, you realize that of course hotel guests want politeness and cleanliness in their service experience.

But such surveys don't tell the story of what fills a customer's emotional accounts. The check-in clerk may have been polite but didn't make

Without a desire to return, customers are not long-term pieces of business on which organizations can count.

the customer feel welcome, didn't recognize the customer even though this guest stays at the hotel several nights a year, and seemed to have a more intimate relationship with the computer than with the customer. Yes, customers may have been satisfied with the degree of politeness. They certainly would think its absence to be important. Customers might return to this hotel out of inertia, because the rates are good, or because of the hotel's location. However, those customers may not feel an ounce of excitement about returning. Such customers are certainly not long-term, dedicated, loyal customers on which the hotel can count.

CHAPTER SEVEN

THE CHALLENGE IN MEASURING CUSTOMER EMOTIONS

Successful organizations understand that quantitative feedback concerning customer judgments about service quality is essential for assessing whether customer needs are being met. Recent and improved technologies have made it relatively easy to measure tangible indices such as telephone hold times, the number of times a customer calls, numbers of abandoned calls, average talk times, and so on. However, because emotions also affect customers' judgments, it would be advantageous to measure and understand their strength in the service equation.

Unfortunately, customer emotional indicators are difficult to quantify and measure. Consider the examples in column 2 in the following chart:

1 Important customer data *Easier to quantify and measure*	**2** Important customer data *Difficult to quantify and measure*
■ Brand recognition	■ Range of customer emotions
■ Numbers of customers	■ Strength of customer emotions
■ Types of customers	■ Customer repurchase intentions
■ Numbers of complaints	■ Customer loyalty tendencies
■ Types of complaints	■ Customer trust
■ Ratio of new customers to old	■ Empathy displayed to customers
■ Retained customers	■ Customer feelings of being respected
■ Number of lost customers	■ Customer level of information
■ Speed of response to customers	■ Customer pride in products/services

Obviously, it is a better idea to measure important customer data than to measure less important business data. Unfortunately, because column 2 factors are difficult to measure, even though they are important, companies tend to have limited data on these metrics. You may also note that they are primarily emotional in nature.

Marsha Richins, professor of marketing at the University of Missouri, after summarizing the literature on customer emotion measurements, states point-blank, "At present, consumer behavior scholars have scant information about the nature of emotions in the consumption environment or how best to measure them."[1] She believes that it would be useful, for example, to know "exactly what it means to feel pride in product ownership, the conditions that create feelings of pride, and the effects of these feelings on other consumer variables such as brand loyalty and word of mouth."[2] These are important factors and yet are not easy to quantify or evaluate.

What are the behavioral implications connected to feeling pride in purchased products or services?

Assessing the Emotional Reactions
of Customers: The Obstacles

There are four challenges to assessing full customer reactions to service:

- Time
- Capturing customers' overall assessments
- Proving results
- Defining satisfaction in the minds of customers

The first challenge of time is easy to describe, but it is, nonetheless, a huge obstacle. Fully understanding customer emotional reactions can require in-depth interviews requiring significant time to administer. These interviews also have to be scored and analyzed.

A second challenge is capturing the *overall* assessment of customers' experiences. Customers tend to mentally evaluate service experiences as a whole, while few research approaches are capable of accurately capturing the total experience of the customer.[3] Surveys are better at measuring component pieces of the service process. William Thomas, national director of human resources for Coopers and Lybrand, identifies the challenge in capturing the concerns that serve as the foundation for long-term customer relationships:

> Real satisfaction, however, is based on much deeper values, which are developed and nurtured by ongoing relationships and experiences between a company and its customers. It is extremely difficult, if not impossible, to truly measure the degree to which customers' experience of a product or service over time matches their dynamic expectations unless the customer is engaged in a way that transcends temporal customer-satisfaction surveys.[4]

Instead, what we get are measurements on survey forms, such as "perceives front desk clerks as polite" or "thinks medical staff cares for patients." Marketing Professor Linda Price, at the University of South Florida, sees these types of measurements as "simplistic" indicators of how service providers are performing their jobs.[5] Customers who have ever filled out such questionnaires do not need to be told by academic researchers that these measurements are inadequate. The authors' experience is that *every time* we have been surveyed, only a small slice of our feelings about the service we just experienced was being reviewed.

The American Management Association cites research in which executives across the United States were asked what business measurements are most important to them. The executives listed financial performance, operating efficiency, *customer satisfaction*, employee performance, innovation/change, and community/environmental issues. Of these metrics, customer satisfaction was chosen as being of most value by the largest percentage of the executives surveyed. But how confident were the corporate executives in the data they received from their staff about customer satisfaction? Very few of them trusted it.[6] We would agree that their skepticism is justified.

A related study by the Juran Institute, the consulting firm founded by quality guru Joseph M. Juran in 1975, suggests that less than 30 percent of executives have any concrete proof that implemented customer satisfaction efforts have added economic value to their bottom lines. Only 2 percent (Yes, that is correct—2 percent!) were able to precisely measure the bottom-line impact of improved customer satisfaction levels.[7] Yet in a survey conducted by Minneapolis-based human resources consulting group Towers Perrin, 90 percent of executives agreed that if they could improve employee customer service performance, it would improve bottom-line results. These executives also recognize the role of staff in their overall business success: 73 percent said that their staffs were their most important investment.[8]

> Most executives don't have any proof that implemented customer satisfaction efforts have added economic value.

The reason why so few companies have proof that customer service programs impact economic results is that they are difficult to scientifically prove. Research on the impact of employee customer service training on customer retention exists, but most of the results point to indirect connections. Ryder Truck Rental, for example, found that employees who attended training programs had a 19 percent turnover rate; for the untrained employees, the rate was 41 percent. Based on other research, it is reasonable to conclude that if staff remain in their service positions longer, then better customer service is offered. But drawing direct cause-and-effect links is problematic.

In a more tightly controlled case study of a New England utility company, researcher Rosanne D'Ausilio found that after a four-hour conflict management training program, the length of complaint calls about bills that were judged to be too high by customers was reduced by 22.3 seconds, saving the utility company $335,000 per year.[9] Nonetheless, we can't say for sure if other operant variables impacted the length of these calls. For instance, the measurements may have taken place when customers were distracted by other issues, or the overbilling may have been significantly less complicated during the period the measurements took place.

A United States client we worked with was able to effectively reduce the size of its escalation service staff because the representatives who first talked with the customers were able to turn situations around before they reached the point where customers wanted to discontinue service. We would like to take some credit for this reduction in costs, but one of the realities we have to accept is that many aspects of business are so complicated that precise proof may be difficult to obtain. Donald Kirkpatrick, training evaluation expert, says to be satisfied with evidence because proof is usually impossible to get.[10]

Challenge number three is that customers tend to score satisfaction survey scales high. Statisticians know that most distributions of measurements will produce a bell-shaped curve. In such distributions, the majority of items measured will fall around the midpoint, with the high and low ends being considerably smaller and not looking much different from each other. Here's how a perfect bell-shaped distribution on a one-to-five scale might look:

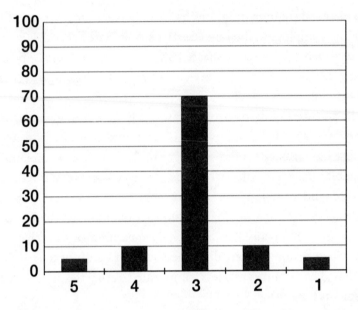

When customer satisfaction surveys are conducted by organizations themselves, however, it is common to find distributions that look like this:

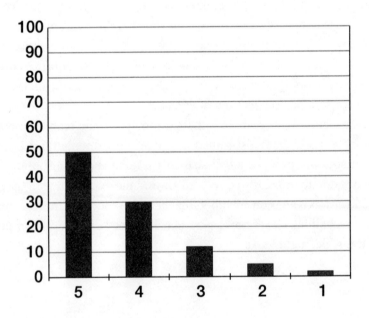

When this happens over and over again, we have to ask ourselves, What exactly are we measuring? Academic researchers are seriously concerned about this skew. If I am a manager and being evaluated for my levels of customer service, I want scales with lots of high-end evaluations, but how useful is the information? What is a scale that looks like the above one really telling me, besides giving me bragging rights?[11] Larry Keeley, president of a Chicago-based consulting firm, harshly judges these types of surveys as a way to find out about your customers: "These surveys are nothing more than tracking studies, designed to measure if customers are a little more or a little less pleased with you than they were last year."[12]

Janelle took a vacation with her family to a famous resort. It was very nice, though there were some problems. A couple of months later she received a telephone call from J. D. Powers asking her to assess her stay. She gave the resort the highest rating on every dimension, even though she didn't experience total satisfaction. All the while she was answering questions, Janelle was aware that she was contributing to this "skew." Why? First, she genuinely likes this hotel chain, and she wanted to "reward" the company. Second, she was in a hurry; someone was waiting in her office to see her, and telling the interviewer to rate everything at the highest level saved considerable time. Finally, the questions were about a specific resort, and she didn't want to get any of the staff there in trouble with their corporate offices. So she didn't discuss any of the problems her family experienced.

Many organizations use feedback reports to gather compliments. The results of many satisfaction scales are, in essence, public documents and extremely useful when companies want to advertise they have higher scores than their competitors. Unfortunately, if an organization uses its survey data this way, it becomes difficult to also use feedback scales as a means to improve. If this is the case, then you had better have another set of "books" that tell you what your customers

Many organizations use feedback reports to gather compliments.

really think of you. It is not a good idea to fool yourself about customer feedback.

In fact, the rosy picture that many companies have of customer satisfaction may lead them to an exaggerated sense of how their customers feel about them. James Morehouse, vice president for supply chain integration at A. T. Kearney, reports, "We have found from our research that most companies grossly overestimate the satisfaction levels they provide to their customers."[13] We wonder if airline personnel get taken in by the warm smiles of disembarking passengers who say "thank you" to the cabin crew and pilots. Realistically, how many passengers are going to stop at that moment and register complaints?

We have talked with representatives of a cruise line that consistently receives 97 to 99 percent satisfaction ratings on a 100 point scale. Those are exceptionally impressive numbers, but what is their message? High scores on that order probably mean that most customers circled the highest number, so the cruise line got a lot of 100s, which then pulled up the averages of those passengers who circled lower numbers.

Now don't get us wrong. This is an exceptional cruise company; it offers a truly exciting, memorable—and expensive—product. If the next cruise, however, receives a 96 percent rating, how does this compare to a 97 or 98 percent rating? Is it possible that weather influenced the scores? The president of this cruise line, while obviously pleased, will also acknowledge his frustration with these scores. He sails on his ships with a yellow legal pad, and by the end of the cruise he has taken pages and pages of single-spaced notes listing items that didn't meet his high quality standards. He says he doesn't want to get lulled by high survey numbers. We like this attitude!

> It is fairly easy to get customers to choose higher ratings by the way the questions are posed.

Satisfaction surveys in the health-care industry are particularly criticized for the way they superficially measure customer attitudes. Since these scales are published on the Internet, it is understandable that health-care corporations want the highest ratings possible. It is fairly easy to get customers to choose higher ratings, not only by the way the questions are posed but also by the choice of the scale itself. For example, if a company uses a four-point scale, instead of a five-point scale, respondents will more likely choose the higher rating off the midpoint, rather than the lower. The use of words to describe the categories can also skew results. If the choices customers have are poor, good, very good and excellent, they may be reluctant to choose poor because it seems in a different universe from good, very good, and excellent. Good is still in the lower half of the scale, but the company will be able to announce to the world that 85 percent of their customers rate their service as "good" or higher.[14]

Let's go back to our "skewed" scale on page 126, where most of the customers rate the organization at the highest levels of satisfaction. Is it possible that useful information could be pulled from such a set of results to get a separate picture of just the highest raters?[15] Of the highest raters, perhaps only 20 percent of these were truly "wowed" by the service they received. Maybe the rest were satisfied because they had no problems, but certainly nothing was added to their emotional accounts. They got problem-free service, perhaps somewhat better than the competitors', but that was all. If this is the case, probably only 20 percent of the highest raters will likely form or deepen loyalty to the business or brand. If 30 percent of the total surveyed population rated service levels at "5," that would mean that perhaps 5 or 6 percent of customers actually deepened their feelings of loyalty.[16] This is a very different picture from that given by a first glance at such high satisfaction scores.

Challenge number four in capturing customer reactions to service is that we have no clear agreement as to the meaning of "satisfaction." One might think that after all these years of studying customer satisfaction, we would know exactly what it means. Actually, there is little agreement about what it means operationally. The dictionary tells us that satisfaction *"implies complete fulfillment of one's wishes, needs, expectations, etc."*[17] That's not a bad definition, but

> *One might think that after all these years of studying customer satisfaction, we would know exactly what it means.*

we do not believe that "complete fulfillment" is what most people have in mind when taking a survey. We suspect most people see "satisfaction" as somehow the opposite of "dissatisfaction," which commonly means "I wasn't contented." If I wasn't *not* contented, then I must have been contented, hence "satisfied," but not necessarily completely fulfilled. Complete fulfillment is actually quite a tall order.

To compound the problem, satisfaction scales have an assumption built into them that the very factors that produce satisfaction will cause dissatisfaction if they are not there. This isn't always the case. Because of the high volume of miles Janelle flies, the flight attendants on her favorite carrier almost always discreetly approach her and ask her what she wants from the menu before anyone else gets to choose. This way, Janelle invariably gets her food selection. Ask Janelle about this, and she will tell you she thinks this is an excellent piece of customer service. But what if the airline didn't have this practice? Would the absence of this benefit cause dissatisfaction in Janelle? No. At the same time, it is these kinds of extras that enhance loyalty, that make regular deposits in emotional accounts.

In an attempt to navigate around the problem of the vagueness of the satisfaction definition, many surveys use gradations of satisfaction, such as the following:

Extremely satisfied   Somewhat satisfied   Acceptable   Somewhat dissatisfied   Extremely dissatisfied

The definition of "extreme" in the dictionary includes phrases such as *"at the end or outermost point . . . to an excessive degree . . . far from what is usual or conventional."* When one looks at a scale like the above, "extremely satisfied" is way beyond "fulfillment of wishes, needs, or expectations." If it genuinely meant this to consumers, we suspect customers would be reluctant to circle "5" with the frequency they do.

Furthermore, satisfaction to one person may have little to do with satisfaction to another. One customer may walk into a place of business expecting little, get more than he or she expected, and give the company high marks on the satisfaction scale. Another customer may walk into this same establishment expecting a great deal more and give the company low marks on a satisfaction sur-

> *Satisfaction to one person may have little to do with satisfaction to another.*

vey. It's conceivable that both customers received the same level of service, but one thought it was great because he or she started out with lower expectations than the other customer.[18]

This raises yet another interesting question. What is the relationship between satisfaction and service quality? Experts in this area suggest "that consumer satisfaction exerts a stronger influence on purchase intentions than does service quality."[19] For this reason, a clearer picture of customer repurchase intentions will be obtained if *both* satisfaction and service quality are considered.[20] (To read more about the elusive link between satisfaction and loyalty, see Appendix C.)

For example, research in health care suggests that customers' judgments of satisfaction are not necessarily based on the quality of care they receive. Patients may like their doctors personally and never switch practitioners, even if a misdiagnosis is made. Satisfaction in health care is mainly a short-term judgment of the last office visit, which may not have a lot to do with the long-term quality of health care the patient receives. Bedside manner may be more important in creating emotionally happy patients and therefore loyalty, while "effective health care" may cause a patient to seek out another physician if it is delivered in a hostile, uncaring manner.[21] This problem extends beyond health care and applies to most professionals—attorneys, accountants, financial advisers, architects, designers, psychologists, and consultants. If customers don't understand how products could be better (computer neophytes, for example), they may judge themselves satisfied, while some other customers with more sophistication (computer specialists, for example) might be disappointed with the same product.

CHAPTER EIGHT

THE GIFT OF EMPATHY

Years ago, Janelle was on an extended business trip that took her around the world, beginning in Hong Kong then continuing to Denmark before returning to the United States. Six hours before she was to return to the United States, she discovered her hotel room had been robbed. Cash, credit cards, passport, and all identification had been stolen. Believe it or not, this was the *third robbery* she had experienced on this trip—once in Hong Kong, where a pickpocket also got her cash, credit cards, passport, and airplane tickets, and twice in Denmark! In a panic, she called the U.S. Embassy very early in the morning. She was told to go to Copenhagen and talk with the embassy duty officer.

Based on how she looked and her accent, Janelle was given a letter indicating that she was a U.S. citizen, that her passport had been stolen, and that the airlines should allow her to return home. Getting through Kastrup Airport in Copenhagen was no problem. However, she had to transfer planes in Heathrow, London's extremely security-conscious main airport. Janelle was pulled from every line she entered and interrogated by several very unhappy Brits before passing on to the next checkpoint. It took her two hours to move from one plane to the next.

When she finally took her business-class seat on a United Airlines plane, she was stressed to the breaking point. Heaving a deep sigh of relief, Janelle broke into tears, not a normal reaction for her. A flight attendant came up to her and asked, "Is there anything wrong?" Janelle responded, "I'm just so glad to be on this airplane." The flight attendant asked: "What happened? Is there anything I can do?" She looked horrified when Janelle told her that she had been robbed three times on this trip, that she had no identification, no credit cards, no cash, nothing. The flight attendant said, "Let me see what I can do." Janelle was puzzled. Was she going to get a glass of champagne? Some peanuts? After a few minutes, the woman returned and said, "Gather up your belongings. We're upgrading you to first class."

That single act of empathic generosity has been the linchpin in Janelle's continuing loyalty to United Airlines. Several hundred thousand dollars in loyalty was nicely entered into Janelle's United Airlines emotional account. This experience raises an obvious question that organizations might ask when looking to build resilient customer loyalty. Does anyone think that United Airlines has scripted policies that read "Empathy Rule # 1: When encountering passengers in business class who are crying, go up and ask them if anything is wrong. If they answer that they have been robbed three times (definitely not just twice!), then you can go out and check if there is room in first class. If there is, upgrade them."

Empathy is as much an effective customer experience tool as asking customers whether they would like help carrying their groceries out to their cars is a good customer service tool. To maximize customer experiences with empathy, we suggest three strategies, covered in depth in the following sections:

1. *Creating a Climate for Generous Empathy.* It is impossible for organizations to precisely define the detailed and specific parameters for when empathy should be used. Staff must be allowed the freedom to implement empathy as they see fit. Organizations need to create a climate for empathy among staff, so staff are inspired to take

advantage of such moments as Janelle presented to United Airlines. This strategy is at the heart of Peter Drucker's statement about "creating customers."

2. *Broadcasting Service Successes.* Organizations have, in their collected history, hundreds of examples of customer experiences that were enhanced through the use of empathy. Organizations need to share these kinds of situations so other staff can learn from them, be encouraged by them, and then attempt to replicate them.

3. *Measuring Emotional Reactions.* Empathy must be measured, at least indirectly, and its impact understood by staff. We consider several approaches for measuring customer emotions, so organizations can communicate this "soft" data to staff, thereby providing staff with guidelines on adding emotional value.

Creating a Climate for Generous Empathy

One of the ways we encourage our clients to create a spirit of generous empathy is by adopting Mahatma Gandhi's view of customers. Gandhi's reflections, reputed to have been made over a hundred years ago while he was practicing law in South Africa, are the strongest we have ever seen about the role of the customer.

Customer is the most important visitor on our premises. He is not dependant on us. We are dependant on him. He is not an interruption on our work. He is the purpose of it. He is not an outsider on our business. He is a part of it. We are not doing him a favour by serving him. He is doing us a favour by giving us an opportunity to do so.[1]

In our own business, we use Gandhi's statement as our organizational quality standard for customer service. While we do not always achieve this level of service quality, we definitely aim for it. We have observed that implementing this standard requires unceasing effort but not necessarily major restructuring.

Implementing this standard requires unceasing effort, but not necessarily major restructuring.

Unceasing effort means day-to-day attention to the little things, the ordinary factors that make up the totality of service offerings. It includes how the phone is answered, how people's names are spelled correctly, the enthusiasm of a "thank you," the behaviors that are called the "relentlessly repetitive responsibility" of customer service. Diana Nelson, chief concierge at the Grand Hyatt in San Francisco, describes the repetition challenge: "You can imagine how many times we're asked about cable cars. And each time you talk about them you have to find the same level of enthusiasm. This is show biz. I can't hang a sign up that says, 'I'm having a bad day, so service will be off by 50 percent.' As a concierge, I have an opportunity to totally make a difference in what kind of visit to San Francisco the guest has. It's an awesome responsibility."[2]

Unisys Corporation, in cooperation with the business magazine *Management Today*, gives annual Service Excellence Awards. Giving these awards has kept Unisys itself focused on service excellence. The Unisys 1998 winner was a United Kingdom food and beverage manufacturer, Nichols Foods, which unabashedly adopts its best ideas from other companies. Nichols Foods recently sent nine managers to visit Ritz-Carlton and UPS, among others. "We came back with about 500 points on our action plan," says Martin Lee, operation manager. "Many of the ideas were simple, such as one from the First National Bank of Carolina for thanking colleagues. It's a simple piece of paper with the picture of an outstretched hand. Employees use it to thank a colleague for a job well done and pin it on the notice board."[3]

A spirit of generosity, as reflected in the simple thank-you described above, will help everyone through his or her day, and its application can be relatively simple and have little cost. Helping customers stay mentally active while waiting to be served will reduce their anxiety and can also be accomplished at little cost.[4] Use of music, television, and environmental design can help time to be perceived as passing faster, thereby shifting moods and making waiting time less frustrating. Customers will also remember better the positive aspects of service offerings if they feel they have not waited too long.[5]

> *A spirit of generosity will help everyone through his or her days.*

Reducing visual signs of staff who aren't helping customers can help as well. Sometimes customers see banking, hotel, or airline personnel standing behind counters working on a computer or register—but not helping customers. The staff may be occupied, though to a customer standing in line it looks like a service failure, and it adds to the feeling of a long wait.[6]

One negative result of viewing customers as interruptions, as outsiders to our business (using Gandhi's language), or as problems in any way is that *all* our customers tend to be seen through the same lens. They can all look like disgruntled cheats if we search for those. Is this reality? No more than to see them as all wonderful friends of our frontline staff. Reality lies somewhere in between.

Most people learn about empathy at home while growing up. They may not, however, know how to apply it to customers or in a business setting. Staff need guidance in how to show empathy toward customers in their *multiple* emotional presentation styles. We have found, as have many others, that people are easier to communicate with if you match their style. In our programs, we teach a simple but effective typology dividing communication styles into four types. This is an eye-opener for many people who have never considered variation in communication styles.

Once people learn the four styles, they understand why some people are easier for them to talk with than others. They also learn how to adjust their own style to match those that are different. This is true empathy, and when staff enhance their skill of empathy, rather than being diminished when they go out of their way for customers, they are flexing their psychological skills and have more opportunities to find joy in their work.

Flow States

Psychologist Mihaly Csikszentmihalyi describes "optimal experience" as a "flow" state.[7] Flow, in his words, involves a seamless connectivity between steps, intrinsic enjoyment of the task that is accompanied by a loss of self-consciousness. Because of its pure pleasure, flow is self-reinforcing. While Csikszentmihalyi does not discuss shared flow states in relationships, it logically follows that the basis for it is empathy. In such a

> *The basis of a shared flow state in relationships is empathy.*

shared customer transaction state of flow, both customers and staff no longer play roles in relation to each other; they mutually cooperate on the tasks at hand. Flow, according to Csikszentmihalyi, results when the challenges one faces exceed normal levels. This can occur when customers complain or have challenging needs but skills are sufficiently developed so the service provider is not overwhelmed.

Shared flow states between customers and providers are easily interrupted, especially if empathy is weak. In Part II, we discussed the necessity of staff autonomy so providers can solve their customers' problems without having to constantly get permission to act. Having to "get permission" will almost always stop the flow experience.

Failing to show customers the kind of respect that Gandhi espoused will also stop empathy, and yet it is remarkable how frequently this happens. *USA Today* reported that although more than half of all cars and trucks are purchased by women, female customers feel that mechanics

- don't show them the same respect as they give to men (57 percent of women);
- treat them as know-nothings (35 percent of women);
- make them uncomfortable about what they don't know (33 percent of women).[8]

Is it possible to teach staff to show the kind of empathy required for shared flow experiences? Director of security Pete Costner, at Advanced Micro Devices (AMD), was motivated to teach his security staff social skills after he noted complaints about customer service skills, including use of inappropriate language. Costner hired a top-notch former hotel concierge, Holly Stiel of Mill Valley, California, who has developed a special customer service program for security personnel. She offers a four-hour course on interpreting and using voice and body language, greeting people by using their names, saying no with empathy, and handling stress.

Holly's efforts resulted in course participants seeing their jobs in a new light. "It's not about being 'nice' or being 'security,'" says Holly. It's seeing things work through the filter of hospitality, which happens after staff attend her program. Within six months, AMD saw a turnaround. Complaint letters became compliment letters. Employees have opened up to the security staff and tell them about critical events that impact security around the facility. Compaq followed AMD's program and saw similar results. Quoting a Compaq spokesperson, "Officers have got the power to put a smile on someone's face." Not only have these two different firms realized the benefits from increased empathy, they have found it is relatively easy to train security people to move from "cops and robbers" to "customer service."[9]

Airborne Express does it another way. In order to support its staff who have to deliver bad news to customers about what has happened to their packages, Airborne focuses on making the agents' jobs seem like fun. Fun gets people in a more generous mood and therefore better able to show empathy. Modern music is piped into Airborne's call centers; agents are put on teams that compete for improved performance. All jobs, part-time and full-time, have full benefits, and Airborne sets up schedules for pay raises and promotions. Grace Safransky, former customer service manager for Airborne's call center in Chantilly, Virginia, says: "We can't change the attitude of the caller, but we can make it a better working environment for our employees. If the agents are happy, they are going to be a lot better with our customers."[10]

Airborne is on to something. As already mentioned, an extensive body of social psychology research supports the notion that positive moods enhance general helpfulness in people.[11] This also applies to the sales role. Once a positive mood has been established, salespeople let this positive feeling affect how they perceive and describe their customers.[12] As we saw in Part I, research demonstrates that people have better inductive reasoning in a positive mood state and are more flexible in their thinking. Salespeople in positive moods are more creative in selling products and services that are personalized and, therefore, more valuable to customers.[13]

Larry Sanders, president and COO of Fujitsu Computer Products of America, Inc., took over his position when Fujitsu was suffering from flat revenues. Among other strategies, Sanders shifted the focus of the company to customers. "I am a believer [that] you organize around your customers, you don't organize around your company."[14] Customer focus, the Gandhi approach to customer service, is the foundation for maximizing customer experiences with empathy.

Nonetheless, it is stunning to find that many companies still create negative mood environments among their sales staffs, primarily by the ways they structure their incentives and place pressure on their staffs. We know several clients that want their brand to be known for customer service, while the sales department engages in high-pressured sales techniques.

■ Application

Schedule a Session with Your Team. Show everyone the Gandhi statement and ask: What if we truly treated all our customers, both internal and external, as if they were the most important visitor on our premises? What if we behaved so that customers were never treated as interruptions of our business? What if we truly considered our customers to be a part of our business? What would we have to do differently? What do we currently do to make our customers feel like outsiders or like interruptions?

Teaching Empathy through Better Listening

Empathy has two aspects: a feeling part (sensing what someone else is feeling) and a thinking part (understanding what someone else is feeling).[15] It is on the cognitive side of empathy that listening plays such a crucial role—especially for the purpose of retaining customers. Based on one of its studies of thirteen large manufacturing and service companies, the Forum Corporation concluded that 70 percent of customer loss happens because of a lack of attention from frontline staff.[16]

> *Empathy has two aspects, a feeling part and a thinking part.*

140

Yet most psychologists believe that it is possible to teach people to be more empathic. Dr. Janet Strayer, of Simon Fraser University, puts it this way:

> Everyone is born with the capacity for empathy—it's part of our biological and cognitive wiring. But there is also a lot of social scaffolding and experiences that can influence how empathy develops, which means we can do something about it.[17]

Rather than tackle empathy head-on, individuals and organizations may find it more accessible by focusing on the role of listening in empathy. Listening skills can be taught, and modern electronic systems can also make listening easier and more immediate. For example, Airborne Express has a new computer telephone system called Customer First. Airborne's system is linked to its automated call system, which customers reach when they first call. By pushing phone buttons, customers indicate whether they need a pickup, package tracking, rate information, or supplies. By the time the customer speaks to an Airborne agent, the agent knows what the customer wants and already has all of the customer's information on a computer screen—and it takes less than two seconds.[18] In effect, the computer "listens" for the agent, so the agent can focus on information of greater interest to customers than spelling out their names, reciting their addresses and phone numbers, and providing their customer identification numbers.

Rather than tackle empathy head on, individuals may find it more accessible by focusing on the role of listening in empathy.

The Five Cs of Intimacy Theory

Customer focus can also be optimized if an organization implements the five Cs of intimacy theory: communication, caring, commitment, comfort, and conflict resolution. All five require active questioning and listening skills and are frequently suggested as critical to relationship building.[19] They certainly impact customers' experiences, which are inherently personal. No two customers will ever taste the same service because experiences are reflective of internal involvement,

No two customers will ever experience the same service, because experiences are reflective of internal involvement.

and this depends on the way people have been engaged. At a minimum, service providers in the experience economy have to ask for and then "listen" for uniqueness, which can be done using the following five Cs.

COMMUNICATION

Communication involves proactive questioning, and the ability to repeat back information accurately; it also includes some degree of self-disclosure. Some people think listening is simply not interrupting. It is much more than that. Communication is facilitated by asking questions and resisting jumping to conclusions. Complete questioning can reduce anxiety because customers know that further delays or mistakes won't be so likely to happen if full information is taken. Sometimes communication involves quiet listening or simply nonjudgmental sympathy. Other times it requires self-disclosure, such as when the service provider says, "Yes, I know what you mean. I've had the same experience myself."

CARING

Caring means valuing another individual for who he or she is, rather than who you would like that person to be. Simply put, it's liking your customers in whatever form they appear. We will never forget an entire group of passengers watching a flight attendant stop to "ooh and aah" over a toddler whose face we could not see. After she walked away, the small child stood up on his seat to watch her leave, at which time we could all see a delighted, smiling—and seriously physically deformed—child. People tend to be more caring and empathic toward people who are similar to them, and customers are not always "normal." Questioning can reveal the ways in which people are similar, thereby increasing likeability and empathy. Listening is also a statement about caring. In effect, if I am willing to listen to you, I must be interested in you.

COMMITMENT

Commitment is taking responsibility for being reliable, for creating a feeling of "we-ness." This means getting back to customers and colleagues in a timely manner and questioning whether everything has been handled. Amazon.com, the giant on-line bookstore, will send you an e-mail indicating it has received your order—within seconds. This speed of response creates an immediate impression that is lasting. Yet it is amazing how many companies do not create this feeling of commitment in their responses to customers. In 1998, Jupiter Communications found that 42 percent of top-ranked Web e-commerce sites either took longer than five days to respond to customer inquiries, never responded, or were unavailable for questioning![20] Commitment also refers to the willingness of an organization to view its customers as long-term relationships and structure interactions that way.

COMFORT

Comfort means reaching out to someone else to create a feeling of compatibility and then doing everything possible to help that person. Complete questioning creates the feeling that the organization is not trying to run away from bad news and that it can handle the answers customers will provide.[21] Comfort also involves supportive comments that service providers can easily provide to customers. Janelle was recently in Manhattan and stopped by a particularly interesting Discovery Shop. Discovery Shops are the kinds of stores you want to go into with a friend

> *Complete questioning creates the feeling that the organization is not trying to run away from bad news.*

so you can talk about the products. Visually, all the displays in the store help customers to experience a level of excitement. Unfortunately, the clerks in this particular store didn't complete the job of transmitting excitement. Instead of walking around the store and commenting favorably on the products being considered for purchase, all the Discovery Shop clerks were in active discussion with their colleagues about what they were going to do the following weekend. No comfort there!

One of Dianna's triplets needed braces. The orthodontist Dianna wanted to see was completely booked, so she was referred to a relatively new dentist, still building his practice. At 7:30 that evening, following her initial visit, Dianna received a call from the orthodontist wanting to know how her son was doing, how much pain he was experiencing. He told Dianna that since they would be working together for about two years on this "project," he wanted to be sure to get to know her. Dianna was so impressed with his concern that the next day, when a friend of the family said one of his children needed braces, Dianna quickly recommended her new orthodontist. He got a second patient within twenty-four hours of showing comfort to a customer.

CONFLICT RESOLUTION

Conflict resolution involves creating trust in relationships so people can work through conflicts. Trust lets customers know their patronage is valued over a period of time and that any specific conflict is not going to result in the end of the relationship. This kind of trust building assumes that frontline staff have been given adequate control to resolve customer problems that may turn into conflicts. Active questioning also helps reduce hostility, as long as the questions are not perceived to be irrelevant. Anger and hostility almost always involve blaming, and questioning can help both the customer and the service provider focus on something other than attribution.

> *Active questioning also helps reduce hostility.*

Apologies Lead to Empathy—and Then to Forgiveness

Apologies, if appropriately offered, generally lead to forgiveness and concern for the person who has just apologized. Continental Airlines went through a customer service transformation between 1994, when it was nearly bankrupt, and 1997, when it once again became profitable, winning service awards along the way. During the recovery period, the president and the chairman, Greg Brenneman and Gordon Bethume, personally called the airline's angriest customers to spell out Continental's vision—and to apologize for previous bad service.

Brenneman noted this about apologies and the humbling experience of talking with upset customers:

> You might think the first step in breaking the doom loop is to fix the product, but that's actually the second step. The first is to beg forgiveness from all the customers you have wronged. Sure, you can skip this step, but you'll miss out on the goodwill it fosters and the relationships it spawns. Confession is good for everyone's soul, and often for the pocketbook as well.[22]

In the last decade, forgiveness has become an almost popular subject of investigation among social psychologists. Among them are Robert Enright, at the University of Wisconsin, Madison, founder of the International Forgiveness Institute, and Michael McCullough, at the National Institute for Healthcare Research in Rockville, Maryland. Both psychologists say that *forgiveness is one of the most fundamental processes that keep relationships functioning.*

McCullough believes apologies motivate empathy, which, in turn, creates a greater likelihood of forgiveness. McCullough's research supports this notion.[23] He found that when a person forgives someone, the forgiver becomes less spiteful and less likely to avoid the other person. McCullough also discovered that after he initially discussed empathy with research subjects, they were more likely to forgive than if empathy had not been discussed. When an organization wounds customers, apologies are essential so customers can forgive the organization—and resume business.

Apologies motivate empathy, which, in turn, creates a greater likelihood of forgiveness.

When service providers demonstrate their concern for their customers with apologies, exchanged empathy becomes part of the communication process. Complaining customers will blame less and show more concern for the service provider if the service provider apologizes. With a sincere apology, psychological equity is restored to someone who has been treated poorly. An apology is more than mere words; it is an appropriate, even necessary, *specific outcome* of the complaint situation.

If delivered well, an apology is something concrete with which the customer walks away.

But the apology has to be genuine. There are few emotional barbs more pointed than an insincere "Sorry." Bernard Marcus, Home Depot's chairman and CEO, on the other hand, got a standing ovation from shareholders—something that doesn't happen every day—after his apology. Marcus had tears come to his eyes at a shareholder meeting when apologizing about customer service complaints. "It's very emotional for me when I hear that customers are not being treated well. I take it in my gut."[24]

Contrast Marcus's sincere apology with an incident reported about a patron of the long-running Broadway show *Cats*. A woman with nine family members in tow was "picked on" and embarrassed by a prowling cat cast member, even though she clearly said "No" to the unfavorable attention she received. The "cat" mussed her hair, made unwanted suggestive sexual gestures, and moved her head from side to side—all while a bright spotlight illuminated her for the rest of the audience to see. The innocent show attendee felt humiliated. When the theater-goer wrote a complaint letter to the show's producers, she received a general written apology—two months later—with a suggestion that she come back to the show![25] Nothing specific was said about her humiliating experience.

■ Application

What is your current "apology culture?" From the customer's point of view, how do you apologize? Do you proactively call customers and apologize in advance of their knowing something has gone wrong? What does an apology mean inside your organization? Do you have legalities in the back of your mind when apologizing? Do these legalities stop your staff from offering sincere apologies?

Focusing on the Impact of Service

One of the most captivating stories told about the beginning stages of the quality movement is the one about Homer Saransohn. When General MacArthur was in charge of the Japanese occupation following

World War II, he understood that the government needed to be able to communicate with the entire population spread across the four main islands of Japan. The radio was determined to be the cheapest, most readily available communication tool. Unfortunately, Japanese electronics manufacturers had extremely poor quality. Ninety percent of the radios that reached consumers' homes ended up not working properly!

MacArthur invited Homer Saransohn, a General Electric (GE) systems engineer, to come to Japan and help the electronics manufacturers with their quality. Saransohn was the first American to discuss quality in Japan. And, as some say, the rest is history in terms of Japanese dominance in home electronics. Saransohn, faced with participants who didn't want to be in his seminars, began his programs with a challenge. He asked his participants to tell him why they were in business—and they weren't allowed to say it was to make money.

By asking this question, Saransohn was getting the electronics manufacturers to look at the impact of their products on customers, rather than focusing on the function of their businesses. We have asked thousands of people in our complaint handling workshops to do something similar by writing what we call a Customer Impact Job Description (CIJD), a one-sentence description of how their work impacts the customer—from the customer's point of view. The best CIJDs are frequently written so totally from the point of view of the customer, it is impossible to guess what the employee specifically does. For example, computer technologists have written that they enable their customers to go home early and sleep well at night. (That's certainly been our experience with our own in-house technologist.) A receptionist said he was the first voice of his company to customers. A support person said, "I make the difficult seem easy to my customers." A secretary said, "I make my boss look great." Others have talked about enabling their customers to be better than the best, taking away the anxiety of working with technology, or creating a competitive advantage.

Most staff, unfortunately, tend to think of their work in terms of functions, and almost always from their own point of view. Work is described in terms

Most staff tend to think of their work in terms of functions.

147

> *From the customers' point of view, however, it is the impact of functions that matters, not the functions themselves.*

such as filing, distribution, drafting, answering questions, filling orders, serving food, collecting money for goods and services, flying airplanes, cleaning hotel rooms, repairing computers, or offering technical advice. From the customers' point of view, however, it is the impact of these functions that matters, not the functions themselves.

Once impact is understood, a foundation for genuine, authentic empathy will have been established. For example, our customers who order Time Manager products from us may become livid if we don't get the products to them in a timely manner or if we send them the wrong product. These mistakes happen from time to time. When customers call our office in a fit of rage (at times even swearing), we try to understand why our customers are so upset. It is tempting to disparage them: "Get a life; it's only a calendar." Rather, we try to understand why the Time Manager calendar is so important to them. When we listen with empathy, we realize that our customers had high expectations of us that we didn't fulfill, and most importantly, they feel they are at a tremendous disadvantage without their Time Manager products.

At such moments, our customers deserve our compassion, our empathy, and not our disparagement. Once we grasp this, then we can react more authentically. Focusing on customer impact makes it easier for our staff to handle customer emotional outbursts. TMI staff tend not to internalize customer attacks as much.

Studs Terkel in his book *Working* writes that Americans are "bigger" than their jobs, suggesting that the spirit of humans is bigger than most of the tasks they perform. He quotes, as proof, American workers describing their jobs:

> "I'm a machine," says the spot welder. "I'm caged," says the bank teller, and echoes the hotel clerk. "I'm a mule," says the steel worker. "A monkey can do what I do," says the receptionist. "I'm less than a farm implement," says the migrant worker. "I'm an object," says the high

fashion model. Blue collar and white collar call upon the identical phrase: "I'm a robot."[26]

We couldn't disagree more. We certainly agree that most people are "bigger" than their jobs if you consider only the functions of work, which is the view the Terkel workers have taken. But when you start looking at impact on other humans, it is arrogant for service providers, or anyone else, to see themselves as "bigger" than the recipients of their work.

> It is arrogant for service providers to see themselves as "bigger" than the recipients of their work.

Recently a television news program ran an interview of a New York City street sweeper. The newly employed worker, a former welfare recipient, was grousing about his work, saying it was boring, repetitive, and worthless. When considered from the impact of clean streets, cleanliness can hardly be seen as worthless. Clean streets mean better hygiene and more attractive communities, which in turn contribute to healthier communities and more tourism, which leads to increased prosperity for all. Finally, clean streets also correlate with reduction in crime levels—hardly a "worthless" impact.

If service workers could understand and also be periodically reminded of the impact of their work on customers, they might be able to deliver these services more wholeheartedly. Emotional labor seems less burdensome when viewed from the perspective of customer impact. Clearly, it need not diminish the provider. The starting point for this approach is the organization's mission statement. Is it written from the customer's point of view? Is the mission statement known to all in the organization? Are the customer service implications of the mission statement understood?

Many clients we work with do not have any idea as to their company's mission. If they do have the mission statement memorized, they find it difficult to put in words what it means to them in their daily work. Many mission statements are filled with admirable high-minded concepts. However, many frustrated staff tell us that if there is any conflict between living the mission and bottom-line results, the dollar value is judged more important, and the mission statement is forgotten.

■ **Application**

Writing a Customer Impact Job Description (CIJD). Keep the description very brief—perhaps one sentence. We have found the best way to "coach" for the best Customer Impact Job Descriptions is to keep asking the question, "So what?" For example, if someone writes, I get products delivered on time, then ask, So what? What does that mean to your customers? Place your CIJD in your desk area so you can be reminded of your impact.

Eliminate Customer Name-Calling

Many organizations engage in what is possibly the most destructive behavior pattern for polluting an emotion-friendly service culture. This is the practice of customer name-calling. We're not referring to the names customers are called to their faces. In fact, rarely do service providers behave so badly as to use disparaging terms when their customers can overhear—unless it is done in fun or with affection. We are talking about the name-calling that goes on when customers cannot hear what is being said about them. Because of the unequal power relationship between customers and staff, with customers supposedly "always right," it is tempting for staff to reassert themselves by name-calling when they think customers are no longer within earshot.

This name-calling can take the form of eye-rolling while listening on the telephone or making lewd gestures that only other colleagues can see. Then it rapidly degenerates into labeling and nasty name-calling. We've heard people called, among other names, idiots, jerks, bimbos, animals, creeps, and retards (just to list the ones we feel comfortable writing in this book). Some companies actually write negative comments in customer files, so *everyone* in the future can form an immediate stereotyped view of a particular customer.

This name-calling sometimes goes on even in the immediate presence of customers, which makes one wonder if managers pay attention to customer name-calling at all. We have heard store personnel berate customers when they use rest rooms set up for both staff and the public. As customers, it makes us feel as if we are giving money to people who think of us as outrageous, stupid interruptions in their busy day. We hear this most frequently from airline personnel waiting to catch buses to employee parking lots. Do they not notice that their customers are standing within hearing distance of these conversations, or do they simply not care?

One of our TMI colleagues saw a description of himself on a hotel function sheet. He was described as a "picky customer." There are so many other, generous words that could have been used, such as "Customer has impeccable standards." We recommend that service organizations discontinue this name-calling immediately. Bring it to zero overnight. In our own consulting/training firm, the worst comment we will ever make about a customer is "That was a challenging telephone call." We try to understand why our customers are upset with us, why we had such a strong impact on them that they got angry. We make it a point to analyze what we can

> *Bring your customer name-calling to zero overnight!*

learn from our "challenging" customers. After all, we have to take some responsibility for the fact that they are our customers. We could turn them away, as can most businesses. We would rather view them, to use Gandhi's terms, as "the most important visitor on our premises."

▪ Application

Discuss Name-Calling at a Group Meeting. Set a standard for no derogatory name-calling behind customers' backs. Then, whenever you hear anyone make a derogatory remark about customers, speak up. Don't let the situation go unnoticed. Name-calling is a delicate situation and demands a careful approach toward those who engage in such a practice. If you attack the name-callers, you'll just drive the practice underground. You want to get everyone to see that name-calling creates an atmosphere of denigration and fosters seeing customers through a filter of negativity. It's difficult to offer world-class service in such an atmosphere. Determine if your staff understand the reasons and feelings beneath this tendency to put customers down. Ask them if there are negative implications for themselves when they engage in this type of labeling.

Broadcasting Service Successes

By focusing awareness on examples of outrageously good service, organizations can increase understanding about the power of extra service effort. This can be easily accomplished by sharing examples of outstanding service efforts and by broadcasting strong examples of service recovery.

The Power of Extra Service Efforts

Extra service efforts can be highlighted by using an exercise we invite our seminar participants to complete. First, we ask participants to identify a five-step level of service for their organization. This could include Poor Service, Minimal Service, Good Service, Excellent Service, and Outstanding Service. We then ask them to choose a specific piece of their service offerings, thinking of it as a Moment of Truth. Third, they are asked to describe how this moment of truth would look at the five levels of service they have identified. *Finally, we ask our seminar participants to indicate what customers are likely to do at each level of the delivered service.*

A description follows of how one client completed this exercise. A hotel operator described a foreign guest asking for the telephone number of a local business.

> **Poor Level of Service.** Tell your guest you don't have external telephone numbers at your station, so you can't help.
>
> **Minimal Level of Service.** Explain to the guest that the local telephone book is in the drawer by the bed.
>
> **Good Service.** Politely explain to the guest that the local telephone book is in the drawer by the bed, and offer to look up the number for the guest.

Excellent Service. Look up the number for your guest and provide it while the guest waits (if this is the guest's preference), or call the guest back as soon as you find the number.

Outstanding Service. Look up the number for your guest and offer to call the number yourself to make sure it is in service. If the offer is accepted and the number has a automated phone menu, tell your guest how to best navigate the menu. Check back fifteen minutes later to make sure your guest was able to get through to the business.

Whenever we conduct this exercise, we are in awe at the creativity staff will bring to figuring out outstanding ways to deliver their service. When we ask them to tell us what customers are likely to do if they receive minimal, good, or excellent service, it becomes quite clear to them that *loyalty is created primarily at the outstanding service level.* No loyalty is engendered with minimal or good service. In fact, little loyalty is created by even excellent service.

> *Loyalty is mostly created at the outstanding service level.*

Once staff understand this, they more clearly recognize the importance of their role in keeping customers. They also understand that outstanding service does not have to be delivered at all times. Indeed, it would be impossible to do so. Time would not permit such lavish levels of service. But a single, strong experience of outstanding service is forever burned in customers' emotional memories.

We also ask seminar participants to list examples of outstanding service they have received. It never ceases to amaze us how people remember examples from years, even decades, ago, and always they are examples of strong empathy. Someone cared for the customer and did something about it. Listening to stories of this type reaffirms one's faith in the basic goodness of humanity.

Broadcasting Stories of Service Recovery

We have listened to legendary service stories over the years in our customer service seminars and are touched by the generosity of spirit in commercial relationships. One we will never forget occurred at the Excelsior Hotel in Hong Kong. A guest was found unconscious in his hotel room and was taken to a hospital. It turned out that he needed a blood transfusion of an extremely rare blood type. One of the members of the concierge staff happened to have the exact blood match. He voluntarily rushed off to the hospital and donated blood to the hotel guest. We'd call that an extreme example of customer service. But until we conducted this "Legendary Service Examples" exercise in a seminar, none of the employees who had been hired over the years since the blood donation had heard the story. Organizations need to create vehicles for discussing their legendary customer service examples.

One way to do this is by starting a "Thorns to Roses" column in your in-house newsletter, so examples of positive and outrageous customer service examples can be shared. Let the entire staff know about the heroics of their colleagues. And then share these stories on your Web site, and in your customer mailings. In fact, tell the entire world! If organizations are serious about retaining their customers, they need to share these examples to inspire everyone to match these levels. It's part of branding.

> *Organizations need to share strong service examples to inspire everyone to match these levels.*

Nordstrom has succeeded in being identified as a department store that offers positive customer service to such a degree that we recently heard a stand-up comic, Steve Bridges, of Los Angeles, relate a humorous story about outstanding Nordstrom service. He didn't have to explain Nordstrom's reputation. Everyone knew. Steve bought a new shirt from a Nordstrom competitor for a gig he was rushing off to, only to discover that his new shirt was very wrinkled. On his way to the parking lot, he happened to pass by a Nordstrom, went inside, and asked a nearby clerk if she could please iron it for him. He explained that he had bought the shirt from a competitor at the opposite end of the mall. The clerk said, "No problem," took the shirt, and brought it back, freshly ironed—in a Nordstrom bag. The comic swears it's a true story. He then delivers his punch line: the following week he took all his laundry to Nordstrom!

Measuring Emotional Reactions

Instead of focusing so intently on customer satisfaction ratings, organizations would benefit by looking at what customers truly value and the factors that deepen their relationships with product and service providers. Since customer loyalty correlates only slightly with satisfaction ratings (see Appendix C), it is important to investigate the aspects of products or services that keep customers coming back. In other words, *measure the product and service characteristics that customers value and think are important.* Value and importance will always have an emotional component. Then spend your time refining the service components that matter the most to your customers.

> Spend your time refining the service components that matter the most to your customers.

A former Fortune 500 CEO of a chemical company highlights this point: "We look for those things that customers perceive as adding value to their relationship with us. That allows us to focus on the critical few issues that affect both our performance for our customer and our profitability."[27] Here's a way to look at this advice.

Critical Customer Factors

1 Adds Value High Performance **Keep Up the Good Work!**	**3** Adds Value Low Performance **Focus on These!**
2 Adds Little Value High Performance **Probably Overkill**	**4** Adds Little Value Low Performance **Low Priority for Change**

The best way to clarify what your customers value is to ask them. One way to do this is to create a list of service attributes for each dimension of your service. Always be sure to ask your customers if there is anything else they consider important, and leave room for them to write their comments in case you have overlooked something. Here's a general list of service dimensions you can use to spark ideas for creating specific attribute lists for your own products and services.

- Clear, reliable information
- Honesty
- Flexibility
- Speed
- No-hassle service
- Accuracy
- Creative ideas
- Options
- Tailored services
- Follow-through on commitments
- Best communication
- Single-source service
- Courteous service
- Knowledge of customer
- Unique giveaways
- Special product features

When choosing attributes, select those that are unique to your brand because they will help refresh your customers' memories. For example, Doubletree Resorts gives hotel guests a warm chocolate chip cookie upon check-in. References to those cookies in a feedback survey help trigger a set of memories about a stay at Doubletree that will result in better response data.

Once you have identified your specific service attributes, ask your customers to rank them in terms of importance, or set up a scale to capture the importance of each attribute, such as the evaluation scale shown on the following page. Finally, ask how well you delivered. Don't be afraid to use emotional ratings, as well as the traditional excellent-to-poor rating, that can help customers have fun with their evaluations.

Always leave room for customers to write their comments.

Keep your surveys simple and provide the customer with space for written comments. Birmingham Midshires Building Society in the United Kingdom sends out a survey that consists of five simple questions on the front side and plenty of free space for comments on the reverse side. At the bottom of the survey, the home telephone number of the chief executive office is listed. The society has found that very few people will actually call the number. They have found, however, that their members take the survey much more seriously when their executive's home telephone number is posted, and if someone does call, he or she is interviewed in depth. The society then makes references to the surveys in its newsletters to members.[28]

How important is this to you?		How well are we doing?
Of utmost importance (I won't come back without this)	5	Outstanding (Truly in a class by yourself)
Very important (I definitely want this)	4	Very good (Better than most)
Somewhat important (I like it)	3	Good (More or less average)
Relatively unimportant (I'll take it if it's offered)	2	Fair (Definitely below the norm)
Couldn't care less (Don't bother)	1	Poor (Get some help!)

Measure Parameters That Are Useful to Your Staff

One way to determine if you are measuring the "right" parameters is to see if staff get excited about the latest data uncovered in your customer surveys. If the surveys are only glanced at when they first come out, are rapidly placed into files, and are not used by anyone to make changes in the organization, you know you aren't measuring the right parameters.

See if your staff get excited about the latest data uncovered in your customer surveys.

Robert B. Woodruff, who holds the Distinguished Professor of Marketing Chair at the University of Tennessee, writes that evaluations "may not provide enough of the customer's voice to guide managers in how to respond."[29] For example, if a satisfaction survey rating decreases from 4.7 to 4.5 in a year's time, it is difficult for staff to use this information to make appropriate changes. But if hotel guests are given an opportunity to specifically comment on check-in waiting time in a meaningful way, for example, strategies can be implemented to address the emotional reaction to waiting. Perhaps more clerks need to be added to the front desk. Perhaps clerks need coaching to remain alert and then implement alternatives when a long line forms. Perhaps clerks need to learn how to reduce irritation among those forced to wait.

Sometimes companies fix problems with costly interventions, such as adding more staff, when displayed emotional competency by existing staff would be more than effective. For example, sometimes all that is

Some companies fix problems with costly interventions, when displayed emotional competency would be adequate.

required to emotionally care for anxious customers is for the clerks to glance at the line to indicate to the people standing in it that they haven't been forgotten and will be attended to quickly.

Greg Brenneman, who was in large part responsible for Continental Airlines' spectacular turnaround, talks about questioning the right customers, specifically the "customers in seat 9C." Brenneman focused on business travelers (who tend to book aisle seats near the front of the airplane; hence "seat 9C"), because Continental, like most airlines, makes most of its profits from business travelers. As Brenneman says, "We're not trying to be a four-star restaurant, just an airline that gives its customers something they'd be happy to pay for. And that's the whole point of asking the customer in seat 9C the right question. In a turnaround situation—or any business situation, for that matter—you can't afford to ask anything else."[30]

Senior-level managers might also consider spending time in the field with their staff to find out if appropriate measurements are being taken. Claude R. Martin, professor of retail marketing at the University of Michigan in Ann Arbor, says, "The further senior management gets away from the point of delivery, the more they have to rely on sophisticated feedback—surrogates—to help inform them about what's going on."[31]

Surveys not only need to measure useful parameters, they need to do it in a way that doesn't create an unnecessary burden on either customers or frontline staff. If senior-level managers do not go out to the field and get involved with the day-to-day operations of their business, they may never know this. One such senior manager, Lamar Bell, CFO of the 451-restaurant chain Golden Corral, has done restaurant duty every year since he joined Golden Corral over a decade ago. "It makes me appreciate what our managers and employees have to go through." He appreciates that store managers frequently "may be completing their paperwork at 2 A.M., after a full day in the restaurant." He says that serving customers is their first priority and that anything corporate asks of them is secondary.[32]

Metaphors Can Capture Emotional Reactions

Because measuring the empathy a customer has experienced is important, measurement approaches that are different and more complex than
standard satisfaction scales may need to be devel-
oped. An easy-to-administer measurement may not
capture customers' experiences, especially of empathy. Market researchers Cathay Goodwin, Stephen
Grove, and Raymond Fisk recommend using
metaphors to more fully capture emotional reactions
of customer experiences.[33]

> *Metaphors can
> more fully capture
> emotional reactions
> of customer
> experiences.*

Most customer service questionnaires ask customers to rate the
attributes of discrete pieces of the service: for example, to what degree
was the check-in courteous, timely, friendly? To what degree was the
front lobby clean? To what degree was your room comfortable? There is
very little room in such a survey for a customer to, for example, express
emotional reactions to interacting with an unhelpful front desk clerk
who summarily told the guest that the hotel was oversold and the guest
would have to stay at another hotel, even though the guest had a guaranteed reservation. This happened recently to Janelle. She was then given
a feedback form that asked about speed of check-in service! It was actually quite fast—even if she didn't get a room. If she had been asked to
describe what the experience was like, which is how metaphors are best
elicited, she would have said, "Front desk clerk behaved like a constipated
dictator." That might have been useful information to the hotel!

Granted, not all customers may be comfortable with this approach,
especially if their vocabulary is as extensive as, "I don't know." But then,
the feedback gathered on a traditional feedback form from such an
uncommunicative customer may be of limited use also. Goodwin,
Grove, and Fisk describe the feedback they receive by using metaphors:
"Particularly important is the fact that metaphors can generate both cognitive and emotional insights regarding customers' perceptions. . . . The
metaphors were vivid and informative, synthesizing complex dimensions and integrating components of the service experience."[34] A smaller

customer sample well measured may be of more use than a huge population poorly measured.

Measuring Key Indicators of Loyalty, Not Satisfaction

While organizations need not be interested in customer satisfaction for its own sake, they need to be consumed by what happens when customers are happy or excited or whatever emotional state is appropriate for them to experience. Namely, do happy customers (1) continue to do business, (2) purchase additional products and services, and (3) tell others? If this is what is interesting, why not focus directly on what customers do when they are happy? In doing so, attention will be placed on the behaviors and reactions of happy customers, which undoubtedly include loyalty and product referrals to others.

" . . . metaphors can generate both cognitive and emotional insights regarding customers' perceptions."

Some organizations do this by asking their customers whether they will recommend their services to someone else. Others, like Bank One of Columbus, Ohio, pay attention to the number of services used by each customer as a measure of retention. This focus, Bank One believes, has enabled it to achieve a return on assets more than double that of its competitors.[35]

Organizational goals also need to target specific customer behaviors—rather than aiming at higher numbers in satisfaction surveys. A customer retention goal, for example, could be to have 25 percent of customers buy a second product. Or set a goal that 10 percent of new business comes from customer referrals.

Measuring Emotional Content of Satisfaction

Michael Edwardson, the Australian marketing professor we introduced earlier, relies on "fuzzy set" theory to identify *patterns* of customer emotions. By pointing out these patterns, he helps companies pinpoint clues as to what customers want in their service situations.

Edwardson has identified "emotional markers" for positive and negative aspects of service in a wide range of industries. Emotional markers are emotions that are unique to a particular service category. Among others, Edwardson has described the emotion profile for the retail clothing sector, the hospitality industry, and banks. Because emotional markers are industry dependent, this approach doesn't fall into the trap of measuring one dimension (namely, satisfaction) across all industries. While Edwardson's lists are longer than the ones provided below, the main emotions for these three industries are as follows:

Emotion Profiles

	Retail Clothing	Hospitality	Bank
Positive	(grateful) relieved happy satisfied excited content	welcome excited warm happy content anticipation (relaxed)	surprised (trusting) encouraged curious happy
Negative	indignant impatient embarrassed annoyed angry (irritated) frustrated disappointing	impatient embarrassed angry annoyed frustrated (disappointed)	anxious nervous angry (powerless) frustrated

The circled words are the emotional markers, and these are the emotions that customers will use to decide whether the service has been positive or negative for them.[36] For example, customers may feel irritated by service they have received from a bank, but irritation is not as critical for banking customers as for retail clothing customers. In order to create loyal customers, retail clothing stories must focus on getting their customers to feel grateful and happy while shopping with them, while avoiding irritation. Banks should focus on establishing trust with their customers while averting situations creating feelings of powerlessness. The hospitality industry should focus on creating feelings of relaxation and stay away from disappointing their guests.

Edwardson is then able to describe how customers play out "scripts" based on these clues. Researching the scripts unique to each industry, he advises companies how to best influence what customers feel. As described in chapter 2, "Managing Emotions Begins with Me," a customer can easily go from being impatient to feeling angry and then to feeling neglected, cheated, and finally upset. However, if the service provider reads the emotions the customer is experiencing and then positively intervenes, the service provider could help the customer go from impatient to encouraged and finally to happy.

Janelle recently experienced these scripts managed to an effective degree at a Ritz-Carlton Hotel in Bali, Indonesia. Relaxation oozes out of every pore of that property. When her luggage was mistakenly not delivered to her room upon check-in, practically the entire hotel staff got into action to minimize the disappointment, above all to avoid anger. The disappointment was rapidly converted into contentment because the staff profusely apologized, "owned the problem," and promised the luggage would be delivered immediately. Finally there was a happy smile on everyone's face as the luggage arrived. Back to relaxation!

Edwardson would be the first to emphasize that this approach to customer service requires emotionally intelligent service staff who can recognize emotional scripts and then influence these scripts in a positive direction. It is our assessment, however, that this approach is a worthwhile investment to better influence future customer behavior in a direction the organization wants.

ASSESSING YOUR ORGANIZATION'S EMPATHY

Answer the following questions:

1. What do you do when your staff or colleagues berate your customers? Do you ignore such remarks, or do you use these opportunities to discuss the role of the customer?

2. Have you considered the implications of berating customers? What does this say about "partnerships with customers?"

3. What "cues" do you send customers that you care for them, that you want to listen to them?

4. What would you have to change in your organization if customers purchased only the "experience" of your organization? What would make them keep coming back, if nothing tangible were received?

5. What is the impression your organization creates by the speed with which you respond to customers?

6. What is the impression your survey tools create on customers?

7. Do you know how well frontline staff listen to your customers? What indicators would tell you when you have a problem?

PART FOUR

VIEWING COMPLAINTS AS EMOTIONAL OPPORTUNITIES

Progress flows only from struggle.

Louis Brandeis

Complaining customers can be converted into loyal customers who engage in less negative word of mouth. As a result, treating complaining customers well is, in many ways, a simple economic decision. It has been estimated, as a general ratio, that it costs five times more to get a new customer than to keep an existing one.[1]

Effective complaint handling can make a major difference to customer retention rates—even after service failures. According to a Technical Assistance Research Programs, Inc. (TARP) National Consumer Survey study, if customers experience minor problems and their complaints are resolved quickly, 95 percent will repurchase from the same organization; 82 percent will buy again even if the problem is major. If the complaint is resolved, but not quickly, only 70 percent will repurchase if they had a minor problem, while 54 with a major problem will repurchase. If the complaint is not resolved at all, 46 percent will repurchase with a minor problem and 19 percent with a major problem.[2] Clearly, there is a lot to be gained in terms of speedy, effective complaint handling.

Emotionality is stronger when customers complain, and these emotions need as much attention as resolving problems. We recommend a variety of strategies that will add positive emotional value to a difficult situation.

CHAPTER NINE

COMPLAINTS: EMOTIONAL OPPORTUNITIES

No aspect of customer service is so replete with emotions as when customers complain. Most don't complain lightly; in fact, most don't complain at all according to dozens of research studies. Consider the emotions expressed in the following poorly handled complaint situation, in which a customer is trying to get his telephone service repaired.

> *Most customers don't complain lightly; in fact, most don't complain at all.*

Service Representative (SR): As long as it is trouble that is outside, we do take care of that for you at no charge. Are you going to be there tomorrow, or is there a number to reach you back tomorrow?

Customer (C): No, I have to work. There is a work number where I work. I went through this one time with you people.

SR: Sir, I don't have any control over that. I just report it.

C: I know, but I just want you to know, I paid my money. The second time they came out, they paid for it because they

167

found out it was their fault. I just had this thing transferred. I don't
want to go through this again. It is too expensive.

SR: If it is outside, there won't be any problem. We will take care of it.

C: I hope it is. We are going to part company if it is not.

SR: That is up to you, sir.

C: You bet it is.[1]

Analysis of the above actual transcribed conversation could fill an entire chapter. Let's consider just a few questions. Does the customer perceive himself to be complaining? Perhaps. Many customers do not like to see themselves as complaining, so this customer may think that he is just "telling" the company his story. Does the service representative hear a complaint or a problem to be solved? Probably a problem to be solved. That is, if the company asked its service representatives to track customers who call in to complain, this conversation is likely not one that would be classified as a complaint. Does a notation of this service failure get communicated to anyone else beyond the person who will do the repair? Again, probably not. Has the service representative learned anything in this exchange that will be applied in his or her next customer exchange? It's doubtful. Does the service representative think that he or she has adequately handled this exchange? Most likely, yes. Does the customer hang up the telephone with a bad feeling about the telephone company? Unfortunately, yes.

One practical way to see complaints is as *an attempt on the part of customers to continue doing business with you.* Reading the above transcript, one can clearly see the customer is working to remain with this company, and the service provider is making little effort to keep the customer. *"That is up to you, sir."* That line reminds us of a couple having an argument. One says, "If that's how you feel, we might as well end our relationship right now." The partner responds, "Okay, if that's what you want. See if I care." Neither really wants the relationship to end, but neither knows how to get out of this tangled web of emotional communication.

> One effective way to see complaints is as an attempt on the part of customers to continue doing business.

Connecting with empathy is the ability to see something from the other person's emotional point of view. Empathy is more strongly called for in a complaint situation than in any other. Yet most companies and their representatives look at complaints from their own points of view. They require customers not only to prove the validity of their complaints but also to prove they did not cause the problem themselves. Organizations frequently make customers go out of their way to express their complaints; and to make matters worse, many companies do little or nothing about the complaints they hear.

In today's high-tech world, responses to complaints are frequently "canned." Computerized responses, while quickly generated and immediately returned to customers by e-mail, can easily miss the mark with their prescribed remarks. When this happens, the negative emotion surrounding a complaint will be reinforced. Dianna recently had difficulty accessing an on-line travel agency. A lot of time was invested trying to get a response from the system, only to receive "system overload" messages, one after another. Dianna sent a note to the travel agency, explaining that while she would like to give the company her business, the service was unusable. The response letter, addressed "Dear User," said that heavy use by members in the evening slowed the whole system down. It recommended using the system any time but seven to nine in the evening. Actually, Dianna was on-line in the midmorning hours, and her initial letter to the company spelled that out. The response letter also gave an invitation to send another e-mail with any additional questions—no doubt so another inappropriate, nonempathic response letter could be computer generated!

Because complaint handling is so unpleasant, many companies try to distance themselves from hearing bad news—or they attempt to eliminate complaints altogether. That is, they believe they can offer their services and products with such consistently high quality that customers will have no reason to complain. It is almost as if managers become schizophrenic about complaints. They know complaints

> *Because complaint handling is so unpleasant, many companies try to distance themselves from hearing bad news.*

are beneficial but at some deep level, they also intensely dislike them to the point they avoid reality by fantasizing they can deliver their service 100 percent correctly.

As a result, one of the most misguided goals we see managers set is to reduce the number of complaints they receive. We frequently speak on the topic of complaint handling based on the material in the book coauthored by Janelle Barlow and Claus Møller, *A Complaint Is a Gift.*[2] When we do, we urge managers to resist setting goals to reduce complaints. We explain that if they do this, their frontline staff and managers will be inclined to not report bad news, particularly if bonuses are paid on reduced complaint statistics. After every speech or seminar, we invariably meet at least one manager who comes forward to talk with us, stunned with the realization that this practice has probably skewed the company's feedback. Once the concept is explained, everyone instantly understands that with few exceptions,[3] it is not a good idea. Nonetheless, the urge to reduce complaints seems to be almost instinctive.

> It is not a good idea to set targets reducing the number of complaints.

When a target is set by managers for complaint reductions, staff will accommodate and very neatly stop hearing or reporting them. This can happen in some almost undetectable ways. One company set up an incentive program that compensated the sales staff not just for sales but also for customer satisfaction ratings. As a direct consequence of this system, some salespeople actually sold less, as they focused on reducing complaints. One salesperson reported that he simply got rid of his dissatisfied customers. "There was a customer who complained a lot and bought products from me. I was concerned about his rating of me and the last time I visited him, I told him that his needs can be better served by one of our competitors." Another said, "I am very careful in choosing customers. If I feel that a customer will not be very satisfied with our products, I stop calling on the customer."[4]

We recently talked with a human resource director who wanted to eliminate complaints. He said, "Yes, we like your approach to complaint handling. However, our desire is to get so good at this business that we never have any complaints." This person is a very sophisticated, experienced hotelier who absolutely knows better than to expect the hotel business to be able to offer 100 percent error-free service. If nothing else, individual preferences will generate some complaints. How on earth do you get the temperature of the swimming pool exactly right for every guest? It's just not possible.

It is this type of thinking that contributes to organizations seeing complaint handlers as part of the "cost" of doing business, rather than a chance to grow the business. We prefer to see complaint handlers as

- customer retention teams who, if they handle complaints well, can retain customers when they are most likely to leave;

- public relations vehicles for controlling negative word of month;

- marketing research departments learning about the wants and needs of the marketplace;

- an extension of the sales department. If a complaint is handled well, many customers feel inclined to repay the organization for how it handled the complaint. One direct way to "repay" is by buying additional products.

According to survey research, customer expectations escalate in complaint situations higher than in ordinary service encounters—especially if the customer is a loyal one.[5] *When problems are experienced, organizations have the most to lose from their best, most loyal customers.* Therefore, organizations would be well advised to staff complaint positions with people at least as qualified and adept as their best salespeople.

Complaint handlers can, in short, be seen as a part of the organization that grows and expands business, rather than as a dreaded cost, a necessary evil, and a dirty secret that has to be talked about in sanitized terms. We believe that complaints are born in a sea of emotions; if they can be turned in a positive direction, they can be seen as the gifts they are.

> *Many companies see complaint handlers as part of the "cost" of doing business, rather than a chance to grow the business.*

171

CHAPTER TEN

FUNDAMENTALS OF COMPLAINTS

The last thirty years has seen a blossoming of research about complaints, some conducted by consulting firms and a great deal more by marketing university professors (see Appendix D). Results definitely vary from one research study to another. Nonetheless, common patterns present themselves throughout the multitudinous studies. These patterns, which we discuss in this chapter, include the following:

- Most customers don't complain when things go wrong or when they are unhappy.
- Service providers aren't very skilled at handling complaints—at least from the customers' point of view.
- Because of their emotionality, complaints tend to be remembered longer than other service experiences.
- A complaint handled well can actually increase feelings of loyalty among customers.

Most Customers Do Not Complain

Customers talk about bad service to just about everyone, but they rarely formally complain. Complaint statistics, which differ depending upon the research study, are all bad and suggest

173

Customers talk about bad service to just about everyone, but they rarely complain formally.

that somewhere from 40 percent to 96 percent of customers do not speak up to someone who can actually do something about their complaints. The percentage range depends upon the type of customer, the severity of the problem, and the accessibility of complaint opportunities—and whether customers believe anything will happen as a result of their complaints. Even when *extreme dissatisfaction* is experienced, many customers do not complain: 49.6 percent for nondurable products; 29.4 percent for durable products, and 23.2 percent for services, according to one study.[1] It can become almost pitiful. Megafax, a New York research company, surveyed thirty thousand utility companies between 1991 and 1995. Some were so bad at complaint handling that customers wouldn't even call to say that they had lost power![2]

If you look at this lack of complaining from the customer's point of view, it makes a lot of sense. Most customers are not wimps who are afraid to speak up. They go through a serious cognitive process that determines whether they will complain or not.

First, customers have to decide if complaining will accomplish anything. In so doing they need to assess the cause of their problem. Without this knowledge, they do not know whom to hold responsible. Not knowing who is responsible may result in the customer concluding that complaining will be a waste of energy. Feeling partially responsible for the problem may initiate a decision to not complain. Second, if customers think that complaining may result in some kind of harm to them, they are likely to cut their losses and not say anything. This factor is particularly significant in the health-care industry.

There are, of course, dozens of other reasons why customers don't complain. If customers lack experience in complaining, come from a social background where complaining is seen as impolite, or psychologically don't feel comfortable with confrontation, they are not likely to complain. Furthermore, consumers tend not to complain when they perceive they have few alternative service providers,[3] or when changing providers is so much trouble that customers perceive themselves as having limited options, such as in changing medical doctors. They may be unhappy, but they will not say anything to the organization, though they are likely to tell family, friends, and colleagues about their experience.

Most Complaints Are Handled Poorly—
According to Customers

Even when customers do complain, statistics show that 50 to 70 percent feel worse than if they had never said anything at all.[4] Customers perceive that their position with the company changes when they are complaining, as compared to when they are purchasing. Charles Martin and Denise Smart found that customers believe they do not receive the same courteous treatment from consumer hot lines when they have problems as when they call for product information.[5]

Even when customers do complain, statistics show that fifty to seventy percent feel worse than if they had never said anything at all.

Events that start off as relatively small examples of service failure can become easily worsened by poor complaint handling. At that point, customers begin to talk. When complaints are handled poorly, the motivation to discuss the event seems to increase. One researcher found that 75 percent of hotel guests would tell twelve other people if their complaints were handled poorly.[6]

Part of the problem is that 65 percent of customers take their complaints to frontline staff, who, in many cases, are poorly equipped to deal with complaining customers.[7] Many frontline staff are not told that complaint handling is part of customer retention and a critical part of their job responsibilities. Instead, many are told to watch out for customers who will attempt to trick them with their complaints. If frontline staff receive little or no training on how to handle irate customers, if they are not supported by fair policies, if they have little flexibility to solve customer problems, then it is hardly a surprise that 50 to 70 percent of customers feel worse after complaining.

Both the authors have had numerous opportunities to observe call-center service representatives sitting with their managers and listening to their previously taped interactions with customers. Time and time again, we hear these representatives say, "I had no idea I was so rude." "I had no idea I sounded so short . . . so bad . . . so heavy handed." When service representatives are inside a complaint situation, they perceive their behavior to be appropriate. It takes some distance for them to see the negative impact of some of their interactions with customers.

Poor complaint handling is particularly rampant when more than one department is responsible for interacting with the same customer, and many organizations are set up so that it is impossible for customers to get their complaints handled by one department or one person. Sales departments handle sales and only sales-related questions. Customer satisfaction departments may handle only product support and related complaints.

Even though customers may call the salesperson to complain about the product they just bought, salespeople commonly believe that when customers are dissatisfied it has nothing to do with them. And for this reason, salespeople will frequently show little urgency in getting back to customers who have already purchased. Salespeople assume that customer dissatisfaction is a result of the behavior of other departments.[8] Apparently it is difficult for *any* staff, including managers, to recognize the role they play in creating dissatisfaction.

Complaints Are Easily Remembered

Memories of complaints tend to be stronger than those of other customer interactions because service failures frequently elicit strong emotions, After a decade of research, Joseph LeDoux, professor of psychology and neuroscience at New York University, has concluded that emotional memories are more intense than other kinds of memories. LeDoux explains that the brain stores the memory of an emotional event in the cortex, the same place it stores other facts. But then it stores the memories of the feelings (for example, a rapid heartbeat in the case of fear) in the amygdala, deep in the interior of the brain. "Memories about emotions are just facts," he says. "Emotional memories give the emotional quality

Memories of complaints tend to be stronger than other service memories.

to those explicit memories, and the brain fuses the two so it makes it seem like they're coming from the same place."[9]

It is as if the brain recalls emotional memories in stereo. And it helps to explain why people remember negative emotional customer experiences so intensely. This may also help to explain why some customers are quick to be upset. Their previous emotional memories instantaneously impact current behaviors. It may take their cortex a while to send information (*"Settle down! This isn't the same situation you experienced last year!"*) enabling them to calm down. This fact alone explains why handling complaints well is so critical in the experience economy, with its foundation of "memorable" experiences. It's not a good idea to have complaints as your organization's memorable experiences!

> *It is as if the brain recalls emotional memories in stereo.*

Complaining Customers Are Potential Loyal Customers

Countless numbers of research studies suggest that customers are more likely to remain customers if they complain and give the organization a chance to fix their problems. In fact, when customer complaints are handled well, they can turn into more positively remembered customer experiences than if there had been no complaint in the first place. One study of seven hundred service incidents from the restaurant, airline, and hotel industries found that 25 percent of all positive memories customers have of service experiences actually started out as service failures.[10] This has led Professor Jagdip Singh at Case Western Reserve University to write,

> Consequently, the counterintuitive notion that the effective encouragement and facilitation of complaints may actually help increase brand loyalty (and profitability) and contain the negative effects of other private actions appears to hold considerable merit.[11]

This is truly one of the greatest anomalies in the complaint research literature. Time and time again, researchers have found that if complaining customers are effectively helped with their problems, in a very high percentage of cases,[12] they become even more loyal customers than

If complaining customers are helped with their problems, they become even more loyal customers than if there had been no problem in the first place.

if there had been no problem in the first place.[13] Research published in the *Journal of Retailing* draws a similar conclusion: "Perhaps the most interesting finding regarding customers' subsequent self-reported shopping behavior is . . . that it is possible to recover from failures, *no matter what type.*[14] However, if complaints are not handled well, only 23 percent of customers will do business with you again.[15] At the same time, even when customers do not get exactly what they asked for, they are less likely to engage in negative word of mouth about the offending company if they have at least complained and gotten something.[16]

Maryanne Rasmussen, vice president of American Express world-wide customer satisfaction, summarized it succinctly, "The formula I use is: Better complaint handling equals higher customer satisfaction equals higher brand loyalty equals high profitability."[17]

CHAPTER ELEVEN

STRATEGIES FOR HANDLING COMPLAINTS

This chapter suggests ten strategies for working with the emotional dynamics of complaints so effective handling can strengthen connections with customers.

Going from Problems to Partners

In their book, *A Complaint Is a Gift,* Barlow and Møller recommend that complaint handlers shift their paradigm about complaints and see them as "gifts," rather than as nuisances, attacks, or whatever other negative views are held about complaints. When people are given gifts, they typically say "Thank you," whether they like the gift or not. Barlow and Møller, in their eight-step "Gift Formula" (see Appendix E), advise service providers to first thank customers for their feedback and then offer an apology. In other words, complaint handlers can be more effective if they phrase their initial responses to complaining customers with emotional words. The complaint

Complaint handlers are best advised to phrase their initial responses to complaining customers with emotional words.

handler should then, and only then, proceed to gather whatever information is necessary to solve the customers' issues.

We have been teaching this methodology around the world for a number of years. The feedback we have heard from our clients who use this emotionally sensitive Gift Formula has been, in many cases, simply astounding. Nonetheless, we do hear objections from some program participants that it is not natural to say "Thank you" when someone is complaining. However, if we can inspire our clients to try the Gift Formula, they almost all report back with dazzling feedback. Literally thousands of people have told us they never could have believed the positive impact of starting a difficult interaction using the emotional words of "Thank you," followed with "I'm sorry"—until they tried it.

One of our major United States clients has reported a significant drop in the amount of time its complaint handlers spend on the telephone with each customer. The service representatives have found that by starting with "Thank you," they avoid time-consuming fights with customers. Many users of the Gift Formula tell us they have heard gasps from their customers, followed by silence when the first words the service provider says are "Thank you for letting us know." Customer tone changes, and in many cases, customers end up apologizing for having begun their conversation in a harsh tone.

Many service representatives do thank their complaining customers for speaking up, but they do it at the *conclusion* of the complaint interaction. We have long argued that these words lose their impact when offered at the end of the conversation. Almost all written responses to complaint letters begin with "Thank you for writing." If it makes sense to start a written response with "Thank you," when the writer has had time to construct the strongest response, then it would be similarly advantageous to use the same methodology in the more heightened emotional situation of a verbally delivered complaint.

After saying "Thank you," we recommend an apology. In practice, apologies are offered in less than half of complaint situations according to the research.[1] And when an apology *is* offered, it is also frequently placed at the end of the conversation, almost as an afterthought. Or it is delivered in a whiny child's tone of voice, "I *said* I was sorry."

Janelle, coauthor of *A Complaint Is a Gift,* had the experience of complaining and hearing "Thank you" from a service provider whose manager had been teaching his staff the Gift Formula. Her experience was to be stunned by the power of the emotional shift she felt at hearing "Thank you" and "I'm sorry" at the beginning of the interaction. She no longer felt in conflict with the organization; in fact, she felt an immediate alliance with the staff member who so nicely thanked her for speaking up.

In analyzing this situation, the authors have concluded that a fundamental shift occurs, directly attributable to hearing emotional language at the beginning of complaints. Emotions are more compelling than mere thoughts. To expect that customers will simply put their emotions aside while they deal rationally with an issue is unreasonable. If emotionality is presented first by customers, then it needs to be dealt with in that same order by the service provider.

> *If emotionality is presented first by customers, then it needs to be dealt with in that same order by the service provider.*

We think that what happens can be illustrated in the following manner. When customers complain, they begin with the belief that the organization and the problem are inexorably linked. Customers see themselves standing in opposition to them. Charted, it looks like this:

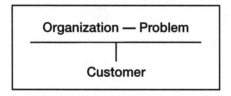

By addressing the inherent emotionality present in a complaint situation, directly, concisely, and at the beginning of the interaction, the service provider takes control of the perception of the event. This helps customers shift attribution so they no longer see themselves in opposition to the organization, but rather *they see themselves in partnership*

with the company, linked against a common enemy—the problem that the customer faces.

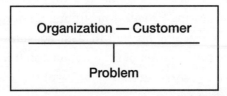

By addressing the emotionality, the service provider takes control of the perception of the event.

Attribution is one of the most difficult aspects of complaint situations. Customers blame the organization for their problems, or they wouldn't likely complain in the first place. Likewise, many service providers seem bent on finding out how customers can be held responsible for their problems.[2] Customers hear this expressed in phrases such as "You should have . . . ," "Why didn't you . . . ?" or "We've never heard that before."

By starting with the strong emotional language of "Thank you" and "I'm sorry," service providers, and the organization they represent, send a strong metamessage that *the most important consideration* is how the customer feels, rather than who did what to create the problem. If customers feel someone cares about them, they are less likely to blame the organization for their problems.[3]

■ Application

Shifting Your Customers' Perspectives. List the concrete advantages you, your staff, and your organization would gain from quickly shifting your customers' perspectives to see that they are in partnership with you to solve their complaint issues. What are all the strategies, including beginning the complaint communication with a "Thank you," you and your staff can use to make this shift occur in the shortest time possible?

Empowering Staff to Handle Complaints
Is More Than Giving Permission

In addition to addressing the emotionality of complaints with polite language, it is vital that complaint handlers have the power to settle complaints quickly and effectively. A United Kingdom car company found that each customer complaint contact cost the company, on average, 60 British pounds in overhead. This same car company found that it could take upwards of three contacts to settle a 10-pound complaint. That's 180 pounds to settle something that potentially benefitted the customers 10 pounds. After being forced to have three contacts with the company, the customers were also no doubt annoyed. They probably made several significant withdrawals from their emotional accounts—even though they may have been compensated.[4]

■ Application

What Does Your Average Complaint Interaction Cost? If you can't calculate it exactly, make a rough estimate. Make sure everyone knows the cost of the average interaction. Encourage staff to use this figure as part of their calculations in shaping responses to complaining customers.

When frontline staff are empowered to settle complaints with customers, they can more quickly handle complaints. This saves both time and money and also helps reduce customer frustration. Responsiveness to complaints is one of the key variables determining how customers feel about complaint handling. As an added benefit, frontline staff feel better about their own work when they can immediately do something for a customer. Pat Brown, vice president of First Tennessee Bank, found that giving her staff training and then more control to settle complaints increased employee job satisfaction enormously. "When you think about it," she says, "it's really a no-brainer."[5]

> *Responsiveness to complaints is one of the key variables determining how customers feel about complaint handling.*

Timothy Firnstahl, with Satisfaction Guaranteed Eateries, has made several attempts to increase customer satisfaction at his Seattle restaurants. He imbued his service culture with an emotional consciousness he and the staff call YEGA—"Your Enjoyment Guaranteed. Always." Restaurant staff know they are in business to make people happy. His staff even speak this language with great enthusiasm. But Firnstahl also found that the same customer complaints kept returning. One day a lightning bolt of inspiration struck Firnstahl while he was driving home from work. "We had given employees responsibility without giving them authority. The result was that they tried to bury mistakes or blame others. I saw it every time we tried to track down a complaint. The food servers blamed the kitchen for late meals. The kitchen blamed the food servers for placing orders incorrectly."[6] After his insight, Firnstahl set up guidelines for his staff to follow, but he did not want these guidelines to result in his staff quibbling over the proper compensation for a dissatisfied customer. Ultimately, staff were to do whatever it took to make sure the restaurant's guests enjoyed themselves.

> "We had given employees responsibility without giving them authority. The result was that they tried to bury mistakes or blame others."

Once Firnstahl's staff grew comfortable with their new authority, they became creative in how they implemented YEGA. In addition, a side benefit occurred: staff became more loyal. Positive experiences for customers created positive experiences for staff.

> Once they got used to the idea, employees liked knowing that the company believed so strongly in its products and services that it wholeheartedly stood behind its work—and theirs. They liked working for a restaurant known for its unhesitating commitment to customer satisfaction. Preeminence in any field gives people feelings of self-worth they could never get from just making a buck. Their power as company representatives increased their pride in the business, and that, in turn, increased motivation.[7]

Stress research literature suggests that tension is reduced in situations when people perceive themselves to be in control. There are four types of control,[8] all relevant in complaint handling situations:

- *Behavioral control:* ability to respond to a threatening situation;

- *Cognitive control:* ability to reduce stress because adequate information is available;

- *Decisional control:* ability to make choices about goals and outcomes;

- *Emotional control:* ability to monitor emotions and then know how to keep them within manageable levels.

When staff believe themselves to possess adequate control to meet the demands of complaining customers, performance improves while emotional integrity remains intact. Staff members can say to complaining customers, "I'm going to take care of this situation for you," and mean it. Customers will hear the conviction in the service provider's voice and will have confidence in that person, thus reducing the likelihood of escalating their complaints. This saves everyone time and money—and emotional distress. Under circumstances of adequate control, complaint situations become manageable job challenges instead of reasons to quit.

> *When staff believe themselves to possess adequate control, performance improves while emotional integrity remains intact.*

Being in control, or being empowered, also helps staff to minimize feelings of shame that happen for some people in service roles. Psychology texts define shame as the "inner sense of being completely diminished or insufficient as a person."[9] This feeling of inadequacy can happen when staff have a picture of how they want to be able to respond to customers but are seriously shackled by organizational policies. This wounding of the ego, we believe, contributes to staff making statements such as "I only work here" or "I don't set policy." Staff want to divorce themselves from their employers, and this is not a pretty picture for customers to behold.

Control also means making sure that staff understand enough about their industry so they can appropriately answer customer complaints that come across in the form of questions. For example, The Institute of Canadian Bankers wanted to ensure that frontline staff could adequately answer questions about service charges, the future of electronic banking, and where the banking industry is headed. These are sophisticated questions, and most people hired into teller or telephone service representative positions could hardly be expected to have ready answers about where the banking industry is heading. The institute developed a course to provide frontline staff with adequate background to answer these types of questions. The director of professional relations for the institute cautioned, "It's not about canned answers to customer complaints. People who complete this course will be able to explain to anyone why the industry works the way it does."[10] That's empowerment! Most staff prefer being able to answer questions as well. They look knowledgeable.

As far as customers are concerned, empowerment also has a dimensionality of speed. If customers have to call twice or return to a store twice to get their complaints handled, they are less appreciative of whatever solutions are offered. The outcome may be just, but inconveniencing customers by slowing them down effectively eliminates the positives of a fair solution.[11]

Slowing customers down effectively eliminates the positives of a fair solution.

Finally, empowerment means that managers must know what their staff are experiencing. Managers can gain this knowledge if they act as coaches. By sitting and listening in on telephone calls with staff, managers will have a more complete understanding of how difficult it is to deal with complaining customers, especially when they are upset. In a call-center environment, managers would benefit by periodically answering the telephone themselves so they have the experience of doing this work for hours at a time. Being on the telephone, hour after hour, for eight hours, is very different from periodically interceding in difficult complaint situations.

This is what Bell Canada is doing. Not only are Answer Centre managers empowering their staff to handle customer problems, they have an extensive system of coaches set up in their offices, with one coach per twenty client representatives. They conduct two coaching sessions per month with each representative. In addition, all the coaches spend each Monday on the phone lines themselves. The results have been notable in terms of contented staff. Staff specifically report feeling better about themselves knowing they have the power to satisfy their customers' needs.[12]

▧ Application

The Continuum of Empowerment. Compose an exhaustive list of everything that your company/department/team does for your customers. Go through your list and put checks by everything staff are already empowered to do. Then analyze the balance of the list. Empowerment does not have to be an "all or nothing" concept. Consider a continuum of empowerment that ranges from suggestion contribution (employees make recommendations) to task contribution (employees take over part or all of a task) to total contribution (complete empowerment). The last category involves a shift in thinking by staff and perhaps a redesign of jobs.

Mark the items that remain on your list with these three levels of empowerment as to where you and other staff are today and where you would like to see them in the future. If your business is a manufacturing-line type of service (for example, fast-food restaurants), there is less opportunity for empowerment. When your business requires spending more time with customers, greater intimacy in terms of shared knowledge with the customer, and closer physical proximity, then empowerment has more impact.

Creating a Craving for Feedback

Customer perceptions of whether an organization will react positively to their complaints influence their decisions about complaining. As indicated earlier, when customers believe they will be treated poorly or nothing will be done about their complaints, they are less likely to speak up.

An organization can influence the number of complaints it receives by its complaint-friendly reputation.

An organization can, therefore, influence the number of complaints it receives by its complaint-friendly reputation. The more willingly the company appears to hear complaints, the more likely customers are to complain—and therefore the more chances an organization has to retain business.[13]

Organizations can influence their complaint-friendly reputation by communicating with well-constructed surveys, even though surveys are not the only way to increase customer feedback. Surveys, nonetheless, can be used as part of the process of emotional bonding with customers and not solely as research tools. They send an implied promise that the organization is concerned about its customers' reactions—that they are cherished customers, not just survey respondents.[14]

Back to restaurateur Firnstahl. As mentioned above, he had groups of his employees call several hundred customers each month and ask them to rate their experiences. Firnstahl notes this about the process: "Aside from the data we gathered, the phone calls were great promotion. Most people were amazed and delighted that we took the trouble to phone them, and many developed enormous loyalty to our restaurants."[15]

Whatever strategies an organization chooses to use to increase customer feedback have to start from a willingness, indeed a craving, to hear from customers. There has to be a willingness to use the Complaint Window of Opportunity, which we have modeled below. Imagine the horizontal axis as the severity of the customers' problems and the vertical axis as the likelihood of the customer to complain. Obviously, the more severe the problem, the more likely the customer is to complain. Each organization will have a slightly different chart, but the important part of the chart is the top portion, the Complaint Window of Opportunity. The more complaint friendly an organization succeeds in being, the larger the Complaint Window of Opportunity to hear more feedback from customers when there are problems. The more an organization can encourage customers to provide feedback, the smaller the Complaint Window of Opportunity will become.

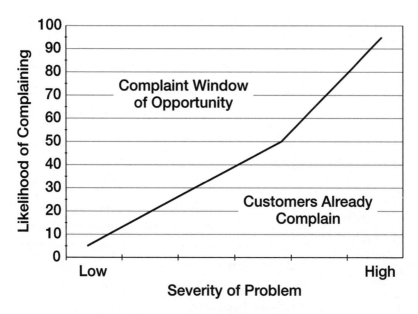

Creating a craving for feedback requires a fundamental shift in how complaints are valued in an organization. It requires frontline staff to use every opportunity to ask questions about service and products. "What do you like best about our store layout?" "How do you think we could organize this section to make our products more available for you?" "I noticed you ordered a vegetarian meal on your flight. How did you like your special meal today? Is there any message I could take back to our chefs to make your next order on one of our flights even better?" As consumers ourselves, we notice how many times we stand next to a service provider and no conversation is struck up. It seems to us a wasted opportunity: a wasted opportunity for soliciting our opinion—for free—and for the organization to tell us it values our opinion. Instead we see organizations spend hundreds of thousands of dollars with surveys that are incomplete in terms of asking relevant questions, surveys that feel like an inconvenience, and surveys that rarely give us a feeling anything is being done with the gathered information.

> *Creating a craving for feedback requires a fundamental shift in how complaints are valued in an organization.*

There are other strategies to receive more feedback from customers. These include

- setting up listening posts, which can be as simple as suggestion boxes;
- marketing the fact that you are looking for complaints/feedback;
- creating and making customer comment forms readily available;
- setting up customer confidants for in-depth interviews;
- randomly asking for feedback from people who call you.[16]

> *For organizations to create this craving for feedback, they have to act on the feedback they receive.*

Of course, for organizations to create this craving for feedback, they have to act on the feedback they receive. This doesn't necessarily mean doing everything customers want. That can quickly bankrupt a company. It means seriously listening to the voice of the customer, and then letting customers know when action has been taken.

Application

How Do We Discourage Complaints? There are several ways organizations shy away from complaints. Compiled below is a list constructed at a client seminar. As you go through the list, check each item that is true of your organization. Then strategize how you can reverse this discouragement of complaints.

- We are vague about where or to whom customers should complain.
- We have limited or no follow-up to the person who complained.
- We pass our customers from person to person.
- We start complaint handling by asking for irrelevant information.
- We signal with our body language that we don't want to hear complaints.
- We don't listen carefully to our customers.
- We deny that problems exist, or we marginalize our customers by claiming that we have never heard their complaint before.
- We don't actively solicit customer feedback.

- We have rigid mechanisms for receiving complaints.

- We set goals to reduce complaints.

- We blame customers when there is a problem.

- We get defensive and show this in our tone of voice.

- We have phone systems that make customers wait unnecessarily.

- We don't quickly share information internally to help our customers.

- We don't actively use the feedback we receive to improve our quality.

Focusing on Lifetime Customer Value

Any single complaint may be costly to handle in terms of time and money. *However, we must never forget that loyalty can be created out of the chaos of complaint situations.* Therefore, all complaint-handling costs must be measured against potential lifetime purchasing power if customers are to remain loyal because of how staff interact with them.

> *We must never forget that loyalty can be created out of the chaos of complaint situations.*

General Electric recognizes this, noting that people buy fifteen major appliances over their lifetimes. As a result, GE has invested in its Answer Center to manage the potentiality of these long-term relationships. GE's Answer Center is open 365 days a year, twenty-four hours a day. Every year, three million people call GE's toll-free lines.[17] For GE, every complaint situation is viewed as an opportunity to convert an upset customer into a fan who will buy his or her next major appliance from GE and say positive things about the company, reinforcing GE's marketing line, "We bring good things to life." GE sees complaints as opportunities to add to customers' emotional accounts.

Application

Calculating Lifetime Value. What is the lifetime value of your average customer? Does everyone know this figure? Do staff understand the meaning of this figure? Is this figure used as one of the drivers of your complaint handling approach?

Listed below is a simple way of calculating lifetime value.

A. Customer's gross purchases $_____ (per year)

B. Profit margin $_____ (per year)

C. Number of purchasing years   _____

Potential Value of Customer (B x C) $_____

Obviously, there are more complicated formulae to use, but this one cuts to the quick and requires knowing only how much different customer categories spend with you during a year's time, the profit margin realized from such expenditures, and how many years the average customer will stay if he or she likes the organization. Rather than focusing on the cost of settling a complaint, every service provider should be encouraged to use this figure as part of the calculations in shaping a response to complaining customers.

The other side of focusing on the lifetime value of customers is complaint management. That is, once complaints have been reported, then someone has to make sure that the system failures or misreading of the market that caused the complaint will be addressed. If service providers are so good at handling complaints that customers are inspired to come back, you cannot continue to repeat the same service failures, or customers will quickly see their complaints as being of little value. In such cases, it will not matter how good your service providers are at handling complaints, customers will stop giving you feedback.

> *You cannot continue to repeat the same service failures, or customers will quickly see their complaints as being of little value.*

While it is reasonable to expect profits to ultimately increase from fixing systems that result in customer complaints, costs may initially increase as an organization invests in fixing immediate problems. Here is our restaurant owner one more time, Timothy Firnstahl, who cautions about financial impact. In his own business, he eventually realized significant increases in sales, a doubling in profits, and significant decreases in system-cost failures, but not without some initial investment in fixing problems.

Remember, costs will go up before they come down, so high system-failure costs and low-phone-survey complaint rates probably mean you're on the right track. Conversely, low system-failure costs and a high rate of "Lousies" and "OKs" from customers almost certainly indicate that the promise is not being kept, that your organization has yet to understand that customer satisfaction is the only reason for the company's existence.[18]

These are figures that an organization should track to see that they are going in the right direction over a period of time. Initially higher investment was required to compensate customers for their ratings of "lousies" or "OKs" in Timothy Firnstahl's case. However, after his staff talked to customers to find out what they really thought, empowered staff to ensure YEGA (Your Enjoyment Guaranteed, Always), and then invested in repairing system failures, Firnstahl reports achieving higher profits.

Talking to the Emotionality of Complaints

To most effectively deal with the emotionality of complaining customers, we recommend *focusing on the customer rather than on the complaint.* Don't ignore the complaint issue, but concentrate on the customer. Too many customer service representatives focus on the complaint itself or on complaint solutions rather than on customer feelings. The measure of success of a well-handled complaint is not necessarily whether a problem is solved but rather how the customer feels about the interaction. Sometimes it is impossible to fix a complaint problem.

> *To most effectively deal with the emotionality of complaining customers, focus on the customer rather than on the complaint.*

Talking to the emotionality of the complaint means that the service provider must be able to recognize the presenting emotions of the customer and then feel sufficiently comfortable to openly discuss these emotions. For example, the service provider can make comments such as, "I'm very sorry. You must feel betrayed." "I can imagine that you are

193

upset. I know I would be." "You must feel awful, and yet you are so calm. I really appreciate that." "Has this happened before?"

The service provider has to look for the inherent emotionality in the situation—and then speak to it. This is called empathy. If this is done, customers will feel as if they have been heard. And for a lot of customers, this is the most important part of the complaint process. Customers will put up with a lot. But they do want to know that someone has noticed and is concerned.

Part of the emotionality in a complaint is a feeling of powerlessness. After all, customers do not know how they will be responded to, whether their problems will be fixed, or whether they will be compensated for their troubles. Marketing professors Stephen Tax and Stephen Brown found in their studies that customers react more positively if they are given options or choices, rather than being told what will happen. Customers are emotionally put back in the driver's seat when they get to choose.[19] The way to do this is by always having two options available: "We can refund your money, or we can give you a store credit that is worth an extra 10 percent over your purchase price. You can spend the store credit at any time." Or "We can guarantee you a seat on the flight that leaves in one hour, or you can fly standby on the flight that leaves in a half hour." Or "You can leave your computer here, and we'll call you to let you know when we can begin to work on it, or you can take it with you since it is still working, and we'll call you to let you know when to bring it in."

◼ Application

Creating Options. Compile a list of your most common complaints. Brainstorm possible options for your customers for each of the situations. Test your options on each other to ensure that they don't annoy but can be seen as legitimate options. Then make sure that everyone has a copy of the suggested options so all service providers are working with the same information.

We also recommend that response letters to written complaints *always* address the emotionality in the situation. It is actually fairly easy to do this with written responses because there is more time to think through a best response. It is more difficult to quickly think of best responses in a live situation. Even with live situations, however, our experience is that with training and role playing, most people get remarkably adept at identifying the inherent emotionality in a situation and then addressing it. It's a matter of modeling it for people who have never even thought about it.

> *Most people get remarkably adept at identifying the inherent emotionality present in a situation.*

The husband of one of the authors wrote an e-mail to his on-line trading company citing numerous problems that had been raised by a rating service for that particular broker. He wanted to know what the trading company was going to do about the publicly identified issues. Within thirty-six hours, he received the following emotionally sensitive response. Only a portion of the letter is reprinted here. We should note that this trading company will continue to get our business, even though twenty other companies had higher ratings.

> First, let me thank you for taking the time to detail your concerns so clearly. To claim that we are without problems right now would be a gross lie. There have been days, since Day 1, where the system has not met the expectation of our customers. That is the bad news.
>
> The good news is, we have been able to decrease the frequency of system issues all the while growing our business exponentially. The technologies used to manage this new method to the oldest game are not without fail. No good technology will ever be without fail. It is from the feedback of the users themselves, that we are able to grow with this new world of trading.

The rest of the letter is sprinkled with strong emotional words, and phrases such as "committed," "we are aware," "working diligently," "expecting fantastic enhancements," "customers have been patient." The letter concludes, "Given this, we are in this together and we will not fail you or our other customers. Your business is our livelihood . . . and we know it!" If these are mere words, they are words that have the power to bind.

Betrayal is one of the dominant emotions customers experience in complaint situations. We have seen betrayal directly stated or implied in most of the hundreds of written complaint letters we have read. Customers pay good money for products and services, and then they don't get what they want. They feel betrayed by the organization and, to a certain degree, ashamed they weren't smart enough to see that coming. Sometimes all it takes is a simple sentence to turn the situation around. "You must feel betrayed. Here you got used to our product, and then we stopped manufacturing it. I know I would feel betrayed." Or "You must feel betrayed. You bought one of our cakes to impress your guests and it didn't taste as good as the last one you bought from us."

> *Betrayal is one of the dominant emotions customers experience in complaint situations.*

Betrayal needs to be addressed if organizations are to have a continuing relationship with such customers. Customers need to know that they are justified in their feelings, which only the organization can truly acknowledge. If service providers do this, more than likely customers will give the organization a second chance.

■ Application

Addressing Feelings in Complaints. When you talk about problems that customers have experienced, always ask staff how they think the customer was feeling. If you regularly ask this question of yourself and your staff, both you and they will soon begin to look for the emotionality in complaints. As a manager, you will know you are on the right track when this information is volunteered in customer complaint reports. Also ask about the emotionality of the customer when the complaint interaction has been completed. With what emotion did the customer walk away? Help everyone to focus on the emotions in complaints. Let staff understand that knowing the customer's emotional state is equally as important as knowing the customer's final decision.

Turning Complaints into Customer Learning Opportunities

Most parents learn very quickly that if they do everything for small children, their youngsters will remain dependent on them for everything. After a while, that's no fun for either. So most parents will take the time and trouble to show their frustrated or complaining children how to do certain tasks for themselves. It gives children a greater sense of control over their lives, provides them the satisfaction of knowing how to take care of themselves, and perhaps most importantly, shows them they don't always need their parents around to get things done.

Service providers, unfortunately, can encourage customer dependency that contributes to emotional frustration and resource utilization problems. If customers can get their needs met only by coming back to the organization, these repeated calls can put undue pressure on staff resources, thereby diminishing capacity to help others. This is particularly true for the computer technology industry. In Part I, "Building an Emotion-Friendly Service Culture," we discussed regulating moods by using five shifts. If service providers see complaints as teaching opportunities for customers and learning opportunities for the organization, they are using the meaning shift.

> *Service providers can encourage customer dependency that contributes to emotional frustration and resource utilization problems.*

When customers are engaged to solve their own problems, complaints are no longer complaints but rather learning opportunities for the customer. Doing something for customers is nice, but emotional freedom can be created by showing them how to take care of their own needs. Then if organizational support is not always available or is overburdened, customers will experience less frustration because they know what to do. The organization will still get the emotional credit! Dick Schaaf, customer service advocate, in *Keeping the Edge*, writes: "Ultimately, profitable and lasting relationships are two-way exchanges that involve mutual value—and even mutual sweat equity. Doing business with today's empowered customers means sharing control."[20]

> *Creating learning opportunities out of complaints places special empathic demands on service providers.*

Creating learning opportunities out of complaints places special empathic demands on service providers, particularly among people who are highly technically trained. Technologists must be able to detect the competence/skill level of their customers so they do not offer a set of instructions that customers will not be able to implement. When this happens, many customers will pretend they understand what is being said to them. When they inevitably call back, sometimes having made their technical situation worse, they are in the embarrassing situation of having to admit they could not follow the instructions they were given. So they may claim they were given incorrect instructions. However they choose to address their lack of knowledge, customers are placed in an uncomfortable emotional box.

■ Application

Guidelines for Turning Complaints into Customer Learning Opportunities. The following guidelines apply not just to paying customers but also to internal customers. Because of the frequency of interaction with internal customers, we recommend that you practice these ideas first with your colleagues, then with your ongoing business customers or distributors, and finally with all your other customers.

- *Listen carefully to insure understanding.* Many times people will say they understand something when they actually don't. This can set up false expectations. Always, always, always check your assumptions. When you "examine" a customer's knowledge, be sure to apologize in advance for any simple questions you ask. For example, you can say, "I'm sure you know the answer to this; I just want to ensure we don't overlook anything."

- *Note danger spots.* If customers choose to take care of their own needs, be sure both of you understand where they can get into trouble. This is particularly true with complex products. We've seen many instances where customers who thought they were following instructions crashed entire computer systems.

■ *Set up checkpoints.* If there is a chance that your customers will create problems for themselves, point out to them "alert" checkpoints along the way. This is the time to come back for help. Let them know you would rather help them with a minor issue than have a major problem created. This could be something as simple as "If you haven't received a response by the 15th of the month, be sure to check back." Or "Let me give you a small word of caution. The order in which you do this is critical. Here's the best way to proceed. If you do it in any other order, you run the risk of. . . . Would you like me to send you an e-mail about that?"

■ *Share information about knowledge levels of different customers.* As most organizations have several service personnel dealing with the same client, it is important that each interaction doesn't involve starting over again. If your system allows for notes to be made, indicate levels of customer competence in your data bank. Be sure to indicate these levels in positive terms. State what customers know rather than what they don't know.

■ *Give customers hints about how to speed up service.* If having certain information available speeds up service, inform customers about that. Make sure this is presented as a service: "By the way, the next time you call, we'll be able to help you even faster, if . . . ." Then tell them how to make that happen. "Just a little hint. Our phone lines are least busy between 8 and 10 A.M."

■ *Finally, be sure to reward your customers when they do handle something for themselves.* Thank them and praise them. You are becoming partners in the truest sense of the word, and it is important to appreciate customers for forming such a relationship with you. After all, you both benefit from this approach to complaint/problem handling.

Taking Complaints Seriously

Too many times customers hear, "Oh, this happens all the time" or "That's nothing." Customers do not want to be measured against an anonymous crowd. They want to hear that their complaints are special. From the customer's point of view, a complaint expresses how he or she feels. When the complaint is belittled, the customer is belittled.

> *If service representatives are to take complaints seriously, they have to listen carefully to customers.*

If service representatives are to take complaints seriously, they have to listen carefully to customers, give them undivided attention, send appropriate valuing communications (such as nodding of the head or concerned facial expressions), and *never compare one customer's complaint with another's—unless it is to validate.*

Part of listening carefully to complaints and simultaneously demonstrating to customers that their complaints are being taken seriously involves note taking. Customers need to see the service provider writing everything down, or they suspect their complaint is going to go no further than the person talking with them.

Service providers also need to learn to give appropriate "taking each complaint seriously" communication indicators, such as "I want to make sure I got this absolutely correct." "I'm writing this down so I don't forget anything." These comments are particularly important on the telephone when customers can't see the service representative writing. Serious listening sends the message that the speaker is valued. We tend not to listen to people we do not value. So the simple act of careful demonstration of listening sends a strong positive metamessage at a time when the emotionality of the customer needs to be engaged.

The total organization can set the stage for the seriousness of complaint handling by formally defining a process that demonstrates the organization's commitment to complaining customers. For example, IBM in Rochester, New York, demonstrates its commitment to complaints by using five customer communication devices that are marketed to both customers and staff:

- User group meetings employing round-table discussions and other forms of feedback that focus solely on the customer

- Customer satisfaction measurements that are linked to key IBM business areas

- Partnership calls and surveys in which customers are asked directly about levels of satisfaction

- Handling of customer complaints through a defined, consistent approach

- Fixing of customer dissatisfactions and then follow-up to ensure that IBM solutions are what the customer wants

> *The total organization can demonstrate commitment to complaining customers.*

Application

Taking Complaints Seriously. Draw a line down the center of a piece of paper. On one side of the line, list everything you do so customers know you take their complaints seriously. On the other side of the line, list everything you do suggesting to customers you don't take their complaints seriously—perhaps even that you find complaints an annoyance. Ask your staff or colleagues to help you make this list. Then talk with some of your best customers and ask them if they agree with your self-assessment or have any other useful feedback about your approach to complaint handling.

Eliminating Blame

When customers complain, they, in effect, blame the provider. There is an equally strong tendency for the provider to blame the customer or, at a minimum, to find out to what degree the customer is responsible for the mishap. "When did you call?" "What did you say?" "Did you read the instructions, first?" All these questions are imbedded with implied distrust of customer behaviors. Mary Jo Bitner, assistant marketing professor at Arizona State University, summarizes the obvious: "Making the

> "Making the customer feel the failure is somehow his or her fault . . . infuriate[s] customers."

customer feel the failure is somehow his or her fault . . . infuriate[s] customers."[21] First, the customer feels victimized by the service failure. To be blamed on top of that seems grossly unfair to customers. Yet that is precisely what happens.

Alan Resnick studied managerial attitudes toward customers by having complaint letters evaluated both by customers and by managers of a Fortune 500 building materials company. Managers were less likely to view complaints as legitimate than were the customers. When they thought the complaint was not legitimate, 34.9 percent of the managers thought the customers wanted something for nothing, 22.9 percent of the managers thought the customers were confused, and 14.5 percent of them thought the customers were dead wrong.[22] A related study indicates that *when customers think this is your perception, it doesn't matter what you do* (give them a refund or give them a replacement product, for example), *customers won't be satisfied.* In short, don't blame your customers. Own the problem of customer service. For example, if your customers do not know how to use the products, then take responsibility for not having explained product use carefully enough.

When *A Complaint Is a Gift* was written, advance copies were sent to reviewers. One reviewer described an example that the authors used as being obviously false. The example involved one of the authors traveling on a Middle Eastern airline from Hong Kong to the Philippines. The reviewer said, "This is obviously a made up example. No Middle East airlines fly this route." Actually, one does. United Arab Emirates flies from Dubai to Hong Kong and then on to the Philippines, and it is possible to book just the portion from Hong Kong to the Philippines. It was tempting to dismiss the reviewer's "complaint" for her lack of knowledge. Rather, we decided that if she had this belief, most likely other readers would have the same reaction. We therefore changed the example to a local Asian airline so that it was less likely to create negative reactions.

If customers don't have adequate background or knowledge to understand or use your products, don't blame them. Fix the situation.

Another reviewer of an early copy of *A Complaint Is a Gift* said that our example of a seven-story department store was ridiculous because they did not exist. That's interesting, because we have shopped in plenty of them. Then we noticed that the reviewer was from a small town in the United States Midwest where obviously seven-story department stores don't exist.

> *If customers don't have the adequate background or knowledge, don't blame them. Fix the situation.*

Don't waste time blaming the customers. Fix the situation for all the other customers. Complaining customers are spokespeople for all the others who are thinking the same but don't say anything. It's an emotional opportunity for deepening relationships.

■ **Application**

Turning Blaming into Questions. Every time you handle a complaint, note the inclination to blame the customer. For example: "They didn't know which product to order." "They called very late, and we couldn't get the product out." Turn these thoughts into questions: "What can we do so our customers don't make these same ordering mistakes?" or "What would we have to do to fix our systems so that customers would be less likely to call too late?"

Expanding the Zone of Tolerance

In a study of the optical industry, researchers found that the difference between customers who were "delighted" and those who were not had to do with *customer service* (reliability, timeliness, and courtesy), *friendliness,* and perceived *fairness*. Researchers Paula Saunders, Robert Scherer, and Herbert Brown concluded: "It is interesting to note that dimensions differentiating customer delight are related to how the client or customer is treated, and these are just as important as those related to expertise."[23]

Friendly and fair customer service is more than a smile and name recognition. It has to do with trust and integrity. (Fairness, as it relates to customer loyalty, is discussed in greater depth in chapter 13.) Friends are friends in great part because they trust each other. When customers have friendly, trusting relations with their providers, they are more forgiving. They are less likely to turn a complaint into an even stronger negative judgment.

This is particularly true when the customer critically needs the service or product. Friendliness is not as emotionally important to customers when they don't depend on your product or service. They can always go someplace else. They are less vulnerable in such situations. If they are dependent on your service, however, they need friendliness to feel secure.[24] Without this friendliness, customers become less tolerant and more difficult.

According to marketing researchers Valarie Zeithaml, Leonard Berry, and A. Parasuraman, complaints occur when customers' perception of adequate service are not met.[25] Customers have two pictures in their minds: a picture of desired service and a picture of adequate service. A "zone of tolerance" separates the two types of expectations as illustrated below.

Desired Service **Zone of Tolerance** Adequate Service

When customers are emotionally upset by the service they have received, the zone of tolerance narrows sharply, so there is little difference between adequate service and desired service in customers' minds. In short, customers become harder to please.

Desired Service Zone of Tolerance Adequate Service

Once you have activated negative emotions in a customer, "adequate" service is no longer adequate. Adequate service and desired service become indistinguishable from each other, and demands on service providers will increase. Another implication of this is that once customers are in a negative frame of mind, they start looking for everything to go wrong. Friendliness helps maintain a broader zone of tolerance, so customer expectations are in a more easily influenced space.

> *Once you have activated negative emotions in a customer, "adequate" service is no longer adequate.*

Unfortunately, many companies betray the trust of their customers regularly. They do it by not responding to their customers, by sending mixed messages, by being inconsistent with their messages so one person tells the customer one thing and another person says something else. You can take friendliness to a new level with heightened trust and integrity and at the same time build a broader zone of customer tolerance.

◼ Application

Increasing the Zone of Tolerance. Tolerance is not something you can demand of customers. However, you can create the mood for tolerance. List ideas for expanding your customers' zones of tolerance. Choose a variety of situations and list ideas for each of them. For example, having candy available to customers on a counter increases friendliness, but it is not something you can offer over the telephone.

Handling Complaints from Corporate Customers

We conclude our ten strategies by considering the special relationships between organizations and their corporate clients. A great deal of research has been carried out on individual consumers and their dissatisfaction. Little has been conducted on industrial buyers, yet the relationships are not the same.[26] Industrial buyers are more likely to get to know their suppliers or vendors very well and frequently form long-term personal relationships with them. Complaining under such circumstances can be difficult for both sides. A critical quality variable for industrial customers, therefore, is how their sales representatives or project managers respond personally when there is a problem.

One of the biggest differences between individual buyers and industrial buyers is that industrial buyers tend to have complaints not only *after* they purchase but also *before* they buy and *while* they are buying. Industrial buyers also *tend to complain more* than individual customers. After all, it is their job to manage the vendor relationship, and part of the success of their company depends on supplier capability.

> *Industrial buyers tend to have complaints after they purchase, before they buy, and while they are buying.*

Corporate buyers will complain more, especially when they conclude

- their supplier is not optimal;
- there are limited options for them to go elsewhere;
- the buyer is larger than the supplier in terms of company size or revenues (to some degree, they think they can afford to push smaller suppliers around);
- they are highly experienced, especially as compared to the supplier;
- the supplier sells itself on high quality;
- the supplier is at fault;
- the cost of complaining is smaller than the benefits to be gained.

Because of the complexity of this type of customer-supplier relationship, two special emotional strategies are called for in this type of relationship.

1. *Carefully manage customer expectations.* Make sure customer goals are always clearly stated and written down. Keep referring back to these written goals as the contract proceeds. Tracking verbal statements with corporate customers is not done to "protect one's backside" but rather to insure a clear, orderly, professional relationship and to inspire trust. Each meeting with the customer should conclude with a summary statement as to everything said and agreed upon, followed by written confirmation, so there are no surprises. Surprises tend to result in withdrawals from emotional accounts. Clear, written summaries allow everyone to relax.

> *Tracking verbal statements with corporate customers insures a clear, orderly, professional relationship.*

2. *Establish easy, uncomplicated communication links with your buyers.* Assign a limited number of people to a contract, so the buyer can enjoy a first-name relationship with company representatives. Special pager numbers assigned to customers will give them a feeling of greater accessibility to the supplier. It will also save everyone a lot of time.

▨ Application

Managing Corporate Customer Complaints. Divide a sheet of paper into three columns. Label the columns "Before Purchase," "During Purchase," and "After Purchase." Describe typical complaints you are likely to encounter with your corporate customers in each category. What steps can you proactively take to minimize the potential damage these types of complaints can do to your long-term relationships with these customers?

ASSESSING YOUR ORGANIZATION'S COMPLAINT FRIENDLINESS

Answer the following questions:

1. Do service providers have to go to someone else to determine whether customers should be compensated for their complaints? What is the degree of empowerment to handle customer complaints in your organization?

2. Do you understand that the purpose of compensating customers by not charging them, or by giving them something, is to *enhance relationships with* customers? Or do you think that the result of your organizational guarantees is to create more rules for you and customers to follow?

3. If you have not fully empowered your staff to handle complaints, what are your fears about empowerment? Are you afraid your staff will "give away the store"? Is this fear justified? How can you find out?

4. Do you actively seek negative feedback from both your customers and your staff?

5. Are you tracking your system failure costs against sales figures and profitability so you understand the ratio between these factors?

6. How do you ensure that your customers know you take complaints seriously?

7. What are you doing to make sure that your "friendliness" level with customers is at its peak?

8. Do staff in your organization understand that listening is a "gift" you give to customers?

PART FIVE

USING EMOTIONAL CONNECTIONS TO INCREASE CUSTOMER LOYALTY

Good words are worth much, and cost little.
—George Herbert, English clergyman
and poet

Using emotional connections to increase customer loyalty requires a carefully thought-out "emotion" retention strategy that every employee understands. It signifies a level of sophistication where staff grasp that the entire purpose of improved service is not simply to make tasks faster, more accurate, or less costly for the customer, but ultimately to honor customers by caring to meet their needs. An article in *US Banker* supports this notion by recommending a mind-set change that we earlier called the Customer Impact Job Description:

> The mind set of bank employees must change. If tellers think they're there to cash checks rather than helping customers realize their financial dreams, they'll act accordingly. There will be little eye contact or personal warmth, because all the tellers see are tallies against their daily transaction quotas—and customers know it.[1]

Throughout this book we have suggested numerous applications related to becoming emotion friendly, embracing emotional competence as a service model, maximizing customer experiences with empathy, and viewing complaints as emotional opportunities to deepen relationships. If implemented, these practices will positively impact customer retention rates. In this final part, we recommend four additional strategies to retain customers:

- Listening to the voice of your loyal customers
- Retaining customers by retaining staff
- Going for impact: that's where emotions reside
- Communicating a message of fairness

CHAPTER TWELVE

LOYALTY IS A BEHAVIOR WITH ITS ROOTS IN EMOTIONS

Most customers would prefer to be brand loyal. It makes their lives so much easier; shopping is quicker because they don't have to ponder which products to purchase; they can feel positively secure about their choices. They have no hesitation about encouraging others to follow their lead. They know they are receiving value for money, and they can trust a business when it asks them to purchase a more developed product or return for another experience. They know if they have problems, they will be helped quickly and with integrity.

Loyalty obviously implies a positive attitude. Perhaps the positive attitude is only about low prices offered or about the organization's incentive programs. Even when prices are rock-bottom, however, customers will still leave if they are treated badly enough. Likewise, incentive programs work well to ensure loyalty, but they are not "loyalty-proof." Airlines know that even their most profitable high-mileage passengers will switch to other carriers if airline personnel are unresponsive to customer needs.

> *When customers are positively inclined, they more willingly tolerate delays, product shortages, mistakes, and many other aspects of poor quality.*

When customers are positively inclined, they more willingly tolerate delays, product shortages, mistakes, and many other aspects of poor quality. Loyal customers become sales staff for companies. Apple's best sales force has been their avid users. Loyal customers are easier to serve; they know how to meet their own needs and how to do that with minimal inconvenience to themselves. When parents love their children, they put up with a whole host of behaviors they will not tolerate from children they don't know. This same type of tolerance occurs when customers feel connected to products and services.

Loyalty, furthermore, is more than just an attitude and nice feelings. It typically means more involvement with products. William Neal, president of Sophisticated Data Research, Inc., puts it this way: "Satisfaction is an attitude; loyalty is a behavior."[1] Car companies have clubs organized around the world based solely on brand ownership. One of the most successful and newest business magazines, *The Fast Company*, is encouraging the formation of local clubs where people gather to discuss *Fast Company* articles. This involvement reinforces customer commitment to repurchase, or in *Fast Company's* case, it probably means readers are exposed to the magazine's advertisements more than once.

Perhaps most relevant to businesses, loyal customers need less incentive to purchase. They are not as price sensitive. While pricing cannot be ignored, committed customers generally do not require sale prices to bring them in the door. David L. Whiting, president of Athletic Bag Co., speaks for many companies when he says, "Loyal customers don't care so much about saving a penny or a nickel or a dollar."[2]

The Value of Retained Customers

Loyalty expert Frederick Reichheld, a director at Bain and Company, cites an oft-quoted but nonetheless jolting statistic: "Good long-standing customers are worth so much that in some industries, reducing customer defections by as little as five points—from say, 15 percent to 10 percent

per year—can double profits."[3] The most loyal customers, according to grocers, are perhaps a thousand
times more valuable to them than infrequent shoppers.[4] To see the figures in yet another light, again
according to Bain and Company, the profit made
from a single interaction with a customer who has

> "Reducing customer defections by as little as five points . . . can double profits."

stayed loyal for seven years is six times more than the profit made from
a new customer.

A *Sloan Management Review* article cites the statistic that approximately 70 percent of all sales come from repeat purchases. As a result, the
authors of the article state that firms must adopt "defensive" strategies to
keep satisfied customers, rather than putting their efforts into "offensive"
strategies that seek out new customers or attempt to turn around customers who have already left.[5]

It is only relatively recently that a significant number of marketing
experts have seriously looked at the importance of focusing on existing
customers to turn them into loyal customers. A long-held definition of
marketing is that it is "the aspect of business that deals with *getting and
keeping* customers." "Keeping" customers has been downplayed because
marketing specialists primarily concentrate on getting new customers—
generally to replace lost customers.[6] With this deeply ingrained bias,
organizations might benefit more from creating vice presidents of customer retention instead of hoping their marketing vice presidents will
change orientation.

Many companies approach customer retention/service/loyalty
issues in a haphazard way. Mary Jo Bitner, marketing professor at
Arizona State University, laments: "A number of companies are unwill-
ing to commit to service-improvement results. They try one thing that
sounds good; then something else comes along that sounds good [and]
then they try that."[7] In our experience, organizations that have a committed interest in retaining customers by upgrading emotional value
have to look at everything: brand recognition, systems, reward structures, processes, product quality—and emotions. And then they have to

look at how all these variables interact with each other to impact customer behavior.

By zeroing in on upgraded services that existing customers value, organizations will likely keep more customers and, in turn, enjoy greater profitability.[8] As the old marketing expression goes, "It's easier to fill a bucket if it's not leaking." Given this, it is surprising how few companies focus on customer retention—beyond lip service and normal customer interaction. Many organizations have no idea how many customers they lose and why they lose them. They keep their eyes instead on cash flow and quarter-by-quarter profitability, which according to Frederick Reichheld does not provide an accurate reflection of how much value a company possesses.[9]

Many organizations have no idea how many customers they lose.

Using a concrete example, consider the impressive numbers of MBNA America, the Delaware-based credit card company, which has one of the lowest customer defection rates in the credit card industry. The average credit card defection rate is ten percent; MBNA's is 5 percent. This 5 percent difference has meant increased profits of sixteenfold for MBNA and an industry ranking that has gone from thirty-eight to four—without acquisitions.[10] Another aspect of retention has to do with how much money a customer spends within a single organization. A British polling firm, the Henley Centre for Forecasting, found that loyal customers, who might normally spend 500 pounds over a five-year period, would spend only 266 pounds if customer service were found wanting.[11]

If an organization does not know whether customers intend to repurchase, money put into customer service improvement cannot be realistically assessed. Managers struggle with inadequate data. We cited earlier a Juran Institute finding that less than 2 percent of managers felt confident in being able to say their organizations experienced bottom-line improvements as a result of their customer service interventions.[12]

To get *bottom-line repurchase information,* customers need to be asked market action questions. These include, What kinds of problems have you experienced with us? What did you do about them? Did our staff help you with these problems? Were you satisfied with their actions? And finally, Will you buy from us again? To receive accurate repurchase information, these questions need to be asked sometime after the initial flush of shopping has faded.

> *To get bottom-line information, customers need to be asked market action questions.*

Immediately after purchasing an item, especially if it is expensive, customers like to psychologically justify their buying decisions. As a result, they will more likely reinforce their positive attitudes right after making a purchase rather than telling you honestly about their future purchase inclinations. To get valid *retention information*, therefore, it's *not* a good idea to ask "Will you buy from us again?" You won't get accurate feedback if that question is asked right after a purchase has been made. To reinforce a *buying decision*, however, it makes sense to reinforce the customer's choice right after purchase. In other words, you have to understand the purposes of your questions and ask the right ones at the right time.

People in relationships tend to be more committed if they believe that the commitment is mutual. The moment customers begin to feel they are just account numbers to organizations, their loyalty weakens. Showing commitment requires focusing and personalizing efforts for existing customers—the bird in hand, as the expression goes. Bob McNeel, president of a Seattle AutoDesk Value Added Reseller (VAR), says his marketing efforts with existing customers make him known throughout the marketplace. "We believe you have to have that customer base so satisfied they essentially replace 95 percent of your sales effort. You should make the customer so happy with what you're doing that they'll go out and sell you constantly over and over again."[13]

A reasonable question is, Where is the best starting point to gain the benefits of loyal customers? The answer is, "It depends . . . ." It depends on how developed or mature the market is. It depends on demand in the marketplace. It depends on what is happening inside each individual company. In this book, we have focused on staff and the impact they can have on customer loyalty when emotional interactions are positively upgraded, ensuring regular deposits into customer emotional accounts. In reality, all three parts of the equation (loyal customers, loyal employees, high quality products and services) need to be considered simultaneously.

Emotional Drivers of Loyalty and Value

Loyal customers come in different intensity packages. Psychologist Leonard Goodstein and Howard Butz, Jr., a defense contractor director of total quality, enumerate five ever-stronger emotional levels of customer "bonding" in easy-to-understand language. Their model provides insight into the emotional drivers of loyalty and value.

> *Loyal customers come in different intensity packages.*

> *Preferential:* Let's try them this time.
> *Favoritism:* "All things being equal, they get the order."
> *Commitment:* "They are our supplier."
> *Referential:* "You ought to buy from these guys."
> *Exclusive:* "No one else has a chance to get an order."[14]

You may prefer other names and descriptions, but Goodstein and Butz make a powerful point. Loyalty doesn't even start until you are at least at the Commitment level. A *Fortune* article describes it this way: "Loyalty rises a bit as satisfaction increases, swooping abruptly up only at the highest levels of satisfaction."[15] On a survey scale from one to five, with one being the lowest, customers at the Preferential level probably mark midline scores (threes) on customer satisfaction surveys. "Fours" might qualify for Favoritism. Unquestionably, it takes scores of "fives" to get to Commitment, Referential, or Exclusive levels. Xerox found that customers who rated the companies as "fives" were six times as likely to repurchase as those who rated Xerox at a "four."[16]

Consider Dianna and Janelle as airline passengers: they both make their judgments of value and are loyal to the degree they are in large part because of their feelings about air travel and their history with a number of airlines. Janelle is at a Commitment/Referential level with United Airlines for a variety of reasons, not the least of which is that the company almost always upgrades her to first class on domestic flights because of the high mileage she flies with it. Janelle likes flying with United. She knows its schedules; she feels comfortable with the way it operates, its safety record, how the staff take care of her, the little gratuities they extend to her. United is "her" airline. She will recommend United to others for specific reasons, one being the landings—very smooth! However, she definitely flies on other airlines as well, particularly when United's scheduling doesn't get her where she needs to be at the time she needs to be there. She has experienced problems on United; by and large, however, the company is good at fixing most service failures. She also knows that she is likely to have the same problems on other airlines as well, so a few delayed or cancelled flights and some instances of lost luggage will not deter her from the comfort she feels flying with United—particularly in light of the way the staff intermittently extend extras to her.

Dianna, on the other hand, is more at the Preferential level with all airlines; she primarily flies according to schedule availability. She does not fly as many miles as Janelle, so she is not committed to one high-volume-flyer loyalty program. She is definitely not forgiving of bad service. There are some airlines she will fly with only if there is absolutely no other choice. Dianna knows good service is not easy to consistently deliver, but she also knows it can be done. She did it at Horizon Airlines where she was a founding director.

Feelings Influence Loyalty

"Produce the highest quality and you will get satisfied customers" was the mantra of the 1980s. Many companies attempted to follow this guideline and were stunned to find that higher judgments about quality didn't necessarily produce more loyal customers. Even today, numerous news releases describe company efforts to upgrade customer service offerings. They include public notification about new phone systems, installation of enhanced computer technologies, and availability of direct ordering on the Web. The assumption of these announcements is that if some aspect of delivery is improved, customers will automatically be more satisfied and inclined to do business. It's an assumption that was made in the early 1980s in business schools around the world. In the last ten years of the twentieth century, this assumption has been widely debated, even to question whether the vast sums of money thrown at enhanced systems has significantly contributed to satisfied customers and the bottom line.

One loyalty expert describes commitment-based companies as those that add customer value by *anticipating* and *responding to* latent or unvoiced needs of the market.[17] In other words, this author says you have to keep moving, looking to the future to determine whether your loyal customers want you to change products and services or whether they would like exactly what you offered last year. You won't get this information by merely using satisfaction surveys, which, by definition, measure the past. In short, it's not easy to assess where the market is moving by looking at data gleaned from satisfaction surveys.

Satisfaction surveys, by definition, measure the past.

Customers may find something that meets their needs better elsewhere, even though they were satisfied with their last purchase. In fact, many academics would argue that service quality and meeting expectations of satisfaction aren't the same phenomenon at all. For instance, if you are single and invited on a dinner date by someone you're not very excited about, your anticipation of quality will be low. If you have a rather mediocre evening, you would hardly end the dinner date saying you were satisfied—because you got what you predicted. And you would not be excited about repeating the experience.

We side with the research that says while the gap between what is expected and what is delivered is important in contributing to customer satisfaction, the gap between what is *delivered* and what the *customer thinks is important* has more to do with creating high levels of customer loyalty. And *loyalty-producing behavior always contains an emotional element.* To put this research in fundamental terms without doing severe damage to its complexity, *high levels of positive customer emotional involvement drive loyalty more than customer judgments about quality.*[18] Company A might have twenty-four-hour service, be capable of quickly accessing decades-old customer data on its computers, and have products that do more than its competitors'. Yet customers could still be more loyal to Company B's products and services because the quality aspects of Company A's products are simply unimportant to them,[19] and because they like Company B personnel better.

Customer repurchase intentions are influenced by a range of variables that is more complex than the simple rational assessment of the satisfaction quality gap between "this is what I expected" and "this is what I got." Customer service and product evaluations are related to immediate specific transaction assessments, while quality judgments are more related to long-term issues, such as, Does my new car still corner as well after a year of ownership? Does my expensive suit still hold its shape after ten dry cleanings? Does my washing machine still get the job done after five years? Long-term attitudes are more of a mental construct, while immediate responses to specific transactions are more emotion based. And it is the *specific transaction assessments* that seem to influence repurchase intention more than do long-term cognitive judgments about service quality. This is one of the reasons why it is hard to get customers to change their minds about an organization's ability to deliver service if it has failed them in the past. As it is commonly said in the service field, it takes twelve experiences of positive service to overcome the damage done by a single strong negative transaction.

> *Long-term attitudes are more of a mental construct, while immediate responses to specific transactions are more emotion based.*

Loyalty, however, as we continue to point out, does require some level of quality. Customers don't care how nice you are if the products they buy from you don't work, create other problems, and wear out just after the warranty expires. If companies focus on consistently providing both *material and emotional value* to their loyal customers over a period of time, customers will likely bond to them.

Basically, judging quality means Did we do what we said we would do? This is an important question, but it is a question for organizations to ask of themselves. It does not answer the question of whether what we did was of value to the customer. The value question must be answered by customers and, in fact, is indicated by repurchase behavior. Quality

> *Value tends to look at what is added and matters to customers—even if it has a few defects in it.*

focuses mostly on errors. Zero defects is the way it is popularly expressed. *Value tends to look at what is added and matters to customers—even if a product has a few defects in it.* A mistake that is fixed by the company can end up adding value to customers that would never have been there if zero defects had been initially achieved.

Loyalty and value are not simple attributes to consider because they open a Pandora's box that contains *both* employee *and* customer emotions. It is easier to measure performance standards or conformance to specifications than emotions. The ISO9000 quality certification, a must in some industries, assures buyers that the producer (mostly of tangible products) will guarantee consistency in production. This way, buyers know for certain that what they are purchasing meets certain specifications. ISO9000, however, does not guarantee that what they buy will meet their needs.

Concentrating on emotional value forces companies to look at customers. Concentrating on quality encourages companies to, in large part, turn in toward themselves, which is undoubtedly easier and the reason it is so attractive. Unfortunately, too strong a focus on quality can produce wonderful products, with only a small number of buyers. We are acquainted with a firm that produces elegant high-tech products. Unfortunately, the customers don't always value these products, or they are willing to get their needs met in a different way at substantially lower costs. As we write this book, many top-notch employees are leaving this company. Not too surprisingly, the company is slowly but surely sinking—but its products win lots of awards. The company has operated under the philosophy that if the products are of sufficiently high quality, customers will come to the company. It downplays the importance of marketing and brand identification.

Emotions Drive Assessment of Value

Value measurements relate to the competitive positioning of products and services. Academic definitions of value say it is the ratio of quality relative to price—compared to what your competition offers. If a customer purchases a quality product (compared to competitors) at a good price (compared to competitors), then the customer receives value (compared to competitors). The higher the quality and the lower the price, the higher the value. While value ratings have a lot to do with customer repurchase intentions, we believe that a simple ratio between quality and price is too narrow a definition of value.

Value must include meeting emotional needs if value is to encompass customer loyalty. Value is also not exclusively a marketing issue; in fact, marketing may have little to do with value. A value "fix" is not achieved quickly and requires emotionally sophisticated staff. Customers can purchase high-quality hair shampoo at a good price, thereby achieving high value, and still not be loyal to the shop where they purchased the shampoo or to the shampoo brand—because they wanted more than sham-

> *Value must include meeting emotional needs if value is to encompass customer loyalty.*

poo. Perhaps they wanted a special feeling of personal care while using the shampoo that was not inspired by their shopping experience. Maybe they wanted advice that they didn't get. Possibly they wanted recognition. Or they wanted rapid, personal attention. We have to consider the full range of what matters to customers, if we are to offer value.

Author John Guaspari offers a simple but expanding definition of value that is very appealing—and includes emotions.[20] He agrees that value is the ratio between what the customer gets and what the customer pays. He calls it the GOT/COST ratio. At this point, Guaspari's idea is not that different from those of other writers in the field. It's how he defines GOT and COST that add dimension to his work. GOT includes the product or service itself, *how it is delivered, and a whole host of intangibles* that are important to the customer. COST includes not only money but also time and other intangibles.[21] Illustrated, it looks like this:

$$\text{Value} = \frac{\text{Product or Service (According to standards that matter to the customer)}}{\text{Cost (Money, time, emotional effort)}}$$

Because of all the variables involved, Guaspari's value is a moving target, but it is *always* expressed in terms of what matters to customers. For this reason, one of the important tools to use in assessing customer value is empathy, the focus of Part III. We have to get into our customers' shoes. We have to find out what matters to them, a both changing and personal target. If we watch emotional reactions, we can receive strong clues about what is important to customers.

> *Value is a moving target, but it is always expressed in terms of what matters to customers.*

CHAPTER THIRTEEN

STRATEGIES FOR RETAINING CUSTOMERS

This chapter suggests four emotion-friendly strategies to increase customer loyalty.

Listening to the Voices of Loyal Customers

If companies are to benefit from loyal customers, they need to focus their energies in a coordinated way on the customers who are already most loyal. This requires being able to identify your loyal customers, seeking out what they have to say, and then implementing what they value. The ultimate goal is one in which service value and relationships are so positive that loyal customers feel

> *Companies need to focus their energies in a coordinated way on the customers who are already most loyal.*

they cannot get their needs met anywhere else. This necessarily involves personal and emotional connections with your customers.

Here is the advice of the British SJB Services, which studies customer loyalty metrics: "Choosing the most profitable customers and accurately targeting them and nurturing them, while virtually deselecting the least profitable customers, is one way of vastly improving bottom-line profits."[1] If too many resources are used to gain new customers or to win back those that have left, there will be fewer financial and staff resources remaining to heighten or maintain loyalty.

Bruce Merrifield, a business consultant from Chapel Hill, North Carolina, advises companies to stop pushing products and focus more on customers. He concludes: "Shouldn't we pursue a customer-centric re-organization of our business instead of fine-tuning our product-pushing past?"[2] In fact, a *Journal of Retailing* article suggests that efforts to attract new customers (by definition less-loyal customers) may not grow your business and may actually negatively affect your loyal, existing customers. The *Journal of Retailing* authors ask, "Who is likely to perceive a benefit from 'Bikini Night' or 'Seance Night' at a sporting event? For those who are attracted by such event sales promotions, what is the likelihood of their returning for future events?"[3]

■ Application

What Do Our Loyal Customers Want? First, gather staff together who really know your customer base well. Ask them to identify your top customers—the ones who are very happy with you, who are currently profitable for you, and who will have greater need for your services or products in the future. Then interview your top customers, making sure you include at least three general service-related questions: (1) How do you define good service? (2) What is irritating about the service you currently receive (not necessarily from our organization)? and (3) When you leave our business, how do you want to feel? Finally, ask yourself, What are the common characteristics of our best customers? What aspects of customer service are most important to them? In this way, you will be able not only to create a template of customers who are a good fit for your offerings but also to know how to meet their needs.

Customer loyalty programs aimed at already-loyal customers are a powerful strategy because they require commitment to and proactivity with existing customers, the point Michael Lowenstein emphasizes in his book, *The Customer Loyalty Pyramid*.[4] Canadian Pacific Hotels (CP), which includes the famous Banff Springs Hotel, has made a proactive, coordinated effort to mark its brand on every aspect of its customer service. One step the company took was to target frequent guests in its surveys. CP executives learned that their loyal customers didn't want a frequent hotel guest program—they wanted airline miles. They also wanted recognition of their individual preferences.

Making the decision to reward their frequent guests was easy for CP executives. Making their systems operationally able to support the small changes they wanted to make was difficult. For example, CP offered a discount to frequent guests in their gift shops. This simple offering required sophisticated technological changes. The results of their efforts, however, have been well worth it for Canadian Pacific. Business travel has increased 3 percent in Canada overall, while CP's room occupancy has increased 16 percent, without adding any new properties. CP's Club members are no longer spreading their stays around to other hotels; they are concentrating on Canadian Pacific Hotels.

United States Automobile Association (USAA), the $7 billion insurance organization primarily catering to former military personnel, builds loyalty "by convincing [customers] we're loyal to them," according to Phyllis Stable, senior vice president of marketing. USAA demonstrates caring to customers in hundreds of different ways. "We make it a point, in all of our materials, to let them know that we're there for them as they make transactions," Stable continues. When a client dies, USAA coordinates all forms, documents, and correspondence through one account executive. Stable says, "Making things easier for widows and widowers is a true service to help people when they need it—on their terms, not ours."[5]

Listening to the voice of customers also refers to individualizing experiences for them, which is easier to do for customers you already know. Computers make this possible and relatively easy today. Ritz-Carlton has a "guest recognition system" that inputs

Listening to the voice of customers also refers to individualizing experiences for them.

225

data on customers' individual preferences. If you request a hypoallergenic pillow, you'll have it without asking on your next visit to any of its more than thirty-five properties.[6] Ritz-Carlton's success has been in utilizing the information it gathers from guests. Some hotels collect detailed information and yet it never seems to be implemented. Janelle has stayed at a hotel in Hong Kong that requests useful and complete information from her—every time she checks into the hotel! When she asks about the information she provided on the last stay in the hotel, she is told, "We need it for our records." It's interesting to watch an organization attempt to do what's right but not have thought the entire process through to completion and considered its impact on customers.

The moment that employees begin to adopt the attitude that customer retention is someone else's job, attention to the customer is reduced.

Abbie Griffin, professor of marketing and operations management at the University of Chicago, identified "best practices" of organizations most sensitive to customer satisfaction. Professor Griffin reported that, in addition to strong top-level management buy-in to the process, acceptance by all employees that every job was related to customer satisfaction was equally critical.[7] The moment that employees begin to adopt the attitude that customer retention is someone else's job, attention to the customer is reduced.

■ Application

How Are You Loyal to Your Loyal Customers? Most companies want their customers to be loyal to them. A more relevant question is, In what ways are you loyal to your customers? List all the ways you are loyal to your customers, then narrow the list down to the three items that are most effective at retaining customers. Then ask your customers if they agree. Finally, choose three other items on your list and ask yourself what you would have to do to make these three strategies work as effectively for you as the top three on your list.

Retaining Customers by Retaining Staff

Sometimes reality is hard. Most firms lose half their customers in five years' time. Even more worrisome, most companies lose half of their employees in only four years, suggesting a relationship between the two figures.[8]

Organizational development pioneer Edgar Schein introduced the idea of a psychological contract to describe the emotional foundation between employer and employee.[9] If the "contract"—the unspoken reality that mutual needs are being met—worked for both parties, then, Schein argued, employment would continue. However, if the terms of the contract were not met, then employees would likely leave the organization.[10]

The idea also applies when considering the relationship between employees and customers. If emotional needs are not met, *both* employees *and* customers will leave, if they have any choice at all. And because customers have greater flexibility in purchasing elsewhere than employees do in getting new employment, this would explain why the rates of customer loss are higher than employee turnover—but not by much.

> *If emotional needs are not met, both employees and customers will leave.*

All this has made social commentators lament about the contemporary short-term transactional nature of employment that has replaced the long-term relational approach that once used to rule. We would suggest that employment is following customer-supplier relationships, which are becoming more and more encounter based rather than relationship based. If organizations (especially those that offer their services and products primarily through short-term customer encounters) create working environments that provide long-term employment opportunities and also make short-term customer encounters take on aspects of customer relationships, they will have a better chance of retaining staff. This takes us to Frederick Reichheld's conclusion: *"[The] fact is that employee retention is key to customer retention."*[11]

Towers Perrin, the human resources research and consulting firm, similarly concludes, "Companies that have practices that create or maintain a highly loyal workforce have superior customer retention."

Focusing on the insurance industry, Towers Perrin concludes that companies having an employee turnover of 10 percent or less enjoy a 10 percent advantage in customer retention rate over companies that lose their employees at anything over 15 percent.[12]

The interplay between high-quality staff (motivated and competent) and the high-quality products and services they produce creates a dynamic economic chain that seeks to attract and hold on to high-quality customers (those who have money, who have an inclination to be loyal, and whose own resources are growing). The longer the high-quality customers remain, the greater an organization's profitability; the longer the high-quality employees remain, the greater the chances of staff producing high-quality products and services and, therefore, of attracting even more high-quality customers. These relationships are the essence of value. If any one part of this attraction fails, the other two suffer as well.

The Economic Link between Employee Retention and Customer Retention

In the early 1990s, the Marriott Corporation attempted to retroactively measure the correlation between employee turnover and customer retention and its impact on profitability. Using conservative numbers, Marriott calculated the impact of a 10 percent reduction in staff turnover in two of its divisions. The conclusion: the savings in rehiring costs from retained staff and the increased revenues from retained customers, from a mere 10 percent reduction in staff turnover, would yield profits greater than the operating profits of both of the divisions considered.[13]

Taco Bell has discovered that its stores with the highest employee retention rates have sales 100 percent higher and profits 50 percent greater than Taco Bell outlets that do not hold on to their employees.[14] Most organizations understand that value, real and emotional, will help retain customers. Many do not understand the same is true for staff.

TMI consultants offer a program to our clients that focuses on customer loyalty—by focusing on employee loyalty. When we have succeeded in getting concrete data, the results have been strong, considering this is a back-door approach to customer retention. One of our international TMI partners, for example, worked with a large Swedish dental-care practice. The company put employees in charge of making structural changes in their own work, for their own satisfaction. This included making decisions about functional roles for both dentists and dental nurses. Since the program and the follow-up implementation, most of the clinics in this system have reported a direct impact on their bottom lines through attraction of more patients.

We also asked every employee of another TMI client, a retail chain with forty shops, to complete an evaluation survey that posed questions about attitudes, relationships within the organization, managerial styles, and willingness to accept change. Individuals, managers, and the entire organization were anonymously assessed. After the results of the survey were shared with the staff, managers were taught a problem-solving method to devise solutions with their store personnel so they could address outstanding areas of staff dissatisfaction. Six months later, the survey was once again administered and showed a dramatic change in staff attitudes toward their employers. A year later, these changes were reflected in improved customer evaluation surveys—and higher gross revenues.

Organizations need to ask what specific emotional value added to staff's lives will inspire them to stay and willingly make deposits in customer emotional accounts. Unfortunately, many ask how they can get staff at the lowest possible costs. Too many companies shop for staff strictly along price lines. According to *Fortune* magazine, as late as the mid-1990s, up to 25 percent of retail stores offered no health insurance policies to clerks, and 40 percent of clerks were paid less than the official poverty level for

Organizations need to ask themselves about the emotional value they add to staff lives.

a family of four. Yet these same organizations expect their staffs to represent their products and services in the best manner possible to the organizations' most important resources—their customers. This has led one consultant to lament, "For the most part, service companies view frontline workers as a disposable resource rather than an economic resource."[15] These statistics explain why Arlie Hochschild may have been

"For the most part, service companies view frontline workers as a disposable resource rather than an economic resource."

inspired to write *The Managed Heart. But low pay is a choice that organizations make, not a requirement.* Organizations must create the environment in which positive emotions can be celebrated by both employees and customers, and this requires, at minimum, a living wage.

Many organizations focus their financial reward systems on sales employees because they are responsible for bringing in new business. At the same time, they fail to provide extra financial rewards to staff who retain customers. Surely they are both selling. Organizations, at a minimum, need to know who in the organization contributes the most to building the customer base. Once this is learned, then the organizations can shift emphasis to where customer retention lives in the organization—or at least pay as much attention to it as to the sales department.

We are acquainted with a research study that contrasted the relative contributions of salespeople and customer service staff to customer satisfaction. The survey reports that in one industrial paper company, customer service added 52 percent toward total customer satisfaction, while sales contributed a mere 20 percent. Customer service added 33.6 percent toward customer satisfaction in the automotive industry, while salespeople contributed only 16.8 percent. In the telecommunications industry—customer service accounted for 40 percent of total customer satisfaction and sales less than 20 percent.[16]

Yet if you ask salespeople, they consistently state they provide excellent service and that customer dissatisfaction is caused by other departments. Our experience from listening to thousands of service staff is that they are all too often left to handle the customer dissatisfaction that results from sales staff overpromising what products can or will do. If salespeople don't always respond to customers who call after they have purchased, they also tend to blame that on their "busy-ness," over which they believe they have no control, or on the customers themselves![17] Isn't it interesting, therefore, that salespeople are generally rewarded at much higher levels than customer service staff. All this has led Peter Jordan, when he writes about the value-added resale business, to conclude, "If a business' primary overall objective is to retain its good customers, then its reward structure needs to be pegged to that objective, rather than heaping glory and reward on the rainmakers who bring in new accounts as in a front-end commission arrangement."[18]

■ Application

Do We See Our Customers as Long-Term Investments? Ask the sales team to list the behavioral implications of the statement "Our customers are sales to be made." Then ask them to consider the statement made by a company CEO: "A customer is an investment, rather than a sale." Compare the two lists of answers. Which approach is likely to result in loyal customers? What kinds of problems will result from taking the first approach? What are the challenges in the second statement?

Job Satisfaction and Staff Retention

The relationship between job satisfaction and loyalty to an organization has been extensively studied. Among salespeople, for example, satisfaction has been consistently found to relate to commitment to the organization and lower turnover.[19]

Numerous shining anecdotal examples can be found of the link between job satisfaction and staff retention. As with examples of outstanding customer service, these examples become part of the legacy of an organization. One such example we are aware of arose out of a nationally covered news incident. A young couple hired a nanny who they eventually suspected of abusing their child. They captured the abuse on videotape, which was widely played on television news shows. The mother was so distraught that she wanted to immediately quit her senior-level position with a managed health-care company so she could take care of her child herself, even though she was the major income contributor to her family and her job provided the best health-care insurance. Her boss told her she was too upset to make such an important decision on the spur of the moment and encouraged her to take time to heal her family—while she worked mainly from home. She did, and is now, some years later, even more committed to her health-care company.[20]

At the same time, other examples sting for their lack of compassion. We are acquainted with a mother whose young daughter developed a severe ear infection. On the same day, the mother had some pressing demands of work that needed to be completed for her boss. So the mother went to her daughter's elementary school, picked her up, and brought her back to her office. She placed a pad under her desk so her daughter could rest while she completed her boss's work before taking her daughter to the doctor. The woman was formally reprimanded for bringing her young child into a "secure" area where her desk was located. Permission was supposed be obtained for any outsiders, and she hadn't gotten it for her daughter. The woman—and her many supportive colleagues—wanted to know why she should show compassion to customers if none was shown to her for her industriousness.

As discussed earlier, if organizations want their staff to deliver the memorable service required to have an impact in the experience economy, work must be designed so it is also a positive experience. A 1995 United States Department of Labor review concluded that innovative workplace practices not only increase current profitability but also indicate future economic success.[21] Since other studies demonstrate a correlation between staff job satisfaction and customer retention, it is undoubtedly a strong starting point for organizations that are interested in improving their customer retention statistics.[22]

The experience economy also requires designing work so it is a positive experience.

Taking emotions into account requires building robust work systems for the following:

- Rewards and recognition (Experiences imply celebrations.)
- Respect for employees (Gandhi spoke of respect for customers; that same respect needs to be shown to staff.)
- Economic value (For employees, it means fair compensation for time invested.)

- Variety (Without periodic changes, even the most professional-minded person will lose his or her enthusiasm.)

- High standards (The organization needs to identify quality standards and then constantly promote them to both customers and staff.)

- Challenging growth (While it is not possible for everyone to reach the top of an organization, every employee can identify a realistic career path.)

▪ Application

Demonstrating Loyalty to Staff. What are the ways you and your organization show loyalty to your staff? What are the five most important reasons your staff want to continue to work with you—besides to earn money? What are the unique ways you add value to your staff's existence?

Going for Impact: That's Where Emotions Reside

Showing attention to detail can be a powerful emotional hook for retaining customers. Ford salespeople still talk about customers who came into showrooms to look at the Taurus when it was just released. Ford was the first to introduce the small trunk net for securing groceries in a moving car. Salespeople were amazed that while customers looked at the total car, they kept coming back to finger the net. Ford is convinced it sold thousands of cars—all for the cost of a three-dollar net. That's an emotional extra, showing sensitivity to an age-old problem of groceries tumbling about inside car trunks.

> *Showing attention to detail can be a powerful emotional hook.*

Extras deepen the feeling of being cared for. One of Ford's most highly rated dealers makes sure that all cars serviced are washed clean at pickup time. If the car isn't picked up as scheduled and sits in the parking lot over the weekend, the staff wash it again before the customer comes in. A valet brings cars to the customers so they don't have to go to the parking lot themselves. And every customer who purchases a car gets a follow-up call.[23]

One man reports buying a new Lexus and on his first drive home from the dealer experiencing extraordinary personalized customer service. He turned on the radio of his brand-new car to find it set to his favorite classical musical station, he pushed another button and found his favorite news station, and so on, through every button, all set to his favorite radio stations. He was curious. How could this happen? Coincidence? Hardly. An enterprising Lexus employee had noted the radio settings on his trade-in car and programmed them into the new Lexus.[24] Now that's elegant personalization of a service experience, and to be sure, this story has been told—over and over again. It's about emotional impact.

■ Application

How Do Your Customers Choose You? To understand how customers think of value, you have to focus on how your customers choose from among the suppliers they know. Value has to do with your competitors, while satisfaction surveys are typically not structured in relationship to competitors. The following three questions can help you to focus on value issues:

- ■ What are the five key value factors your customers use when choosing to buy the kinds of products or services you offer?
- ■ Rank the five key value factors and assign percentages to each.
- ■ List your top competitors. How do you and your competitors rate—in your customers' eyes—on these five key value factors?

But one hook won't do it. Companies need to identify a handful of preferences customers want and then consistently deliver them. Brian Richardson, vice president of marketing for Canadian Pacific Hotels, operates on the assumption that a brand is not one promise but many. "When you put together six or seven preferences and do it consistently, you suddenly have people who think you're listening and responding."[25]

Listening and responding to customer needs are the essence of brand value. Mintel International, a London-based global market research firm, found that after quality and price, *customer service, staff behavior,* and *complaint handling* are the critical elements of a brand reputation.[26]

> *After quality and price, customer service, staff behavior, and complaint handling are the critical elements of a brand.*

We have asked groups to list brand features of a handful of well-known brands, such as American Express, Disney, Toyota, Macintosh, Microsoft, and Nike. Almost always, the descriptors are consistent across the groups. And it is this consistency that creates the sense that the brand has empathy with its customers.

Amazon.com works hard at this. Dianna recently ordered two books on Amazon, and the next morning ordered a third. She asked if the orders could be combined. Less than twenty-four hours later, she received a return e-mail saying that the first shipment had already been sent but that Amazon, under the circumstances, would not charge for shipping the third title. The letter was signed with a person's name, instead of the title "Customer Service Representative." Dianna replied with a strong positive letter in which she said, "I am truly amazed at the complexity and speed of your operation and the high-value personalized customer service you provide." Immediately, she received another Amazon.com response, again signed by yet another Amazon.com employee, with the comment, "We want to provide service on a level that customers will remember, and it is very gratifying to receive such a nice compliment." Computer generated? Perhaps, but speedy and personalized enough to make substantial deposits into Dianna's emotional account with Amazon.com.

Customers expect core features or services to be available. At the same time, it's the peripheral services that customers notice and frequently talk about.[27] We have never heard anyone mention Doubletree Resorts' quality of mattresses or size of rooms, but we certainly have heard people talk about the warm chocolate chip cookies offered upon check-in. When you ask customers what they want when they say they want better service, United Kingdom researchers found they speak about

It's the peripheral services that customers notice and frequently talk about.

three factors, all three of which are emotional. They want their opinions respected, they want to be assisted by people to whom they can relate on an equal level, and they want sincere concern and kindness.[28] None of these desires are core features, but they all have impact.

Customer safety and on-time performance are core business factors in the airline industry. They are expected. If an airline continually crashed its planes and was never on time, it would have a hard time attracting customers. But most customers don't comment on core services unless they are missing. A customer will more likely disembark from an airplane and talk about a joke the pilot told than comment, "Hey, we didn't crash! These pilots are something!"

In fact, customers do not want more core services than they need. Otherwise, they will be forced to financially support something they feel is excessive. If customers buy a product that is gold plated on the inside and this plating makes absolutely no difference for the functioning of the product, doesn't extend its life, and never gets looked at, it is too much for all but a tiny niche of people who like everything gold plated. However, most customers will welcome peripheral services, such as a shipping company that (1) sells postal stamps at cost, (2) sends notification of a problem *in advance* of the customer finding out about it, or (3) makes payments easy to remit. We subscribe to a daily customer service electronic newsletter that reprints customer letters. Virtually every positive situation customers write about deals with something peripheral.[29]

■ Application

Core Services and Loyalty. At a staff gathering, ask them to list all your core services. Make sure everyone understands that core services need to be consistently delivered. Now list your organization's peripheral services, especially the emotional peripherals. Ask where the group thinks loyalty is formed.

Again we return to the notion that emotions are created in the moment and quality perceptions are created over a period of time. Obviously, organizations must work to provide the best core offerings. When failures occur in core offerings, however, it is the established emotional relationships with customers and the generosity of feeling and empathy

> *Emotions are created in the moment, and quality perceptions are created over a period of time.*

that have been created because of the small favors done for them that create the emotional flexibility for customers to forgive organizations for their quality errors. As Toby Wagner, national sales manager of the Troy, Michigan–based American Speed Printing, emphasizes,

> We compete in four areas: price, quality, location and service. We don't emphasize the first three because that's what the customer expects. We focus on service because it's the least expensive and the most effective and fastest way to differentiate ourselves from the competition with our customers.[30]

■ Application

Peripheral Services. What peripheral services can you add to your service offerings? A good way to bring fresh ideas to this question is to periodically schedule a brainstorming session with your staff or colleagues. Bring music, so everyone is in a more creative frame of mind, perhaps catalogs and magazines to stimulate thinking, and then let everyone suggest ideas. After you have accumulated a number of ideas, set criteria for determining which ones might be appropriate for you to implement. For example, you may want to set limits on costs, time involved, complexity, and so on. Then decide if you want to make these peripheral services available to everyone at all times or whether you would like to use them intermittently.

Communicating a Message of Fairness

It is almost instinctive for humans to react strongly when they feel a fairness norm has been violated.

Children hear thousands of times in their childhood "That's not fair," and they rapidly learn to repeat the phrase from an early age. It becomes almost instinctive for adults to react strongly when they feel a fairness norm has been violated. Some people will fight to the death for what is fair, and customers who feel they have not been treated fairly are inclined to get even. Some will become consumer terrorists, even willing to pay a high personal price to restore "justice."

Unfairness feels like injustice, and when customers face injustice they are motivated to seek justice, especially if they have grown up in a system that espouses justice as a high value. When customers believe they have been treated unfairly, they are first surprised, then disappointed. This feeling converts to anger and indignation, emotions that can be held onto for a long time.[31] Anger wrought from unfairness leads to a desire to punish and is probably the emotional justification for customers who go out of their way to punish an organization they believe has treated them unfairly.[32] Trust and fairness are intimately related. The basis for trust is perceived fairness. Without trust, a shaky foundation exists for service exchanges.[33]

Fairness is such a strong motivator that perceptions of unfairness will cause some customers to take a high-handed approach—even if they are the ones who will pay the price. One of the authors observed a fellow lap swimmer at her public swimming pool who became indignant when he was forced to swim in a circle because of overcrowding. "This is totally unfair and I'm never coming back," he said in a huff and left, not completing his swim that day and cutting himself off from future high-value swimming. It's a great swimming pool, very reasonably priced, and only rarely is it so crowded that swimmers are forced to swim in a circle.

When customers buy services, fairness is expected. Poor service is not necessarily unfair, but unfair service is almost always judged as poor quality.[34] Being fair is particularly important for organizations whose services are intangible, since customers can't easily evaluate the service before using it and are forced to rely on trust.

Research suggests that when customers perceive themselves to be treated unfairly, they experience immediate, emotional reactions, which dramatically affect their satisfaction judgments. Customers also seem to remember service encounters that have an element of unfairness in them longer than when this is not the case.[35]

> *Customers remember service encounters longer when they are unfair.*

According to marketing researchers, unfairness consists of a number of elements, including a lack of caring, lengthy processes to resolve complaints, procedures that require repeating information, and an unwillingness to take responsibility for the customers' problems or inconvenience. Lack of fairness is notably commonplace. In one study, customers were asked to evaluate the fairness of service recovery procedures. *Less than half judged them to be fair.* Fair service recovery procedures were those rated as clear and easy to understand, quick, and without hassles.[36]

Perception of fairness is most critical when there is a service failure because customer expectations rise under failure conditions—especially if the customers are loyal customers.[37] We described this as a narrowing of the "zone of tolerance" in chapter 11. Loyal customers are most likely to emotionally exacerbate the situation they are in by arousing themselves with such words as "My gosh. How can they treat me this way, after all the business I give them? Don't they know who I am?" Loyal customers get on their so-called high horses and ride away. Onetime customers are less likely to place as high a value on fairness as loyal customers.

Automobile servicing is a field that is beset with an additional "fairness" challenge. Researchers have found that when customers judge themselves to be not technically competent, the element of fairness increases significantly. In fact, fairness becomes the single most important predictor of service quality when customers feel at the mercy of someone else's knowledge.[38]

▧ Application

How Do Our Systems and Policies Rate on Fairness? List all the ways your customers might find your policies and/or systems unfair. Put yourself in the role of the customers as you do this exercise. What is your response when your customers complain about a lack of fairness?

Lack of Fairness Shows Up in the Small Things

Lack of fairness is many times experienced in relatively minor situations—when a service provider helps one person more quickly than another, closes a service window when the customer reaches the front of the line, or offers observably different standards of treatment to another customer. Customers also feel vulnerable when they are not treated fairly—even if the issue is relatively unimportant.

When airlines book themselves very tightly on their shuttle flights between major metropolitan areas, such as San Francisco and Los Angeles, they open themselves up to a lack-of-fairness charge. The tight time crunch forces airlines to rush passengers onto the planes, especially when they are making up for lost minutes. Many of these flights are sold out, so the number of people who need to take their seats and get belted in is at maximum. Passengers are subjected to flight attendants who say, "If you don't sit down immediately, you will be forced to leave the airplane." The authors have even heard them say, "If you don't take your seats immediately, you will be responsible for us losing our place in the takeoff line." Under these circumstances, everyone on the whole plane grouses about the unfairness of that remark. The airline has created the situation of overcrowding and then attempts to blame the passengers when they don't move quickly down narrow aisles. An entire planeload of emotional withdrawals is simultaneously made. And the customers, with nothing much to do for the next hour, can spend all that time reinforcing their negative moods. That's not the way to build loyalty!

Listed below is a "fairness susceptibility" chart that shows the relationship between customer knowledge and product complexity and where fairness is most crucial to customers. In this case, fairness plays the most critical role in the upper-left-hand quadrant.

Fairness Susceptibility Quotient

1 Customer Not Knowledgeable Product Complex, Expensive Customer feels most vulnerable High anxiety Fairness element most critical Product guarantees very important Greatest opportunity for loyalty building if fairness issue handled well	**2** Customer Knowledgeable Product Complex, Expensive Relatively high degree of customer control Fairness element somewhat critical Customer demands still high because of product cost
3 Customer Not Knowledgeable Product Simple, Low Priced Customer may need some help Fairness element not too critical	**4** Customer Knowledgeable Product Simple, Low Priced High degree of customer control Fairness element least critical

---

■ **Application**

The Fairness Susceptibility Chart. Where do your customers and products fit on the above chart? Describe a typical customer from each of your various customer categories and the products they are likely to purchase. Place them in the above quadrants and then evaluate your policies and procedures for your products on their fairness quotient.

Some organizations discourage staff from taking responsibility—which they see as admitting guilt and carrying legal implications—especially when customers complain about unfairness. Wally Bock, in his e-letter "Monday Memo," copied an e-mail response he received from an American newspaper institution, now an interactive product available to subscribers over the Internet. Wally names the newspaper and describes its unwillingness to take ownership of the problem of its service being unavailable. He calls the company arrogant and accusatory and wonders if it was fearful he would ask for a refund of one-twentieth of the five dollars or so he spends each month for his subscription.[39]

Marketing researchers Kathleen Seiders and Leonard L. Berry found, however, that when organizations both offer an explanation for what

happened and compensate customers who feel unfairly treated, customer perceptions become strongly positive. The two practices "offered
simultaneously" are very influential in eliminating customer feelings of
unfairness.[40]

Sometimes perceived unfairness stays with a customer for a very
long time. Jeremy Dorosin has paper and videotape files of public reports
about his lack of fair treatment by Starbucks so big they fill several boxes.
In fact, everything is up on the Internet and can be accessed by visiting
www.starbucked.com. The ostensible offense was a single transaction of
product failure in 1995 and Starbucks' accumulated poor handling of the
situation. Jeremy felt so indignant about the situation that he took out
an ad in the *Wall Street Journal* asking anyone who had experienced similar treatment to call him at a toll-free number. He received hundreds of
calls. Here are Jeremy's words:

> They (Starbucks) talk about such great people-oriented service, but
> when it's time to deliver a tremendous inconsistency arises. *They weren't
> being fair.* . . . I told the guy I was prepared to take out a sizable display
> ad in the *Wall Street Journal* with an eight hundred number for other dis-
> pleased customers to call in with their Starbucks problems. He said he
> was sorry I felt that way. Guess he didn't believe I'd take out the ad.[41]

When the unfairness bug bites, it doesn't easily let go. Many years
later, Jeremy has not given up the fight. He has written a book, *Balance
at Middlefork,* describing the situation and continues
to generate volumes of publicity about his settlement
fight with Starbucks. He has personally invested over
$45,000 in his fight. A University has written a case
study about the event, and Starbucks refuses to dis-
cuss the matter anymore. Starbucks has painted Jeremy as a "nut," which
only reinforces his feelings of unfairness. Jeremy isn't going away. And his
event *started* with a clerk who wouldn't give him a pound of coffee that
Starbucks advertises as a benefit when purchasing an espresso machine.

Angry customers today get on the Internet, download graphics, and
create pages that are virtually indistinguishable from company Web

> *When the
> unfairness bug
> bites, it doesn't
> easily let go.*

pages. Angry customers will punish the "unfair" company by listing their Web sites on all search engines. One such Web site, attacking a car dealer, received twelve thousand visits and hundreds of supporting e-mails in the first two weeks of its existence.[42] To protect themselves, some companies buy Internet addresses that negatively relate to their names, such as www.Compaqsucks.com.

The converse also holds true. Perceived fairness enhances trust and can be a solid emotional basis for service exchanges. And once again, it many times occurs over small items. It's the emotional rush customers experience when the service provider points out something they wouldn't have noticed and the business takes the responsibility to fix it—at no charge. It's the gratitude customers experience when company representatives defend you and protect your interests, especially when you know they didn't have to do that. And it's the compromises you work out with service providers when they say, "Here's what I think is fair from our point of view. What do you think would be fair?"

> *Perceived fairness enhances trust and can be a solid emotional basis for service exchanges.*

■ Application

Fairness and Empathy. Fairness takes a generous heart to deliver. It frequently requires bending the rules a bit. It takes the emotional competency skill of empathy. How can unfairness be prevented? We recommend three strategies:

- *Ask your customers if they ever feel they are unfairly treated by you or by any other company. You can frequently learn from examples your customers tell you about the competition.*

- *Ask your employees to notice when customers experience intense emotions. Chances are, high emotions signal feelings of unfairness.*

- *Ask your staff to identify customer-unfriendly systems. These are systems where the goals or policies of your company run head on into your customers' needs or desires.*

ASSESSING YOUR ORGANIZATION'S FOCUS ON CUSTOMER RETENTION

Answer the following questions:

1. Does your organization pay as much attention to customer retention as to acquiring new customers? What specific ways do you focus on sales at the expense of customer retention?

2. Are your customer-retention activities regularly assessed and evaluated for effectiveness?

3. How do you ensure that all the needs of your customers and staff are addressed physically and emotionally?

4. Does the complexity of your products or services require high levels of trust by your customers? How does this affect your "fairness"?

5. Do your staff ever blame other departments or people when customers complain about unfairness?

CHAPTER FOURTEEN

FINAL THOUGHTS

There's no one simple answer to the complex challenge of attracting and retaining customers. Implementation is also not easy. But the rewards are significant. According to the Strategic Planning Institute of Cambridge, Massachusetts, offering service that is focused on caring for customers results in customers staying up to 50 percent longer, which, in turn, reduces marketing costs by between 20 and 40 percent and ultimately leads to better net returns of between 7 and 17 percent.[1]

Ultimately, an organization that is successful at customer retention is successful at what Peter Drucker, whom we quoted earlier in this text, wrote almost fifty years ago: "The purpose of a business is to create a customer."[2] A "created" customer is one that not only has been won but also has been retained. To emphasize this point one final time in concrete dollar terms, a Towers and Perrin survey reports that in the insurance business, increasing customer retention *by just 2 percent* can add approximately $60 million of value to an agency with a billion dollars in current premium levels.[3] These are bottom-line assets asking for a home. We have no doubt that adding emotional value can easily increase customer retention by this 2 percent.

If staff are to "create" customers in the service/experience economy, they require a level of emotional sophistication not widely found or supported in the modern world. In order for organizations to meet this challenge, they cannot expect that old approaches will bring success in the changed environment. At the same time, they do not need to completely reinvent themselves. The process of human development is a gradual one. As long as organizations commit themselves to incorporating the emotional aspect of their work into their structures, systems, policies, and procedures, they will have taken that first step toward adding emotional value to the workplace, to staff, and ultimately to customers.

EMOTIONS: RESEARCH BACKGROUND

If emotions are difficult to define and measure, they are also difficult to name. One psychologist has listed 213 different emotions,[1] while another combed through Roget's *Thesaurus* and identified 400 emotion words.[2] Not to be outdone, yet another identified 500 emotion-related words.[3]

Within the field of social psychology, much time and effort has been spent on simplifying these lengthy lists of emotions. Paul Ekman, at San Francisco State University, for example, spent years reducing these cumbersome lists to just six. Ekman maintains that his basic emotions—anger, fear, surprise, disgust, happiness, and sadness—are experienced by everyone.[4] He also argues that this six-pack of emotions is expressed in identifiable and universal facial expressions. Part of Ekman's contribution to the field of psychology has been to demonstrate that people can read these six emotional states of others—in split seconds. This has interesting implications for service encounters.

Ekman is not the only psychologist who has attempted to reduce long lists of emotions to a set of "basics." Several other researchers have identified slightly different emotions as being part of the "basic" pack.[5] Psychologist Robert Plutchik, for example, lists eight basic emotions; he adds anticipation and acceptance to Ekman's list.[6] He theorizes that other emotions come from blends of these eight basic emotions, similar to the idea that three primary colors combine to create all other colors.

It is important to note that satisfaction, which is the emotion that most customer surveys measure, is *never* listed as part of the "basic" emotion packs. Even in the longer lists, satisfaction appears low on the lists when they are ranked in frequency of occurrence. For example, when Northwestern University Professor Andrew Ortony rank ordered his list of five hundred emotion-related words, satisfaction appeared seventy-ninth.[7]

Dynamics of Emotions

When customers interact with service providers, whether for sales or for support, both providers and customers experience emotions. And it is this human interaction that is the source of most strong emotions.

- *Human interaction is of central emotional concern.* Researchers have found that more than 75 percent of the time emotions are experienced, human interaction is the central concern.[8] Viewed from this perspective, emotions can be seen as a positive or negative communication system between people. Psychologist Brian Parkinson writes, "Evidently, many of the things that people get emotional about relate to other people in some way."[9]

- Both *service providers and customers are influenced by emotional factors.* Service providers' emotions are shaped by the same factors that influence customers' emotions. In addition, service providers are influenced by factors frequently not directly viewed by customers: organizational policies, managerial style, training, coaching, available support, coworkers' attitudes, and marketing promises.

- *Human emotions are a part of all products.* When the service experience is intangible and personal, rather than concrete and material, the delivery of service is the simultaneous interaction of customers and providers. Even when the service experience is about concrete products, emotions play a role, albeit a smaller role. Business leaders recognize the ever present role of human interaction in *any type* of quality. Arthur Andersen Company and New York University, in a jointly conducted survey, found that 87 percent of business executives believe that human beings are the *key* to high quality.[10]

Some of the assumptions inherent in the great variety of definitions of "emotions" are also worth reviewing. We have summarized them below without attribution.

- Emotions are ways of talking and acting; they happen between individuals.

- Emotions are what we think about what we are doing or what is happening, though they are stronger than simple thoughts.

- Emotions are the result of bodily reactions to events and, as such, are part of our survival response.

- The system that underlies emotions is unconscious. By and large, we do not choose our emotions; they happen to us.

- We have little direct control over our emotions, though we can cultivate certain emotional habits.

- Emotions are powerful motivators for future behavior.

- Emotions are more easily remembered than facts or data.

Whether you agree with these definitions or not, they speak to a variety of psychological theories about emotions and all add depth to the concept of emotions.

WHAT DOES MARKETING RESEARCH TELL US ABOUT CONSUMER EMOTIONS?

A number of important studies have been conducted by marketing experts defining the parameters of emotions associated with consumption. Six parameters suggest that evaluation of service by customers is a lot more complex than perhaps many have previously thought.

1. *Different industries elicit different emotions.* Australian psychologist Michael Edwardson and others have discovered that certain emotions are more likely to be experienced with specific kinds of consumer experiences. For example, automobiles are more likely to create strong, positive feelings of joy and excitement rather than love and nostalgia. When there is a problem, automobiles are more likely to create the strong, negative feelings of frustration and worry rather than anger.[1]

Edwardson himself has mapped the emotional profiles for some thirty service industries. He finds more positive, strong emotions in retailing and restaurants than in banking. In other words, customers are more likely to be emotionally neutral while using banking services than while eating a meal. For this reason, Edwardson recommends that banks work to eliminate the strong, negative feelings that can be associated with banking, such as feelings of powerlessness, anger, anxiety, nervousness, and frustration, rather than focusing on creating strong, positive emotions. Edwardson describes the results of 368 in-depth interviews with consumers, in which over 220 different emotion words were used by the people being interviewed.[2] The top 10 emotions recalled were as follows:

Anger	30 percent
Happiness	21 percent
Frustration	21 percent
Annoyance	13 percent
Disappointment	10 percent
Satisfaction	10 percent
Impatience	9 percent
Relaxation	8 percent
Excitement	8 percent
Irritation	6 percent

Note where satisfaction appears on this list. It is perhaps more relevant to look at anger, happiness, frustration, annoyance, and disappointment, which, no doubt, are going to be more influential in creating loyal or disloyal customers. Edwardson further points out that you rarely find customers using the word "delight" to describe their consumption experience, even though this is a word popularized by dozens of speakers and authors.[3] We believe that businesses need to create happy, enthusiastic, and appreciative customers, i.e., create customers around the emotions that they, in their own terms, remember.

2. *Quality variables all have an emotional component.* Five service variables are identified in the SERVQUAL model (developed by service marketing researchers Valerie Zeithaml, A. Parasuraman, and

Leonard L. Berry) as being most important to customers when receiving service. The five variables are well known in the customer service field and include *tangibles* (physical quality), *reliability* (whether the organization follows through on its promises), *responsiveness* (how quickly the organization gets back to you), *assurance* (feeling of confidence), and *empathy* (caring for the customer).[4] The foundation for all five of the SERVQUAL variables, *including physical quality*, is emotional. For example, a customer can view a sturdy, dependable car that is a good value for the money and not purchase it because there is no "wow" factor. Ted Levitt, at Harvard Business School, puts it this way: "There is no such thing as service industries. There are only industries whose service components are greater or less than those of other industries. Everybody is in service."[5]

3. *Emotions do not run along a continuum.* Emotions do not run along a continuum, according to researchers of customer emotions. This is one of the biggest challenges to the usefulness of the satisfaction/dissatisfaction continuum, a continuum used by most businesses to measure customer reactions. On a continuum scale, it is assumed that the very factors that produce satisfaction will, in their absence, produce dissatisfaction. There are dozens of simple everyday examples that suggest otherwise. For instance, a plane leaving on time generally produces satisfaction while one leaving late normally produces dissatisfaction. But that does not mean that a plane that leaves on time makes me happy, and one that leaves late makes me sad.

My sadness or happiness can depend upon my attitude toward the event—or how the service provider handles the delay. A plane that leaves late might make me happy if I happen to arrive late to the airport or if the flight crew makes the delay a pleasant one. And one that leaves late might make me feel secure if the reason for its lateness is that something mechanical has to be fixed or if I want to have more time at the gate talking with a friend before my flight leaves.

4. *Emotions matter with advertising, as well.* There are two camps about the use of emotions in advertising. One view has it that customers

respond with higher purchase intentions when ads provide more information rather than trying to excite customers.[6]

The other camp takes the exact opposite point of view. It says that feelings are more important for consumer decision making than thinking. Tim Ambler, senior fellow at London Business School, states his point of view: "Must ads be informational? If you are of a cognitive or rational disposition then you will believe that ads are rational and humans are rational and the economy is rational and the choices are rational. Therefore advertising must be about information."[7] Ambler argues that this point of view benefits the researcher and not the consumer. In fact, he says this is a myth, and it's time to put it away. Ambler explains that when ads evoke feelings, they also activate the part of the frontal lobe that is the center for decision making. Therefore, emotional ads make it easier for the customer to link buying decisions to positive feelings.

5. *Emotions are dependent on space and temporal demands.* Service encounters that are of short duration are experienced by customers differently from those of long duration. For example, customers have more time to experience emotional states on an international flight that is several hours long than they do going into a bank for five minutes. The more complex the service transaction is, the more opportunity there is for emotions to be experienced. The same is true depending on how physically close the service provider and the customer are. A medical appointment with a gynecologist or proctologist is very different from a luggage porter bringing suitcases to your hotel room.[8]

6. *Customer knowledge affects emotional states.* Emotions differ depending on the knowledge the customer brings to the service experience. For example, when customers need car servicing or repair and they feel technically challenged by what they are told, fairness emerges as the most important emotion that will predict how customers evaluate the service they receive. Otherwise, empathy, responsiveness, reliability, and convenience are more important to customers in such situations.[9]

THE ELUSIVE LINK BETWEEN CUSTOMER SATISFACTION AND CUSTOMER LOYALTY: A SUMMARY OF THE RESEARCH

Conventional wisdom would tell us that there must be some kind of link between customer satisfaction and customer loyalty. And to a limited degree that does seem to be the case. But where exactly does loyalty get formed on the scale from extremely dissatisfied to extremely satisfied? We don't know beyond the suggestion that it happens primarily at the highest reaches. Xerox found in its pioneering work in the early 1990s on customer satisfaction and loyalty that on a satisfaction one-to-five scale, customers who give a "four" rating of satisfaction are six times more likely to leave than those who rate Xerox at "five."[1] Satisfaction scales also don't tell exactly what causes the loyalty. At Doubletree Resorts is it the comfort of the beds or the chocolate cookies that cause loyalty? Or do the cookies merely increase satisfaction ratings?

Yet most organizations persist in trying to link the two phenomena as if they were dependent variables. Loyalty, after all, is an organizational goal and not necessarily a customer goal. Some consumers can be completely satisfied, even "extremely" satisfied, without forming a bit of loyalty. This is particularly true with products and services that can offer pleasure from variety; that is, different cars, hotels, styles of clothing, or cuisine. Here are some points to consider:

- Several strong studies reported in marketing journals show very weak relationships overall between satisfaction and customer repurchase intentions.[2] Researchers at Harvard University Graduate School of Business Administration, for example, found that it is only at the highest levels of satisfaction that loyalty is created.[3] For this reason, it means very little to simply show an increase in satisfaction scales from one year to the next. The improvement may have occurred at the lowest levels of the scale, where virtually no loyalty is created. Yet we continually see organizations brag about how their satisfaction scores went from 4.1 to 4.3 or even 3.7 to 3.9.

- While people who choose the highest satisfaction numbers to describe their experience will likely be more loyal than those who don't, an increase in satisfaction numbers doesn't necessarily guarantee loyalty. This is especially true when considering an individual customer.[4]

- On a five-point satisfaction/dissatisfaction scale, customers who choose the lower ratings (one and two), exhibit zero loyalty. You might think, therefore, that customers who choose the higher ratings (three, four, and five) would exhibit loyalty. This is not the case. In one study of the health-care and automotive industry—and we're not sure that the health-care and automotive industries are typical of other industries—loyalty was measured at 23 percent when customers checked the midpoint rating on a satisfaction scale. At the four-point level, loyalty was only 31 percent in both the health care and automotive industries. When customers rated themselves as "extremely satisfied," their *average* loyalty was still only at 75 percent.[5]

- The greater the competition within any industry, the less likely that satisfaction and loyalty are correlated. When customers have many choices, it is only at the very highest levels of satisfaction that loyalty is strengthened. With monopolies, of course, satisfaction doesn't matter, which has led one commentator to muse, "Neuter (your) competition or satisfy customers completely."[6]
You can, in effect, create pseudo-monopolies by locking your customers into benefits that come from loyal patronage, such as the airlines have done. We have both observed that business air travelers will put up with a tremendous amount of trouble rather than switch carriers because they have become addicted to upgrades and special treatment. Grocery stores are beginning to do the same with special shopping privileges, special lines, and special prices for big shoppers. It works for at least a period of time, but what if airlines were willing to accept other airlines' mileage points in exchange for the passenger's transfer to their elite flyers club? We might see more switching.

- Satisfaction is a moving target. Because satisfaction is related to customers' perceptions, if a company delivers service that customers are excited about, the next time it will not necessarily move them in the same way. The unexpected becomes the expected. If regular shoppers' grocery store clerks recognize them when they shop, that is nice but not necessarily for all shoppers. And the times they don't recognize loyal customers by name may also represent a problem to certain shoppers.[7]

- Most service is so complex that measurements of single events in the service process are the only data that tell us anything meaningful about what we need to do to get better. For example, if customers are asked how they feel about a repair service, what is being measured: courtesy, speed, price, or accuracy? Which dimension triggers customers' evaluations? Which dimension do customers hold to be most important in determining whether they will return?[8]

- The satisfaction/dissatisfaction scale may actually be measuring totally different items at the top of the scale as compared to the bottom ratings. Researchers have found that when customers mark lowest ratings, this has little to do with service quality and a whole lot to do with customers' experiences of incivility, rudeness, or lack of common courtesy. Furthermore, if your product has serious flaws in it but your service staff are extremely friendly and courteous, you will probably have much higher ratings than your product quality actually deserves. It is impossible for customers to separate out hard product quality from the way the service provider delivers it. In fact, it may be emotional factors that cause the low overall correlation between satisfaction and customer loyalty.[9]

- Negative experiences are more meaningful to customers than positive ones. Research shows that when a customer has a negative experience, it has a stronger impact on overall satisfaction and repurchase intentions than if the customer has a positive experience. Another way to say this is several positive experiences can be outweighed by one negative experience. On a feeling level, it is easy to understand: you are invited to a friend's house and everything is perfect—except your friend becomes drunk and behaves rudely. All the positives of the evening could easily be overshadowed by the inappropriate behavior of your friend.

This is a challenge for organizations because, in effect, customers can be simultaneously satisfied and dissatisfied with different parts of the same product or service. Service is multidimensional, and relationships between satisfaction and its antecedents *and* consequences are complex. Loyalty may be more related to overall satisfaction, while useful feedback for organizations may be more related to specific attribute judgments.[10]

COMPLAINT HANDLING: WHERE DOES THE LATEST RESEARCH TAKE US?

The last twenty years have seen a dramatic increase in the number of articles written about customer complaints. Many are solid, research-based articles; others offer mostly advice about this difficult subject. When *A Complaint Is a Gift* was published in 1996, Barlow and Møller plotted the sheer number of articles published on complaint handling. Since then, Barlow and Maul have gone back to see what additional articles have been written since 1995, once again using the Dialog database as a basic source. Here's what we found.

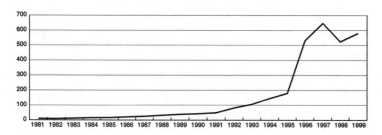

Clearly, the interest in this topic has not waned, though the increase in articles on complaint handling does seem to be leveling off. Recent articles range in topics from the simple and direct, "How to Handle Customer Complaints," to the complex and research based, "Why Don't Some People Complain? A Cognitive-Emotive Process Model of Consumer Complaint Behavior."[1] Within this growing body of printed research and advice, however, there is little discussion of the verbal interaction between service representatives and complaining customers. Since this is precisely where the highest component of emotionality resides, there clearly is room for more research in this area.

Most of the complaint research of the last decade has focused on written complaints. The research is, by and large, solidly designed. After all, research based on written documents is a lot easier to conduct than research based on a live interactive process between customers and company representatives. However, studying written complaints is limiting since most formal complaints since the early 1990s are expressed live on toll-free lines.[2]

Furthermore, almost all the research that has been conducted in the last thirty years has been an analysis of how organizations *respond* to complaints, rather than how they emotionally *interact* with customers when they are in this critical customer service moment. All this has led Marquette University and University of Wisconsin-Milwaukee researchers Dennis Garrett and Renee Meyers to conclude: "In sum, even though dissatisfied consumers are encouraged to complain directly to company service representatives via telephone, relatively little is known about the nature of these important verbal interactions."[3]

Garrett and Meyers's research on live interactions stands as an exception to the trend of analyzing written complaints or customer-remembered complaint situations. After audiotaping, dividing each call into conversational units, and then analyzing 461 live interactions between complaining customers and company representatives, Garrett and Meyers have reached some important conclusions.[4]

Both parties, consumers and company representatives, perform distinct communication roles in complaint telephone calls. Company representatives basically obtain information, identify the problem, attempt to understand its causes, and then resolve the customer problem. Customers, on the other hand, primarily explain their problem and attempt to seek resolution. This conclusion is pretty much as one would expect. The topics not discussed, however, are perhaps the significant concerns for customers.

Garrett and Meyers found that customer expectations were almost never discussed—only in 0.5 percent of the conversational units, the segments into which the researchers broke the conversations. When expectations were discussed, customers brought up the subject 85.4 percent of the time. We have defined emotions as being about things that matter. If this is the case, then to be emotionally sensitive, eliciting and then discussing customer expectations would seem to be in order. And this is not happening—at least according to this research.

Garrett and Meyers also found that customers were most likely to discuss how well the company performed (83 percent of the time), while the organization stayed away from performance topics (17 percent of the time). Because company performance directly impacts customers, organizations can show empathy to customers by initiating conversation on this topic. Instead, Garrett and Meyers found that company representatives *dominated* the discussion when attempting to determine where the blame lay and what was a fair solution.[5] As Garrett and Meyers say, both "have a stake in the final resolution," but mostly the representatives describe what they will do, and in most cases, "consumers passively accept(ed) the proposed solution without debate or counter proposal."[6]

There appears to be little standardization in terms of how individual representatives communicate with their customers. This is an interesting point because several researchers have argued that in order to measure the efficacy of complaint handling, standardization is necessary.[7] Garrett and Meyers conclude that standardization may, in fact, be difficult and perhaps not even desirable. The representatives they studied had undergone identical training procedures but they did not respond to customers the same way. They conclude, "In fact, this individualized communication approach may be beneficial if it yields greater customer satisfaction with the resolution of complaints."[8]

EIGHT-STEP GIFT FORMULA

1. Say "Thank you." Don't think about whether customers have a legitimate complaint or not. Just consider the complaint valuable information—a gift. We need to create immediate rapport with our customers and we need to meet them on their ground. There is no better way to make someone feel welcome than to say "Thank you."

2. Explain why you appreciate the feedback. "Thank you" by itself can sound empty. You need to qualify it by saying something about how hearing the complaint will allow you to better address the problem. "Thank you for telling me. It gives me a chance to fix it for you."

3. Apologize for the mistake. You create more powerful rapport with customers by saying, "Thank you. I appreciate your telling me about this." Then comes the apology: "May I apologize? I'm really sorry this happened."

4. Promise to do something about the problem immediately. This step is perhaps the easiest to take. "I promise you I'll do my best to fix this situation as soon as possible." Hearing this makes customers relax because they know

you are going to do something. Then, of course, you have to do something. If you can't fix the problem, then tell the customer what will happen next.

5. Ask for necessary information. Ask only for the information that is necessary. Make certain you ask for enough information, or you will have to call back for more.

6. Correct the mistake—promptly. Do what you said you would do. A sense of urgency will be greatly appreciated by the customer. Rapid responses say you are serious about service recovery. A sense of urgency lets you get back in balance with the customer.

7. Check customer satisfaction. Follow up. Call your customers back to find out what happened. Ask them directly if they are satisfied with what you did for them.

8. Prevent future mistakes. Make sure the complaint is known throughout the organization so this kind of problem can be prevented in the future. And fix the system without rushing to blame someone else.[1]

NOTES

Preface

1. Joel L. Swerdlow, "Global Culture," *National Geographic* 196, no. 2 (August 1999): 4–5.

Introduction: Adding Emotional Value to Your Customers' Experience

1. As discussed in Howard E. Butz and Leonard Goodstein, "Measuring Customer Value: Gaining the Strategic Advantage," *Organizational Dynamics* 24 (1 January 1996): 63–78.

2. For a recent and complete summary of the role of building profits by focusing on people as assets, see Jeffrey Pfeffer, *The Human Equation* (Boston: Harvard Business School Press, 1998). Pfeffer makes a compelling case that the way an organization manages its people is its real competitive advantage.

3. We recommend *The Experience Economy* as the best current summary on the subject. Joseph Pine II and James H. Gilmore, *The Experience Economy, Work Is Theatre & Every Business a Stage* (Boston: Harvard Business School Press, 1999). The quotation is from page 12.

4. The term Moments of Truth was popularized in Jan Carlzon, *Moments of Truth* (Cambridge: Ballinger Publishing Co., 1987).

5. See George T. Silvestri, "Occupational Employment Projections to 2006," *Monthly Labor Review* 120 (1 November 1997): 58–84; Mike Meyers, "More Brain, Less Brawn," *Minneapolis Star Tribune*, 11 April 1999, p. 04D; and Ellyn Ferguson, "Expanding Economy Seeing Rebirth of 'Rust Belt,'" *Garnett News Service*, 16 February 1999, pp. ARC.

6. As quoted in Peter Carbonara, "Preaching What They Practice," *Your Company* (April/May 1998): 44.

7. Research by Forum Corporation as cited in Leonard A. Schlesinger and James Heskett, "The Service-Driven Service Economy," *Harvard Business Review* (September/October 1991): 71.

8. Harvey Miller, as quoted in *Nation's Business* (March 1988), as cited in Lewis Eigen and Jonathan Siegel, *The Manager's Book of Quotations* (New York: Amacom, 1989), 273.

9. *Wall Street Journal,* 16 October 1997, p. 1.

10. Some companies obviously did better than others. But one utility actually used a cheap answering machine to take messages, one voice system took seven minutes and thirty seconds to connect to a human, and one utility hung up on a caller when it came time to offer a solution. Mark Abernethy, "A Break in the Holding Pattern," *The Bulletin* (20 November 1998): 53.

11. Survey by Net Effect and reported in *USA Today,* 1 June 1999, p. 8a. Julie Schoenfeld, CEO of Net Effect, says that e-commerce needs to learn as much about customer service as "bricks and mortar" businesses. She concludes, "The bottom line is that customer service ought to be managed by a dedicated function with the [e-commerce] business."

12. Herb Kelleher, "Customer Service: It Starts at Home," *The Journal of Lending & Credit Risk Management* 54, no. 3, (May/June 1998): 68–73.

13. Researchers L. L. Berry, A. Parasuraman, and V. Zeithaml found that, on average, companies score higher on "tangible" items than on "intangibles." Berry, Parasuraman, and Zeithaml, "Improved Service Quality in America: Lessons Learned," *Academy of Management Executive* 8, no. 2 (1994): 32–44.

14. Peter Senge, *The Fifth Discipline: The Art and Practice of the Learning Organization* (New York: Doubleday/Currency, 1994).

15. Robert Rabbin, *Invisible Leadership, Igniting the Soul at Work* (Lakewood, Colo.: Acropolis Books, 1998), 29.

16. Sara Lawrence-Lightfoot, *Respect: An Exploration* (Reading, Mass.: Perseus Books, 1999).

Part I: Building an Emotion–Friendly Service Culture

1. For a complete discussion of the differences between product and service offerings, see Valarie Zeithaml, A. Parasuraman, and Leonard L. Berry, "Problems and Strategies in Services Marketing," *Journal of Marketing* 49, no. 1 (1985): 33–46.

2. As quoted in Sharon Nelton, "Emotions in the Workplace," *Nation's Business* 84 (1 February 1996): 25.

Chapter 1: The Customer Is Always Emotional

1. Adrian Furnham and Michael Argyle, *The Psychology of Money* (London: Routledge, 1998).

2. Charlotte LeCroy, associate broker with Prudential Atlanta Realty in Marietta, Georgia, quoted in Donna Espy, "Holidays Can Help Sell a House: Decorations, Cozy Fire, Cookies Can Lure Buyers," *The Atlanta Journal and Constitution*, 7 December 1995, p. G/04.

3. Jan Morris, "Confessions of a Hotel Addict," *San Francisco Examiner Magazine*, 11 October 1998, pp. 8–9.

4. Jay A. Conger, "The Necessary Art of Persuasion," *Harvard Business Review* (May/June 1998): 84 ff.

5. Emphasis added. Quoted in "Friendly's Persuasion," *Nation's Restaurant News* 2, no. 2 (31 August 1998): 55–58.

6. Michael Stocker with Elizabeth Hegeman, *Valuing Emotions* (New York: Cambridge University Press, 1996), 84–85.

7. *USA Today*, 19 October 1998.

8. As quoted in Rebecca Eisenberg, "Brighter Mood Prevails as Apple Rolls Out New Products at Macworld Expo," *San Francisco Examiner*, 10 January 1999, pp. B5–6.

9. As quoted in *Fortune* (9 November 1998): 96.

10. *USA Today*, 19 October 1998, Money section, p. 10B.

11. Quoted in Ronald B. Leiber, "Storytelling: A New Way to Get Close to Your Customer; Surveys and Focus Groups," *Fortune* (3 February 1997): 102 ff.

12. As cited in Oren Harari, "Ten Reasons TQM Doesn't Work," *Management Review* 86 (1 January 1997).

13. Jeremy Kahn, "The World's Most Admired Companies," *Fortune* (26 October 1998): 218.

14. J. Hornik and N. Melt, "The Effect of Mood States on Consumer's Time Perception and Orientation," in *Advance Research in Marketing*, ed. H. Muhlbacher and J. Jochum (Proceedings of the 19th Annual Conference of the European Academy, Innsbruck, Austria, 1990).

15. B. Fehr and J. A. Russell, "Concept of Emotion Viewed from a Prototype Perspective," *Journal of Experimental Psychology: General* 113, no. 3 (1984): 464–86.

16. P. R. and A. M. Kleinginna, "A Categorized List of Emotion Definitions with Suggestions for a Consensual Definition," *Motivation and Emotion* 5 (1981): 345–79.

17. Definition used by Gerald L. Clore, Andrew Ortony, and Mark A. Foss, "The Psychological Foundations of the Affective Lexicon," *Journal of Personality and Social Psychology* 53 (October 1987): 751–55.

18. To complicate matters, psychologists distinguish between affective traits, moods, and emotions. Moods and emotions are both transient; that is, they normally don't persist for long periods of time, though moods generally last longer than emotions. Affective traits, to use popular language, constitute our personality. They are the "stable predispositions" that underlie how we respond emotionally. We talk about people having a "sunny disposition" or being "very fussy," which are examples of affective traits. Customers show up with their predispositions and moods and then experience emotions.

19. Erik Rosenberg, "Levels of Analysis and the Organization of Affect," *Review of General Psychology* 2, no. 3 (1998): 250. This definition shares the bias of the father of American psychology, William James, who believed that emotions *are* physical feelings. That is, without some kind of concomitant physical sensation, there is no emotion. In other words, I know I am happy because I "feel" happy, and I can describe that physical sensation. We also like the definition used by Bagozzi, Gopinath and Nyer: "Emotions are mental states of readiness that arise from appraisals of events or one's own thoughts." See Richard P. Bagozzi, Mahesh Gopinath, and Prashanth U. Nyer, "The Role of Emotions in Marketing," *Journal of the Academy of Marketing Science* 27, no. 1 (spring 1999): 184–206.

20. Researchers also report that when there is an audience, customer emotions intensify for most people. For example, service in a crowded environment evokes more intense emotional responses than when customers are by themselves—such as when they are in front of an automatic teller machine with no one around. For example, R. E. Kraut and R. E. Johnston found that bowlers tended to display more observable reactions when they thought someone was watching them. "Social and Emotional Messages of Smiling: An Ethological Approach," *Journal of Personality and Social Psychology* 37 (1979): 1539–53.

21. See Linda L. Price, Eric J. Arnould, and Sheila L. Deibler, "Consumers' Emotional Responses to Service Encounters," *International Journal of Service Industry Management* 6, no. 3 (1995): 49.

22. Richard S. Lazarus, *Emotion and Adaptation* (New York: Oxford University Press, 1991).

23. See Michael Edwardson, "Emotional Profiling in Service Encounters" (paper presented at IIR Conference, Sydney, Australia, August 1997). See also Fehr and Russell, "Concept of Emotion"; and J. Fitness and G. O. Fletcher, "Love, Hate, Anger, and Jealousy in Close Relationships," *Journal of Personality and Social Psychology* 65, no. 5 (1993): 942–58.

24. Edwardson's work is cited throughout this book. This particular summary comes from a speech delivered at a TMI Breakfast Briefing in Sydney, Australia, in December 1998.

25. Michael Edwardson, "Measuring Emotions in Service Encounters: An Exploratory Analysis," *Australasian Journal of Market Research* 6, no. 2 (1998): 34–48.

26. Michael Edwardson, "Emotion Prototypes in Service Encounters," *Australian Journal of Psychology* 49 (1997 supplement): 33.

27. Emphasis added. William G. Austin, "Justice, Freedom, and Self-Interest in Intergroup Relations," in *The Social Psychology of Intergroup Relations*, ed. William Austin and S. Worchel (Belmont, Calif.: Brooks/Cole, 1979), 20–37.

28. Stocker, *Valuing Emotions*, 139.

29. Marcy Wydman, CEO of Witt Co., a sheet-metal fabrication and galvanizing business in Cincinnati, Ohio, as quoted in Nelton, "Emotions in the Workplace."

30. This is the notion popularized in Daniel Goleman's book, *Emotional Intelligence: Why It Can Matter More than IQ* (New York: Bantam Books, 1995).

31. See, for example, Martin A. Johnson, "Variables Associated with Friendship in an Adult Population," *Journal of Social Psychology* 129 (March 1989): 379–89.

Chapter 2: Managing Emotions Begins with Me

1. Goleman, *Emotional Intelligence*, 47.

2. A. Rafaeli, "When Clerks Meet Customers: A Test of Variables Related to Emotional Expressions on the Job," *Journal of Applied Psychology* 74 (August 1989): 385–93.

3. There is considerable research on this topic. For example, see B. A. Stead and G. M. Zinkhan, "Service Priority in Department Stores: The Effects of Customer Gender and Dress," *Sex Roles* 15 (November 1986): 601–12; and G. M. Zinkhan and L. F. Stoiadin, "Impact of Sex Role Stereotypes on Service Priority in Department Stores," *Journal of Applied Psychology* 69 (April 1984): 691–93.

4. As described in *USA Today*, 11 June 1999, p. 9A.

5. Psychologists Demaree and Harrison use empirical research as a basis for developing a neuropsychological model to explain the relationships between hostility and lack of self-awareness. Heath A. Demaree and David W. Harrison, "A Neuropsychological Model Relating Self-Awareness to Hostility," *Neuropsychology Review* 7 (December 1997): 171–185.

6. George P. Prigatano [St. Joseph's Hospital and Medical Center, Barrow Neurological Institute, Phoenix, Arizona], "The Problem of Impaired Self-Awareness in Neuropsychological Rehabilitation," in *Neuropsychological Rehabilitation: Fundamentals, Innovations and Directions,* ed. Jose Leon-Carrion (Delray Beach, Fla., St. Lucie Press, 1997), 301–11.

7. We have summarized this research in the main text in very simple terms when we say that there were only two groups. Actually, participants were 171 female and 60 male undergraduates who were randomly assigned to *one of six conditions* in a 2 (Mirror versus No-mirror) by 3 (Control vs. Velten manipulation vs. Music manipulation) design. This article discusses the potential benefits of using small mirrors as a substitute for explicit instructions about the expected impact of mood-induction procedures. John M. Govern and Lisa A. Marsch, "Inducing Positive Mood without Demand Characteristics," *Psychological Reports* 81 (December 1997): 1027–34.

8. As cited in "The Write Way to Get Healthy," *Health* (July/August 1999): 30.

9. Church found that other variables, such as gender, management level, age, and tenure, did not relate to higher performance among the 124 high-performing managers and the 470 average-performing managers he studied. Allan H. Church, "Managerial Self-Awareness in High-Performing Individuals in Organizations," *Journal of Applied Psychology* 82 (April 1997): 281–92.

10. Ram Charan and Geoffrey Colvin, "Why CEOs Fail," *Fortune* (21 June 1999): 78.

11. Susan Fournier, Susan Dobscha, and David Glen Mick, "Preventing the Premature Death of Relationship Marketing, *Harvard Business Review* (January/February 1998): 42–52.

12. See Bernard J. Baars, *In the Theater of Consciousness: The Workspace of the Mind* (New York: Oxford University Press, 1997).

13. See Peter Sifneos, "Affect, Emotional Conflict, and Deficit: An Overview," *Psychotherapy and Psychosomatics* 56 (1991): 116-22.

14. Fournier, Dobscha, and Mick, "Preventing the Premature Death of Relationship Marketing."

Chapter 3: Positive Emotional States Are an Asset

1. Barbara L. Fredrickson, "What Good Are Positive Emotions?" *Review of General Psychology* 2, no. 3 (1998): 300–19.

2. Scott W. Kelley and Douglas K. Hoffman, "An Investigation of Positive Affect, Prosocial Behaviors, and Service Quality," *Journal of Retailing* 73 (fall 1997): 407–27.

3. Once psychologists begin to study positive states, they quickly find more ways to differentiate subtleties. Paul Ekman, for example, says that there may be as many as eighteen different kinds of smiles. All one has to do is to look at photo albums to see the wide range of emotions expressed in different smiles. See Paul Ekman and Wallace V. Friesen, *Unmasking the Face: A Guide to Recognizing Emotions from Facial Clues* (Englewood Cliffs, N.J.: Prentice Hall, 1975).

4. Load factor statistic cited in *The Asian Wall Street Journal*, 9 June 1999, p. 12.

5. Actually, researchers are a little confused about action tendencies and positive emotions. They know that negative emotions tend to lead to predictable and specific action tendencies: for example, anger tends to lead to attack, fear to escape, disgust to expel, guilt to make amends, sadness to make amends. Because positive emotions tend to open up possibilities, it is difficult to predict exactly what someone will do after experiencing joy, but likely the tendency is more or less to repeat the situation to reexperience joy. See B. L. Fredrickson and R. W. Levenson, "Positive Emotions Speed Recovery from the Cardiovascular Sequelae of Negative Emotions," *Cognition and Emotion* 12, no. 2 (March 1998): 191–220.

6. A. M. Isen, K. A. Daubman, and G. P. Nowicki, "Positive Affect Facilitates Creative Problem Solving," *Journal of Personality and Social Psychology* 52, no. 6 (1987): 1122–31.

7. These five shifts are based on the descriptions summarized in James J. Gross, "The Emerging Field of Emotion Regulation: An Integrative Review," *Review of General Psychology* 2, no. 3 (1998): 271–99.

8. As quoted in Nelton, "Emotions in the Workplace," 25–29.

9. Brian Parkinson, "Emotions are Social," *British Journal of Psychology* 87 (1 November 1996): 663–84.

Part II: Choosing Emotional Competence

1. Arlie Russell Hochschild, *The Managed Heart, Commercialization of Human Feelings* (Berkeley: University of California Press, 1983), 17.

2. Goleman, *Emotional Intelligence*, 149.

Chapter 4: Emotional Labor or Emotional Competence?

1. Interviewed in *The Fast Company* (September 1998): 54.

2. Ibid., 7.

3. Linda Price, Eric Arnould, and Patrick Tierney, "Going to Extremes: Managing Service Encounters and Assessing Provider Performance," *Journal of Marketing* 59, no. 2 (1995): 83–98.

4. Ibid., 95.

5. Numerous articles have been written to help organizations terminate staff who poison their workspace with negative attitudes. The reason for all these articles is that firing staff is very difficult, let alone "firing for attitude." As one example, see Gillian Flynn, who lays out an involved set of steps that employers must take if they are to minimize the risk of counter legal action. "You Can Say Good Riddance to Bad Attitudes, *Workforce* 77, no. 7 (July 1998): 82–84.

6. As quoted in *The Fast Company,* (September 1998).

7. Goleman, *Emotional Intelligence,* 135.

8. Parkinson, "Emotions are Social," 663–84.

9. *Webster's New World Dictionary,* 2nd college ed.

10. A special thank you to Bill Oden, our colleague, for this phrase.

11. The concept of "internal customer" has been around for some time. By 1979 there are regular references to corporate customers and branch customers. For example, see Richard J. Matteis, "The New Back Office Focuses on Customer Service," *Harvard Business Review* (March/April 1979): 146 ff. Jan Carlzon in his popular book *Moments of Truth* wrote extensively about internal customers based on the course that TMI conducted company wide for Scandinavian Airlines (SAS) in the early 1980s. By the late 1990s, the term is being used without explanation. It has become part of our vocabulary.

12. For an interesting and thorough discussion of this topic, see Barbara A. Gutek, *The Dynamics of Service, Reflections on the Changing Nature of Customer/Provider Interactions* (San Francisco: Jossey-Bass Publishers, 1995).

13. Sandi Mann, *Hiding What We Feel, Faking What We Don't: Understanding the Role of Your Emotions at Work* (Boston: Element Books, 1999), and *Annals of the American Academy of Political and Social Science* 561 (January 1999).

14. As reported by Patricia B. Seybold, *Customers.com: How to Create a Profitable Business Strategy for the Internet and Beyond* (New York: Times Books, 1998).

15. Janelle Barlow and Claus Møller, *A Complaint Is a Gift* (San Francisco: Berrett-Koehler, 1996), 141–42.

16. Statistic cited by Debra Boelkes and Patrick O'Rourke, "10 Steps to Increase Sales, Service, and Satisfaction through Your Call Center," *Telemarketing & Call Center Solutions* 16, no. 11 (May 1998): 86.

17. As quoted in Lorrie Grant, "Spotty Service Hinders On-Line Retailing," *USA Today,* 1 June 1999, p. 8A.

18. Maslach and Jackson labeled the three signs of burnout as emotional exhaustion, depersonalization, and diminished personal accomplishment.

Christine Maslach and S. E. Jackson, "The Measurement of Experienced Burnout," *Journal of Occupational Behavior* 2 (1981): 99–113.

19. "Cathay Pacific Passengers Could Face Service with a Frown," *South China Morning Post*, 6 January 1999.

20. Hans Selye, M.D., *The Stress of Life* (New York: McGraw Hill, 1956).

Chapter 5: Managing for Emotional Authenticity

1. V. A. Thompson, *Bureaucracy and the Modern World* (Morristown, N.J.: General Learning Press, 1976). Thompson is also the author of *Without Sympathy or Enthusiasm: The Problem of Administrative Compassion* (University: University of Alabama Press, 1975).

2. As far as the authors are aware, there has been only one quantitative study conducted that considers the relationship between regulated emotional labor and sales performance. Researchers found a weak, but significant, *negative* relationship between regulated emotional display and service quality. In other words, when emotions were "regulated," service quality suffered. See R. I. Sutton and A. Rafaeli, "Untangling the Relationship between Displayed Emotions and Organizational Sales," *Academy of Management Journal* 31 (1988): 461–87.

3. As cited in Esther Dyson, "Wanted: Brilliance and Attitude," *Computerworld* (10 November 1997): 82.

4. Ibid., 83.

5. Ronald Henkoff, "Managing, Finding, Training, and Keeping the Best Service Workers," *Fortune* (3 October 1994). This is an excellent discussion of practical examples of how to hire and manage staff to retain them.

6. Leonard A. Schlesinger and James L. Heskett, "The Service-Driven Service Company," *Harvard Business Review* (September/October 1991): 71 ff.

7. A recent article reported a statistically significant link between human resource (HR) orientation and sustainable competitive advantages in manufacturing organizations. Specifically, the researchers looked at effective recruitment of valued employees, above-average compensation and fringe benefits, and extensive training and development programs. See Long W. Lam and Louis P. White, "Human Resource Orientation and Corporate Performance," *Human Resource Development Quarterly* 9, no. 4 (winter 1998): 351–64.

8. Leonard L. Berry, *On Great Service: A Framework for Action* (New York: The Free Press, 1995).

9. Frederick E. Webster, Jr., The Changing Role of Marketing in the Corporation," *Journal of Marketing* 56 (October 1992): 117.

10. For a complete discussion of this subject, see Barbara B. Stern, "Advertising Intimacy: Relationship Marketing and the Services Consumer," *Journal of Advertising* 26, no. 4 (winter 1997): 7–19.

11. Emphasis added. Ibid., 8.

12. In personal conversation with O'Hara, December 1998.

13. Paco Underhill, *Why We Buy, The Science of Shopping* (New York: Simon and Schuster, 1999).

14. Among others, see Robert Saxe and Barton Weitz, "The SOCO Scale: A Measure of Customer Orientation of Salespeople," *Journal of Marketing Research* 19 (August 1982): 343–61; and Dhruv Grewal and Arun Sharma, "The Effect of Salesforce Behavior on Customer Satisfaction: An Interactive Framework," *Journal of Personal Selling and Sales Management* 9 (March 1991): 13–23.

15. Michael Hepworth and Paula Mateus, "Connecting Customer Loyalty to the Bottom Line," *Canadian Business Review* 21 (December 1994): 40–44.

16. As cited in Timothy W. Firnstahl, "My Employees Are My Service Guarantee," *Harvard Business Review* (July–August 1989): 28–32.

17. Arlie Hochschild, in her focus on service providers, forgets that customers frequently hold in their "true feelings." They grit their teeth to maintain a level of civility when they would many times rather lash out at incompetent service providers. Both customers and service providers have a choice—to repress their feelings or transmute them into civil behavior as the airline passengers in the above situation demonstrated.

18. Retaining staff is almost always a major challenge whenever unemployment rates fall below 5 percent. PR Newswire via News Edge Corporation, 12 September 1998.

19. As cited in "Why Rivals Quaking as Nordstrom Heads East," *Business Week* (15 June 1987).

20. Oren Harari, "Out of the Mouth of Babes," *Management Review* 85 (1 March 1996): 33–36.

21. The foundation for this concept was stated by marketing experts A. Parasuraman, Valerie Zeitnmal, and Leonard L. Berry in a frequently quoted statement: "For most services, the server cannot be separated from the service." Parasuraman, Zeithaml, and Berry, "A Conceptual Model of Service Quality and Its Implications for Future Research," *Journal of Marketing* 49, no. 4 (fall 1986): 41–50.

22. This point of view was emphasized by Mary Jo Bitner, Bernard H. Booms, and Lois A. Mohr, "Critical Service Encounters: The Employee's Viewpoint," *Journal of Marketing* 58, no. 4 (October 1994): 95–106.

23. As concluded by Jaclyn Fierman, "Americans Can't Get No Satisfaction," *Fortune* (11 December 1995): 187.

24. Research would suggest that it is better to hire staff who have less difficulty being in situations of emotional dissonance. See J. Andrew Morris and Daniel C. Feldman, "Managing Emotions in the Workplace," *Journal of Managerial Issues* 9, no. 3 (fall 1997): 257–74.

25. PDP, Inc., Woodland Park, Colorado, interviewed in David Beardsley, "These Tests Will Give You Fits," *The Fast Company* (November 1998): 88–90.

26. Kelleher, "Customer Service: It Starts at Home."

27. Placement of many of the items on the following two lists is supported by research conducted by Andrew Morris and Daniel Feldman. See Morris and Feldman, "Managing Emotions."

28. This is particularly true when high amounts of emotional dissonance is experienced; that is, when the staff feel one way toward customers but are expected to behave in another way. This is where the greatest amount of emotional exhaustion occurs, and managers need to address these specific issues. See Morris and Feldman, "Managing Emotions."

29. See Mann, "Becoming a One-Minute Friend—How to Manage Your Emotions to Get the Job and Keep the Job," Chapter 4 in *Hiding What We Feel*, 55–66.

30. As reported in William Davidow and Bro Utall, *Total Customer Service* (New York: Harper & Row, 1989), 91.

31. Robert Kegan, *In Over Our Heads: The Mental Demands of Modern Life* (Cambridge: Harvard University Press, 1994), 5.

32. Ibid., 70.

33. Ashfort and Humphrey, for example, have demonstrated that when bank tellers are allowed more flexibility in their emotional styles with customers, they have higher job satisfaction than bank tellers who are given emotional scripts. See B. E. Ashfort and R. H. Humphrey, "Emotion in the Workplace: A Reappraisal," *Human Relations* 48 (1995): 97–125. Hackman and Oldham argue basically the same point. J. R. Hackman and G. Oldham, "Development of the Job Diagnostic Survey," *Journal of Applied Psychology* 60 (1975): 159–170.

34. This conflict between felt and displayed emotions is labeled Emotional Dissonance by D. R. Middleton, "Emotional Style: The Cultural Ordering of Emotions," *Ethos* 17 (1989): 187–201.

35. The research behind this idea is fully examined in Morris and Feldman, "Managing Emotions in the Workplace," 257–74.

36. For a more complete and excellent discussion of this issue, see Ingebjorg Folgero and Ingred H. Fjeldstad, "On Duty—Off Guard: Cultural

Norms and Sexual Harassment in Service Organizations," *Organization Studies* 16, no. 2 (1995): 299–313.

37. Several studies have demonstrated that emotional labor is less difficult for staff who have greater job autonomy. For example, see Pamela Kathryn Adelmann, "Emotional Labor and Employee Well-being" (unpublished dissertation, University of Michigan, 1989); Rebecca Jane Erickson, "When Emotion Is the Product: Self, Society, and Authenticity in a Postmodern World" (unpublished dissertation, Washington State University, 1991); and A. S. Wharton, "The Affective Consequences of Service Work," *Work and Occupations* 20 (1993): 205–32.

38. As reported in Ellen Earle Chaffee, "Listening to the People We Serve," in *The Responsive University*, ed. William G. Tierney (Baltimore: The Johns Hopkins University Press, 1998), 37.

39. As quoted in Thomas A. Stewart, "How to Lead a Revolution," *Fortune* (18 November 1994): 48 ff.

40. From an interview conducted by 9 to 5, Working Women Education Fund, cited in Ellen Alderman and Caroline Kennedy, *The Right to Privacy* (New York: Knopf, 1995): 316–17.

41. Ibid., 317.

Part III: Maximizing Customer Experiences with Empathy

Chapter 6: Satisfaction Isn't Good Enough—Anymore

1. Michael Edwardson, "Emotional Profiling in Service Encounters" IIR Conference paper, Sydney, Australia, August 1997, page 2. Janelle presented at a customer service conference in Sydney, Asutralia, to which she was first exposed to this new approach. For those interested in additionl work by Edwardson, other references include "More Than a Feeling," *Australian Leisure Management* (August/September 1997): 40–41; "The New Era in Satisfaction Research: Consumer Emotions," in *Customer Service Excellence*, ed. B. Whitford (Sydney: Beaumont Publisher, 1998), 11–23; and "Emotion Knowledge Structures in Service Encounters" (American Marketing Association—Frontiers in Services Conference, Nashville, Tennessee, October 1997).

2. Thomas O. Jones, and W. Earl Sasser, Jr., "Why Satisfied Customers Defect," *Harvard Business Review* (November/December 1995): 88 ff.

3. Russ Alan Prince, "Attending to the Emotional Aspects: The Process of Grief," *Trust and Estates* 134, no. 4 (1 April 1995): 82–87. Prince found that 15 percent of the population liked the "official distance" type of behavior. They thought this was the mark of a "true professional." Clearly, one approach is not

going to work for all customers. Figuring out the best approach is the key to empathy.

4. Janine L. Smith and Gaylon E. Greer, "The Trust Industry Takes Time Out for Human Services, *Trust and Estates* 135 (1 February 1996): 54–60.

5. Ibid., 56.

6. Ibid., 60.

7. Firnstahl, "My Employees Are My Service Guarantee," 28.

8. Marsha L. Richins (professor of marketing at the College of Business and Public Administration at the University of Missouri), Linda Price and Eric J. Arnould (College of Business, University of South Florida), and Sheila Deibler (College of Business at the University of Colorado at Boulder). See also Bagozzi, Gopinath, and Nyer, "The Role of Emotions in Marketing"; V. Lililjander and T. Strandvik, "Emotions in Service Satisfaction," *International Journal of Service Industry Management* 8, no. 2 (1997): 148–69; Richard L. Oliver, Roland T. Rust, and Sajeev Varki, "Customer Delight—Foundations, Findings and Managerial Insight," *Journal of Retailing* 73, no. 3 (1997): 311–36; and, finally, the seminal work of Richard L. Oliver, *Satisfaction: A Behavioral Perspective on the Consumer* (New York: McGraw-Hill, 1997).

9. Edwardson, "The New Era in Satisfaction Research," 16.

10. Emphasis added. Prashanth U. Nyer, "A Study of the Relationships between Cognitive Appraisals and Consumption Emotions," *Journal of the Academy of Marketing Science* 25, no. 4 (fall 1997): 296–304.

Chapter 7: The Challenge in Measuring Customer Emotions

1. Marsha L. Richins, "Measuring Emotions in the Consumption Experience," *Journal of Consumer Research, Inc.* 24 (September 1997): 127.

2. Ibid., 144.

3. See Christian Gronroos, *Services Management and Marketing: Managing and Truth in Service Competition* (Lexington, Mass.: Lexington Books, 1990).

4. William Thomas, "Customer Satisfaction: Turning Temporary Scores into Permanent Relationships," *Quality Progress* 31, no. 67 (June 1998): 87–90.

5. See Price, Arnould, and Deibler, "Consumers' Emotional Responses to Service Encounters," 35.

6. John H. Lingle and William A. Schiemann, "From Balanced Scorecard to Strategic Gauges: Is Measurement Worth It?" *Management Review* 85 (1 March 1996): 56–62.

7. As reported by Hepworth and Mateus, "Connecting Customer Loyalty to the Bottom Line," 40.

8. As cited in Rosanne D'Ausilio, "The Impact of Conflict Management Training on Customer Service Delivery," *TeleProfessional Magazine* 10, no. 9 (October 1997): 66–72.

9. Ibid.

10. Donald L. Kirkpatrick, *Evaluating Training Programs: The Four Levels,* 2d ed. (San Francisco: Berrett-Koehler, 1998).

11. See Arum Sharma, "Customer Satisfaction-Based Incentive Systems: Some Managerial and Salesperson Considerations," *Journal of Personal Selling and Sales Management* 17, no. 2 (spring 1997): 61–70.

12. Larry Keely, president of the Doblin Group, quoted in Leiber, "Storytelling: A New Way to Get Close to Your Customer."

13. As cited in Peter Jordan, "There's No Business Like Return Business," *VARbusiness* 11, no. 20 (15 December 1995): 113.

14. For a complete discussion see Barbara Sande Dimmitt, "The Power of Words," *Business and Health* 15, no. 11 (November 1997): 18-24.

15. See Paula M. Saunders, Robert F. Scherer, and Herbert E. Brown, "Delighting Customers by Managing Expectations for Service Quality: An Example from the Optical Industry, *Journal of Applied Business Research* 11, no. 2 (spring 1995): 101–9.

16. One way to get in-depth information from your highest ranking customers is to ask those who marked their scales at your highest rating additional questions. For example, the highest raters could be asked: How likely are you to recommend our products or services to someone else? How likely are you to use our products or services again? Please check which words describe your feelings about our service: happy, delighted, excited, thrilled, trusting, contented. Be sure to choose words that are relevant to your industry.

17. *Webster's New World Dictionary.*

18. A number of academicians argue this point. Perhaps the most closely identified with this subtle but important issue are Zeithaml, Berry and Parasuraman. See Valarie A. Zeithaml, Leonard L. Berry, and A. Parasuraman, "The Nature and Determinants of Customer Expectations of Service," *Journal of the Academy of Marketing Science* 21 (winter 1993): 1–12.

19. J. Joseph Cronin, Jr., and Steven A. Taylor, "Measuring Service Quality: A Reexamination and Extension," *Journal of Marketing* 56, no. 3 (1992): 55–68.

20. Steven A. Taylor and Thomas L. Baker, "An Assessment of the Relationship between Service Quality and Customer Satisfaction in the Formation of Consumers' Purchase Intentions," *Journal of Retailing* 70, no. 2 (summer 1994): 163–79.

21. See Steven A. Taylor and J. Joseph Cronin, Jr., "Modeling Patient Satisfaction and Service Quality," *Journal of Health Care Marketing* 14, no. 1

(spring 1994): 34–44. McAlexander et al. suggest that over time, service quality will have a stronger impact on purchase intentions than will satisfaction that is measured immediately. See James McAlexander, Dennis O. Kaldenburg, and Harold F. Koenig, "Service Quality Measurement," *Journal of Health Care Marketing* 14, no. 3 (fall 1994): 34–40.

Chapter 8: The Gift of Empathy

1. Attribution of this quote to Gandhi is not without some controversy. The original document came to us complete with a picture of Gandhi and inscribed "Gandhiji." We have been told by one Gandhi expert that he is not aware that Gandhi made such a statement, but Gandhi wrote thousands of pages in his lifetime. We found the quotation in the 1 July 1999 *Business Line (The Hindu)*, which indicated that Gandhi made the statement in 1890 during the period when he was practicing law in South Africa. Part of the article goes on to say, "The Father of our nation was not considered a visionary in marketing. Probably, at the time when he advocated this wisdom, marketing as a discipline did not even exist. But viewed in retrospect, there is no doubt that the Mahatma hit the bull's eye with this insightful thought. More than a century later, companies have found themselves in deep trouble for neglecting the very reason for their business—the customer."

2. As cited in Austin Murphy, "You've Got Questions, The Concierge, She's Got Answers, *Via* (July/August 1999): 47–49.

3. "Service Excellence Awards—Winner Business to Business Category: Nichols Foods," *Management Today* (October 1998): 92–93.

4. See G. Burnside, "Judgments of Short Time Intervals Performing Mathematical Tasks," *Perception and Psychophysics* 9 (February 1971): 404–21.

5. Jean-Charles Chebat et al., "The Impact of Mood on Time Perception, Memorization, and Acceptance of Waiting," *Genetic, Social and General Psychology Monographs* 121 (1 November 1995): 411 ff. Richard C. Larson cites the classic case of the time spent waiting for elevators passing more quickly when customers have full-length mirrors to distract them. Richard C. Larson, "Perspectives on Queues: Social Justice and the Psychology of Queuing," *Operations Research* 35, no. 6 (1987): 895–905. Managing waiting time is a simple idea and easy to implement, but it is also psychologically complex. Two Hong Kong researchers found that how an organization best manages waiting time depends on the length of the wait. One size doesn't fit all. Here's what Michael Hui and David Tse found: short waits (less than five minutes) require no information to elicit a positive customer affect. For medium waits (between five and ten minutes), the best customer response is had when the length of the wait is

told to the customer: "You will be helped in seven minutes." Long waits (ten minutes or longer), however, were most positively judged when customers were regularly updated on their position in the queue. "There are five people ahead of you," was received more positively than "You will be helped in approximately thirty minutes." Michael K. Hui and David K. Tse, "What to Tell Consumers in Waits of Different Lengths: An Integrative Model of Service Evaluation," *Journal of Marketing* 60, no. 2 (April 1996): 81–90.

6. Julie Baker and Michaelle Cameron, "The Effects of the Service Environment on Affect and Consumer Perception of Waiting Time: An Integrative Review and Research Propositions," *Journal of the Academy of Marketing Science* 24, no. 4 (fall 1996): 338–349.

7. Mihaly Csikszentmihalyi, *Flow: The Psychology of Optimal Experience* (New York: Harper & Row, 1990).

8. "USA Snapshots: Lady You Need a New Engine," *USA Today*, 7 January 1994, p. 1.

9. Based on personal conversation with Holly Stiel. Also, see Michael Gips, "The Softer Side of Security," *Security Management* 42, no. 4 (April 1998): 11.

10. As reported in Kristin S. Krause, "Forward to the Past," *Traffic World* 255 (31 August 1998): 23.

11. For example, see D. Aderman, "Elation, Depression, and Helping Behavior," *Journal of Personality and Social Psychology* 24 (January 1972): 91–101.

12. J. A. Morris and D. C. Feldman, "The Dimensions, Antecedents, and Consequences of Emotional Labor," *Academy of Management Review* 21, no. 4 (1996): 986–1010.

13. A. M. Isen and R. A. Baron, "Positive Affect as a Factor in Organizational Behavior," in *Research in Organizational Behavior,* vol. 13, ed. B. M. Straw and L. L. Cummings (Greenwich, Conn.: JAI Press, 1991): 1–54.

14. As quoted in Kelly Spang, *Computer Reseller News*, 8 December 1997, p. 33.

15. This distinction is summarized by Beth Azar, "Defining the Train That Makes Us Human," *American Psychological Association Monitor* 18 (November 1997): 1.

16. As reported by Rosanne D'Ausilio, "The Impact of Conflict Management Training," 68.

17. Azar, "Defining the Train," 15.

18. As reported in Krause, "Forward to the Past," 22-23.

19. See Stern, "Advertising Intimacy," 7–19.

20. As reported in Justin Hibbard, "Web Service: Ready or Not—Businesses Brace for a Sharp Increase in Online Buying," *Information Week* 18 (16 November 1998).

21. Complete questioning is particularly important in the insurance business. See Brenda French-Mullins, "Golden Opportunities," *Canadian Insurance* 102, no. 12 (November 1997): 22–23.

22. Greg Brenneman, "Right Away and All at Once: How We Saved Continental," *Harvard Business Review* (September/October 1998): 162 ff.

23. As reported by Beth Azar, "Forgiveness Helps Keep Relationships Steadfast," *American Psychological Association Monitor* 18 (November 1997): 14.

24. Mario Saporta, "Home Depot Execs Spend Day on Firing Line," *The Atlanta Journal and Constitution*, 1 June 1995.

25. As reported by Linda Winer, "Limelight: Amid the Bragging, A Case of Betrayal," *Newsday*, 7 June 1996, p. B03.

26. Studs Terkel, *Working: People Talk about What They Do All Day and How They Feel about What They Do* (New York: Pantheon, 1974).

27. Quoted in Joan Fredericks and James M. Salter, "What Does Your Customer Really Want?" *Quality Progress* 31, no. 1 (January 1998): 63–65.

28. Anita van de Vliet, "Are They Being Served?" *Management Today* (February 1997): 66-70.

29. Robert B. Woodruff, "Customer Value: The Next Source for Competitive Advantage," *Journal of the Academy of Marketing Science* 25, no. 2 (spring 1997): 139–53.

30. Brenneman, "Customer Value."

31. As quoted in Roberta Maynard, "Back to Basics, from the Top: Executives of Growing Firms Find Ways to Stay Close to Front-Line Employees and Their Customers," *Nation's Business* 84 (1 December 1996): 38–40.

32. Ibid.

33. See Cathay Goodwin, Stephen J. Grove, and Raymond P. Fisk, "'Collaring the Cheshire Cat': Studying Customers' Services Experience through Metaphor," *Service Industries Journal* 16, no. 4 (October 1996): 421–42.

34. Ibid., 440.

35. As cited in Mark W. Morgan, "Improving Business Performance: Are You Measuring Up?" *Manage* 49 (1 February 1998): 10–13.

36. From Michael Edwardson, "The New Era in Satisfaction Research: Consumer Emotions" (paper presented at 1998 Market Research Society of Australia, 22 April 1998).

Part IV: Viewing Complaints as Emotional Opportunities

1. The original figures were first set in 1983: $20 to keep a customer satisfied and $118 to get a new one. Larry J. Rosenberg and John A. Czepiel, "A Marketing Approach for Customer Retention," *Journal of Consumer Marketing* (fall 1983): 45–51.

2. National Consumer Survey data by TARP. A minor problem is defined as between $1 and $5 in losses; a major problem is anything over $100 in losses.

Chapter 9: Complaints: Emotional Opportunities

1. From Dennis E. Garrett and Renee A. Meyers, "Verbal Communication between Complaining Consumers and Company Service Representatives," *Journal of Consumer Affairs* 30, no. 2 (winter 1996): 444–75.

2. Barlow and Møller, *A Complaint is a Gift.*

3. At times it is useful to set targets for complaint reduction if they are a quality-improvement measurement. For example, a clothing manufacturer might set a target to reduce the number of complaints about cloth shrinkage because that would reflect improvement of that quality factor. If a company was interested in reducing wait time at counters, setting targets for that specific purpose would indicate that organizational interventions to reduce waiting time were working.

4. Sharma, "Customer Satisfaction-Based Incentive Systems."

5. Stephen S. Tax, Stephen W. Brown, and Murali Chandrashekaram, "Customer Evaluations of Service Complaint Experiences: Implications for Relationship Marketing," *Journal of Marketing* 62, no. 2 (April 1998): 60–76.

Chapter 10: Fundamentals of Complaints

1. As reported in William O. Bearden and Jesse E. Teel, "Selected Determinants of Consumer Satisfaction and Complaint Reports," *Journal of Marketing Research* 20 (February 1983): 21–28.

2. Rebecca Piirto Heath, "The Marketing of Power," *American Demographics* 19, no. 9 (September 1997): 59–63.

3. See Albert O. Hirschman, who looked at complaint behavior in the health-care industry, "Exit, Voice, and Loyalty: Further Reflections and a Survey of Recent Contributions," *Social Science Information* 24 (1973): 7–26.

4. For example, see Christopher Hart, James Heskett, and W. Earl Sasser, Jr., "The Profitable Art of Service Recovery," *Harvard Business Review* 65 (July/August 1990): 148–56.

5. Charles L. Martin and Denise T. Smart, "Consumer Experiences Calling Toll-Free Corporate Hotlines," *Journal of Business Communication* (31 July 1994): 195–212.

6. Tax, Brown, and Chandrashekaram, "Customer Evaluations."

7. S. Morris, "The Relationship between Company Complaint Handling and Consumer Behavior" (master's thesis, University of Massachusetts, Amherst, 1985).

8. See Arun Sharma, "Customer Satisfaction-Based Incentive Systems."

9. Joseph LeDoux, Ph.D., as quoted by Beth Azar, "LeDoux Outlines His Theory of Emotions and Memory," *American Psychological Monitor* (15 July 1998).

10. Mary Jo Bitner, Bernard H. Booms, and Mary Stanfield Tetreault, "The Service Encounter: Diagnosing Favorable and Unfavorable Incidents," *Journal of Marketing* 54, no. 1 (January 1990): 71.

11. Jagdip Singh, "Industry Characteristics and Consumer Dissatisfaction," *Journal of Consumer Affairs* 25, no. 1 (summer 1991): 51.

12. TARP first reported this statistic in 1980 in its U.S. government-commissioned report, *Consumer Complaint-Handling in America: Final Report* (Washington: White House Office of Consumer Affairs, 1980).

13. See Claes Fornell and Birger Wernerfelt, "Defensive Marketing Strategy by Customer Complaining Management: A Theoretical Analysis," *Journal of Marketing Research* 24 (November 1987): 337–46, and George R. Walther, "Complaints Good for Most Companies," *Peoria Journal Star*, 28 November 1985, p. B-5.

14. Emphasis added. Scott W. Kelley, K. Douglas Hoffman, and Mark A. Davis, "A Typology of Retail Failures and Recoveries," *Journal of Retailing* 69, no. 4 (winter 1993): 429–53.

15. TARP statistics, as cited by Sarah Kennedy, "Waking Up to the Realities of Customer Satisfaction," *CMA Magazine* 71 (2 January 1997): 28.

16. See Marsha L. Richins, "Negative Word-of-Mouth by Dissatisfied Consumers: A Pilot Study," *Journal of Marketing* 47 (winter, 1983): 68–78, and John E. Swan and Richard L. Oliver, "Postpurchase Communications by Consumers," *Journal of Retailing* 65 (winter 1989): 516–33.

17. As quoted by Patricia Sellers, "Service: How to Handle Customers' Gripes," *Fortune* 24 (October 1988): 88.

Chapter 11: Strategies for Handling Complaints

1. Among others, Ron Zemke and Chip Bell found that, on average, companies apologize for only 48 percent of their errors. See Ron Zemke and Chip

Bell, "Service Recovery: Doing It Right the Second Time," *Training: The Magazine of Human Resources Development* (June 1990): 43.

2. Folkes and Kotsos suggest that retailers, in particular, seem bent on blaming their customers for product failures. See Valarie Folkes and Barbara Kotsos, "Buyers' and Sellers' Explanations for Product Failure: Who Done It," *Journal of Marketing* 50 (April 1986): 74-80.

3. See Mary Jo Bitner, "Evaluating Service Encounters: The Effects of Physical Surroundings and Employee Responses," *Journal of Marketing* 54 (April 1990): 69–82.

4. Statistics cited in "SJB Services: Comprehensive Study of Customer Loyalty Published Today," *M2 Press WIRE*, 2 December 1996.

5. Brown also gave her staff greater control over how their own work was structured to make their jobs easier. Pat Brown, interviewed on *All Things Considered*, National Public Radio, 18 June 1996.

6. Firnstahl, "My Employees Are My Service Guarantee," 28–54.

7. Ibid.

8. Averill delineates the three mentioned forms of control. The authors have added emotional control. See J. R. Averill, "Personal Control over Aversive Stimuli and Its Relationship to Stress," *Psychological Bulletin* 80, no. 4 (1973): 286–303.

9. Merle A. Fossum and Marilyn J. Mason, *Facing Shame: Families in Recovery* (New York: Norton, 1986), 5. Perhaps this feeling of inadequacy is foundational to Arlie Hochschild's emotional labor concept. Perhaps staff workers don't necessarily want to attack their customers, but they feel caught between customer demands and organizational policies, and customers happen to be handy and ultimately less damaging to someone's career than one's manager.

10. Can a Bank Give Me Answers?" *CA Magazine* 131, no. 1 (January/February 1998): 10.

11. Stephen S. Tax and Stephen W. Brown, "Recovering and Learning from Service Failure, *Sloan Management Review* 40, no. 1 (fall 1998): 75–88.

12. Vicki J. Powers, "Measuring Up," *Ivey Business Quarterly* 62, no. 3 (spring 1998): 52–57.

13. Mary C. Gilly and Betsy D. Gelb, "Post-Purchase Consumer Processes and the Complaining Consumer," *Journal of Consumer Research* 9 (December 1982): 323–28.

14. For a complete discussion, see Terry G. Vavra, "Is Your Satisfaction Survey Creating Dissatisfied Customers?" *Quality Progress* 30, no. 12 (December 1997): 51–57.

15. Firnstahl, "My Employees Are My Service Guarantee."

16. Barlow and Møller, *A Complaint Is a Gift*, chapter 10.

17. Tax and Brown, "Recovering and Learning from Service Failure."

18. Firnstahl, "My Employees Are My Service Guarantee."

19. Tax and Brown, "Recovering and Learning from Service Failure."

20. Richard Schaaf, *Keeping the Edge: Giving Customers the Service They Demand* (New York: Dutton, 1995).

21. Mary Jo Bitner, Bernard H. Booms, and Mary Stanfield Tetreault, "The Service Encounter," 76.

22. Alan J. Resnik and Robert R. Harmon, "Consumer Complaints and Managerial Response: A Holistic Approach," *Journal of Marketing* 47 (winter 1983): 86–97.

23. Delight was inferred when customers selected "very satisfied" on a five-point survey scale. Saunders, Scherer, and Brown, "Delighting Customers by Managing Expectations for Service Quality."

24. Amy Ostrom and Dawn Iacobucci, "Customer Trade-Offs and the Evaluation of Services," *Journal of Marketing* 59, no. 1 (January 1995): 17–28.

25. Zeithaml, Berry, and Parasuraman, "The Nature and Determinants of Customer Expectations of Service."

26. As far as we know, only three papers have attempted to analyze organizational complaint behavior. See Scott Hansen, Thomas L. Powers, and John E. Swan, "Modeling Industrial Buyer Complaints: Implications for Satisfying and Saving Customers," *Journal of Marketing Theory and Practice* 5, no. 4 (fall 1997): 12–22; I. Fredrick Trawick and John E. Swan, "Complaint Behavior by Industrial Buyers: Buyer Roles and Organizational Factors," in *Southern Marketing Association,* ed. Carol H. Anderson, Blaise J. Bergiel, and John H. Summey (Carbondale, Ill.: Southern Marketing Association, 1982), 81–83; and Alvin Williams and C. P. Rao, "Industrial Buyer Complaining Behavior," *Industrial Marketing Management* 9 (1980): 299–304.

Part V: Using Emotional Connections to Increase Customer Loyalty

1. JoAnna Brandi, "Earning Customer Loyalty," *US Banker* 108, no. 3 (March 1998): 89–91.

Chapter 12: Loyalty Is a Behavior with Its Roots in Emotions

1. William Neal quoted in Kevin T. Higins, "Coming of Age," *Marketing News* 3, no. 22 (27 October 1997): 1–12.

2. As quoted in Michael Barrier, "Building Your 'Customer Portfolio,'" *Nation's Business* 84 (1 December 1996): 45.

3. Frederick Reichheld, "Learning from Customer Defections," in *The Quest for Loyalty*, ed. F. Reichheld (Boston: Harvard Business School Press, 1996): 234.

4. SJB Services is a British independent business information provider. *"The Customer Loyalty Report,"* SJB Services, 1997.

5. Abbie Griffin, Greg Gleason, Rick Presiss, and Dave Shevenaugh, "Best Practices for Customer Satisfaction in Manufacturing Firms," *Sloan Management Review* 36, no. 2 (winter 1995): 87–98.

6. Laura A. Liswood, "Once You've Got 'Em, Never Let 'Em Go," *Sales and Marketing Management* 139, no. 7 (November 1987): 73–77. Liswood argues that the classic four *P*s of marketing (price, product, promotion, and place) are focused almost entirely on acquiring customers rather than on retaining them. She argues that retention marketing has to do with individualization of the customer, rather than with the broad-based descriptions of customers in acquisition marketing.

7. Mary Jo Bittner, "Building Service Relationships: It's All about Promises," *Journal of the Academy of Marketing Science* 23 (fall 1995): 246 ff. We should note that some companies have such high retention rates that emotionally upgrading their cultures is probably not going to have much of an impact on their customer retention rates. USAA, the insurance company headquartered in San Antonio, Texas, for example, has defection rates of only 1.5 percent per year with some of its products! You can't get much higher than 98.5 percent customer retention rates. After all, some customers die! As USAA's competitors become more emotionally sophisticated, however, taking emotional upgraded service offerings to an even higher level will help USAA and other companies like it to retain dominance in their niches, enhancing their long-term value. On the other hand, some companies experience "churn" rates of over 20 percent a month. Emotionally upgraded service can have a tremendous and immediate impact on those dismal figures.

8. Reichheld, "Learning from Customer Defections," 233–56.

9. Frederick F. Reichheld, "Zero Defections: Quality Comes to Services," in *The Quest for Loyalty*, A Harvard Business Review Book, 129–142.

10. van de Vliet, "Are They Being Served?" 66.

11. As reported by Hepworth and Mateus, "Connecting Customer Loyalty to the Bottom Line," 40–44.

12. Robert McNeel, president of Robert McNeel and Associates, in Jordan, "There's No Business Like Return Business," 114.

13. Jordan, "There's No Business Like Return Business," 113–18.

14. Howard E. Butz, Jr., and Leonard D. Goodstein, "Measuring Customer Value: Gaining the Strategic Advantage, *Organizational Dynamics* 24 (1 January 1996): 63–78.

15. Thomas A. Stewart, "Smart Managing: The Leading Edge, A Satisfied Customer Isn't Enough," *Fortune* 21 (July 1997): 112.

16. Statistics cited in Morgan, "Improving Business Performance," 13.

17. Michael W. Lowenstein, *The Customer Loyalty Pyramid* (Westport, Conn.: Quorum Books, 1997).

18. The article that best summarizes our views is Joseph J. Cronin and Steven A. Taylor, "SERVPERF versus SERVQUAL: Reconciling Performance-Based and Perceptions-Minus-Expectations Measurement of Service Quality," *Journal of Marketing* 58, no. 1 (January 1994): 125–131.

19. This point represents a complicated debate that deals with two models: SERVPERF versus SERVQUAL. Both are "gap" measurements. SERVQUAL assumes that the judgment of service quality is the gap between what customers expect and what they receive. The larger the gap, the lower the judgment of service quality. SERVPERF is a performance-based gap measurement and assumes there are more variables that determine judgments of satisfaction than service quality. The two original articles that have laid the groundwork for these models are A. Parasuraman, Valarie Zeithaml, and Leonard Berry, "SERVQUAL: A Multi Item Scale for Measuring Consumer Perception of Service Quality," *Journal of Retailing* 64 (spring 1989): 12–40; and Cronin and Taylor, "Measuring Service Quality."

20. His books include *I Know It When I See It* (New York: Amacon, 1991) and *Theory Why: In Which the Boss Solves the Riddle of Quality* (New York: Amacon, 1986).

21. See John Guaspari, "A Cure for 'Initiative Burnout,'" *Management Review* 84 (1 April 1995): 45–50.

Chapter 13: Strategies for Retaining Customers

1. James H. Barnes and Kirk L. Wakefield, "Retailing Hedonic Consumption: A Model of Sales Promotion of a Leisure Service," *Journal of Retailing* 72, no. 4 (winter 1996): 409–28.

2. Bruce Merrifield, "Reorganize around the Customer," *Food Service Distributor* (1 March 1998).

3. Barnes and Wakefield, "Retailing Hedonic Consumption."

4. Lowenstein, *The Customer Loyalty Pyramid.*

5. Quoted in Geoffrey Brewer, "The Customer Stops Here," *Sales and Marketing Management* 150, no. 3 (March 1998): 30–36.

6. Cited in Mary E. Thyfault, Stuart J. Johnson, and Jeff Sweat, "The Service Imperative," *Informationweek*, no. 703 (5 October 1998): 44–55.

7. Abbie Griffin et al., "Best Practices for Customer Satisfaction in Manufacturing Firms."

8. *Financial Times*, 12 April, 1996, p. 3.

9. See, among other books, Edgar H. Schein, *Organizational Culture and Leadership*, 2d ed. (San Francisco: Jossey-Bass, 1992).

10. Research by David E. Berlew and Douglas Hall at AT&T found that employees were likely to leave a company in the next year if the terms of contract were not met. As reported in Douglas Hall and Jonathan E. Moss, "Helping Organizations and Employees Adapt," *Organizational Dynamics* 26 (1 January 1998).

11. Frederick F. Reichheld, "Loyalty-Based Management," in *The Quest for Loyalty*, 8.

12. "Customer Retention and Financial Performance," New York: Business Wire Features, 11 May, 1998.

13. Leonard A. Schlesinger, and James Heskett, "The Service-Driven Service Company," 71 ff.

14. Morgan, "Improving Business Performance."

15. Jeffrey Zornitsky, vice president of Abt Associates, Cambridge, Massachusetts, quoted in Ronald Henkoff and Ann Sample, "Finding, Training, and Keeping the Best Service Workers, *Fortune* (3 October 1994): 110 ff.

16. Daniel P. Finkelman, "Crossing the Zone of Indifference," *Marketing Management* 2, no. 3 (1993): 22–31.

17. See research of Arun Sharma, "Customer Satisfaction-Based Incentive Systems."

18. Jordan, "There's No Business Like Return Business," 116.

19. For a complete overview, see Emin Babakus, David W. Cravens, Mark Johnston, and William C. Moncrief, "Examining the Role of Organizational Variables in the Salesperson Job Satisfaction Model," *Journal of Personal Selling and Sales Management* 16, no. 3 (summer 1996): 33–46; and Steven P. Brown and Robert A. Peterson, "Antecedents and Consequences of Salesperson Job Satisfaction: MetaAnalysis and Assessment of Causal Effects," *Journal of Marketing Research* 30 (February 1993): 63–77.

20. Snetsinger and Pellett found a relationship in the office equipment industry between customer retention and staff satisfaction. Douglas Snetsinger and Gret Pellett, "Making Employee Research Pay Off," *CMA Magazine* 70 (17 July 1996): 13–16.

21. Sarah C. Mavrinac, Neil R. Jones, and Marshall W. Meyer, *The Financial and Non-Financial Returns to Innovate Workplace Practices: A Critical Review* (Boston: Ernst and Young, 1995).

22. As cited in Sue Shellenbarger, "Sometimes Compassion Is at Work," *San Francisco Examiner and Chronicle*, 11 October 1998, p. CL29.

23. Describing the Tasca Lincoln-Mercury dealer in Seekonk, Massachusetts. Reported by Thomas Moore, "Selling: Would You Buy a Car from This Man?" *Fortune* 11 (April 1988): 72.

24. Reported in Denny Hatch, *Target Marketing* 19, no. 3 (March 1996): 3.

25. Richardson quoted by Stewart, "Smart Managing," 112 ff.

26. As cited in Stewart, "Smart Managing," 113.

27. For a complete discussion, see Edward A. Morash and John Ozment, "The Strategic Use of Transportation Time and Reliability for Competitive Advantage," *Transportation Journal* 36, no. 2 (winter 1996): 35–46.

28. David Hall and Simon Haslam, "How to Achieve—and Measure—Customer Delight," *Business Marketing Digest* 17, no. 4 (fourth quarter 1992): 17–20.

29. For a discussion of how this concept relates to the health-care industry, see "James D. Hutton and Lynne D. Richardson, "Healthscapes: The Importance of Place," *Journal of Health Care Marketing* 15, no. 1 (spring1995): 10–11.

30. As quoted in Crystal Laurie, "Staffing the Front Lines," *Franchising World* 30, no. 5 (September/October 1998): 8–10.

31. As discussed by Kathleen Seiders and Leonard L. Berry, "Service Fairness: What It Is and Why It Matters," *Academy of Management Executive* 12, no. 2 (May 1998): 8–20.

32. For a complete discussion of activist behavior, see Barlow and Møller, *A Complaint Is a Gift*, 43–50.

33. See R. M. Morgan and S. D. Hunt, "The Commitment-Trust Theory of Relationship Marketing," *Journal of Marketing* 58 (1994): 20–38.

34. For a complete discussion of fairness in service, see Kathleen Seiders and Leonard L. Berry, "Service Fairness."

35. For one of the better articles on consumer reactions to fairness, see R. L. Oliver and J. E. Swan, "Consumer Perception of Interpersonal Equity and Satisfaction in Transactions: A Field Survey Approach," *Journal of Marketing* 53 (1989): 21–35.

36. C. Boshoff, "An Experimental Study of Service Recovery Options," *International Journal of Service Industry Management* 8, no. 3 (1997): 110–30.

37. Scott W. Kelley and Mark A. Davis, "Antecedents to Customer Expectations for Service Recovery," *Journal of the Academy of Marketing Science* 22, no. 2 (1994): 52–61.

38. Syed Saad Andaleeb and Amiya K. Basu, "Technical Complexity and Consumer Knowledge as Moderators of Service Quality Evaluation in the Automobile Service Industry," *Journal of Retailing* 70, no. 4 (winter 1994): 367–382. Andaleeb and Basu considered automobile service and repair exclusively in their research.

39. *Wally Bock's Monday Memo*, 9 August 1999.

40. Seiders and Berry, "Service Fairness."

41. Emphasis added. Jeremy L. Dorosin, *Balance at Middlefork* (Berkeley, Calif.: Celestial Arts, 1999), 70.

42. Bern Stauss, "Global Word of Mouth: Service Bashing on the Internet Is a Thorny Issue," *Marketing Management* 6, no. 3 (fall 1997): 28–30.

Chapter 14: Final Thoughts

1. Zemke, "The Service Revolution: Who Won?" *Management Review* 86, no.3 (March 1997): 11–15.

2. Peter Drucker, *The Practice of Management* (New York: Harper and Row, 1954).

3. "Customer Retention and Financial Performance."

Appendix A: Emotions: Research Background

1. P. Shaver, et al., "Emotional Knowledge: Further Exploration of a Prototype Approach, *Journal of Personality and Social Psychology* 52, no. 6 (1987): 1061–86.

2. Davitz (1969), as cited in Richard M. Sorrentino and E. Tory Higgins, *Handbook of Motivation and Cognition* (New York: The Guilford Press, 1986).

3. Clore, Ortony, and Foss, "The Psychological Foundation of the Affective Lexicon," 751–66.

4. Paul Ekman, "An Argument for Basic Emotions" *Cognition and Emotion* 6 (1992): 169–200. There is considerable disagreement as to whether it is possible to reduce emotions to a list of "basic emotions." Ortony and Turner conclude, after reviewing the research, that "there is no coherent nontrivial notion of basic emotions as the elementary psychological primitives in terms of which other emotions can be explained." Andrew Ortony and Terence J. Turner, "What's Basic about Basic Emotions?" *Psychological Review* 97 (July 1990): 315.

5. We are aware of fourteen such lists, none of them identical, each including certain emotions for different reasons. For an excellent review, see Ortony and Turner, "What's Basic about Basic Emotions?" 315–31.

6. Robert Plutchik, *Emotion: A Psychoevolutionary Synthesis* (New York: Harper & Row, 1980).

7. Ortony and Turner, "What's Basic about Basic Emotions?"

8. P. R. Shaver, S. Wu, and J. C. Schwartz, "Cross-Cultural Similarities and Differences in Emotion and Its Representation: A Prototype Approach," in *Review of Personality and Social Psychology* 13, ed. M. S. Clark (1992): 175–212.

9. See Brian Parkinson, "Emotions Are Social," for a complete discussion of how emotional significance is defined interpersonally.

10. As reported in Howard Feiertag, "Technology Delivers, but Salespeople Are Here to Stay," Computer Technology, vol. 211 of *Hotel and Motel Management* (3 July 1996): 16.

Appendix B: What Does Marketing Research Tell Us about Consumer Emotions?

1. Marsha Richins, "Measuring Emotions in the Consumption Experience," page 141.

2. Michael Edwardson, "Emotional Profiling," *Tempus* (winter 1998): 5.

3. Peter Donovan, *Delighting Customers: How to Build a Customer-Driven Organization* (London: Chapman and Hall, 1995), and Roderick McNealy, *Making Customer Satisfaction Happen: A Strategy for Delighting Customers* (London: Chapman and Hall, 1996).

4. Valarie Zeithaml, A. Parasuraman, and Leonard L. Berry, *Delivering Service Quality* (New York: The Free Press, 1990).

5. Theodore Levitt, as cited in Brenda French-Mullins, "Golden Opportunities," 22.

6. For an excellent review of the literature on this viewpoint, see Marla Royne Stafford, "Tangibility in Services Advertising: An Investigation of Verbal Versus Visual Cues," *Journal of Advertising* 25, no. 3 (1996): 13–28.

7. For a complete overview, see Tim Ambler, "Myths about the Mind: Time to End Some Popular Beliefs about How Advertising Works," *International Journal of Advertising* 501 (November 1998).

8. For a complete discussion see Price, Arnould, and Tierney, "Going to Extremes."

9. Syed Saad Andaleeb and Amiya K. Basu, "Technical Complexity and Consumer Knowledge," 367 ff.

Appendix C: The Elusive Link between Customer Satisfaction and Customer Loyalty: A Summary of the Research

1. Stewart, "Smart Managing."

2. Among others, see T. Hennig-Thurau and A. Klee, "The Impact of Satisfaction and Relationship Quality on Customer Retention: A Critical

Reassessment and Model Development," *Psychology and Marketing* 14, no. 8 (1997): 737–64. One study measuring satisfaction with business-to-business services and loyalty actually demonstrated a strong link between satisfaction and repurchase intentions. It may be that business-to-business services are different from other relationships. If this is the case, the companies that provide services to other business groups need to pay particular attention to satisfaction survey information. See Paul G. Patterson, Lester W. Johnson, and Richard A. Spreng, *Journal of the Academy of Marketing Science* 25, no. 1 (winter 1997): 4–17.

3. See Jones and Sasser, "Why Satisfied Customers Defect," 88–99.

4. See, for example, Daniel P. Finkelman, "Crossing the Zone of Indifference."

5. See Banwari Mittal and Walfried M. Lasser, "Why Do Customers Switch? The Dynamics of Customer Loyalty" (presented at the AMA Frontiers in Services Conference at Nashville, Tenn., 5–7 October 1995).

6. Stewart, "Smart Managing."

7. This is a particular challenge for health care, where regular "service improvements are needed to continue to impress the patient," even though the result of the health-care product is something that is enjoyed outside the doctor's office. See James H. McAlexander, Dennis O. Kaldenburg, and Harold F. Koenig, "Service Quality Measurement."

8. See Susan J. Devlin and H. K. Dong, "Service Quality from the Customers' Perspective," *Marketing Research* 6, no. 1 (winter 1994): 4–13.

9. See Linda L. Price and Eric J. Arnould, and Sheila L. Deibler, "Consumers' Emotional Responses to Service Encounters," 34–63.

10. For a complete discussion of a study that considers the asymmetric and nonlinear nature of the relationships among overall satisfaction, repurchase intention, and attribute-level performance, see Vikas Mittal, William T. Ross, Jr., and Patrick M. Baldasare, "The Asymmetric Impact of Negative and Positive Attribute-Level Performance on Overall Satisfaction and Repurchase Intensions," *Journal of Marketing* 62, no. 1 (January 1998): 33–47.

Appendix D: Complaint Handling: Where Does the Research Take Us?

1. Nancy Stephens and Kevin P. Gwinner, "Why Don't Some People Complain?" *Journal of the Academy of Marketing Science* 26, no. 3 (summer 1998): 172–89.

2. See Society of Consumer Affairs Professionals in Business (SOCAP), "SOCAP 800 Number Study: A 1992 Profile of 800 Numbers for Customer

Service," (Alexandria, Va.: SOCAP, 1992), and Carl Quintanilla and Richard Gibson, "'Do Call Us' More Companies Install 1-800 Phone Lines," *The Wall Street Journal*, 20 April 1994, p. B1.

3. Dennis E. Garrett and Renee A. Meyers, "Verbal Communication between Complaining Consumers and Company Service Representatives," *Journal of Consumer Affairs* 30, no. 2 (winter 1996): 444–475.

4. It should be noted that the limitation of Garrett and Meyers's research is that it involved the local telephone service, more or less a monopoly at the time of their research. They conclude that different research might be obtained in a more competitive environment. Ibid., 457–58.

5. With regard to blame, 57.4 percent of the coded communication units were spoken by company representatives; with regard to equity, 62.3 percent were spoken by company representatives. See *Ibid.*

6. Ibid., 459–60.

7. See Valarie Zeithaml, Leonard L. Berry, and A. Parasuraman, "Communication and Control Processes in the Delivery of Service Quality," *Journal of Marketing* 52 (April 1988): 35–48.

8. Ibid.

Appendix E: Eight-Step Gift Formula

1. For a complete description, see Barlow and Møller, *A Complaint Is a Gift*, chapter 6.

INDEX

ABOUT THE AUTHORS

Janelle Barlow, Ph.D., is president of TMI, USA, a partner with Time Manager International, a Denmark-based multinational training and consulting group. Her keen sense of diverse ideas and approaches to management has been shaped by working extensively in Asia for the past fifteen years.

Janelle speaks on the subjects of customer service, complaint handling, strategic planning, stress management, and creativity. Her decades of moving audiences to implement behavioral changes have ignited her passion to look at the emotional demands that the shift to an experience economy will have on customer service. A member of the National Speaker's Association, she has earned the designation of Certified Speaking Professional.

She is coauthor with Claus Møller of the bestselling business book *A Complaint Is a Gift: Using Customer Feedback as a Strategic Tool*, published by Berrett-Koehler. Her book *The Stress Manager* is used in the popular TMI course by the same name. She also developed a management training program, *Creativity Power: Unbind Your Mind*, which uses 365 skill-building mental aerobic exercises called "mind flexors."

Her doctorate is from the University of California, Berkeley. A licensed clinical marriage and family therapist, she has two master's degrees, one of which is in psychology. Janelle is married and has a son.

Dianna Maul is vice president of marketing for TMI, USA, and manages TMI's Pacific Northwest office. Dianna's ability to assist clients in implementing practical solutions to customer service needs is the result of over twenty years of operational experience. Dianna gained her footing in customer service working with Nordstrom and studying with W. Edwards Deming and Disney University. A founding director of

Horizon Airlines, widely regarded for its outstanding customer service, Dianna conceptualized and directed the Horizon Air Training Academy in her role as vice president of customer service.

Dianna is coauthor of "Maintaining Superior Customer Service during Periods of Peak Demand" in *Best Practices in Customer Service,* edited by Ron Zemke and John Woods. Dianna has honed her emotional abilities managing a full-time career while raising five children, including a set of triplets.

TMI, USA's Web page is at www.tmius.com. Janelle's telephone number is (415) 499-5508, and her e-mail address is JaBarlow@aol.com. Dianna's telephone number is (253) 428-0133, and her e-mail address is DiannaMaul@aol.com.

Coming in June 2000 from

Berrett-Koehler Communications!

Emotional Value in Customer Service

Janelle Barlow, Series Editor

EMOTIONAL VALUE IN CUSTOMER SERVICE uses five concise, convenient, action-oriented handbooks to help employees apply the powerful message of Janelle Barlow and Dianna Maul's book *Emotional Value*.

Emotional Value in Customer Service focuses on the emotional side of employees' relationships with customers. Even if you have the best product in the world at the best price, if there is no emotional connection made with your customers, it will be very easy to lose them to another supplier.

These engagingly illustrated handbooks feature stories, exercises, and examples that show how to build a bond with customers that will continue to pay off for years to come. Not just in increased sales, but also in reduced employee stress, greater job satisfaction, and reduced turnover.

The *Emotional Value in Customer Service* handbooks are perfect for individual study or for group training and discussion sessions. They're an entertaining and effective way to help your entire workforce apply the vital lessons of the *Emotional Value* book.

The handbooks in the series are:

1. **Emotional Competency: Creating Memorable Customer Experiences**, *Bill Oden* Helps employees realize the benefits of using emotional competence in their work—rather than toiling under emotional pressures. ISBN 1-58376-121-7

2. **Self-Awareness: Managing the Tone of Customer Interactions**, *Janelle Barlow* Outlines five steps for helping employees harness the power of emotional self-awareness to help customers deal with their emotions. ISBN 1-58376-122-5

3. **Empathy: Connecting with Customers**, *Alan Milham* Teaches five skills that will enable employees to use empathy to build loyal customer relationships. ISBN 1-58376-123-3

4. **Complaints: Finding the Treasure in Customer Feedback**, *Janelle Barlow and Paul Holden* Presents five powerful guidelines that enable employees to actually derive benefit from customer complaints, rather than merely "handling" them. ISBN 1-58376-150-0

5. **Loyalty: Creating Emotional Partnerships With Customers**, *Janelle Barlow and Dianna Maul* Offers tools and techniques for examining emotional relationships with customers and determining what can be done to create happier long-term customers who are more pleasant to serve. ISBN 1-58376-124-1

Handbooks are 6" x 9", approximately 48 pages. For more information, see the Berrett-Koehler website at bkconnection.com.

Berrett-Koehler Communications
PO Box 565, Williston, VT 05495-9900
Phone toll-free 7am-12 midnight **800-929-2929**
Fax to 802-864-7627 or order online at **www.bkconnection.com**

BK